# IN THE MOMENT

# IN THE MOMENT
## Jazz in the 1980s

FRANCIS DAVIS

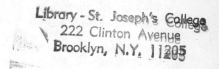
NEW YORK    OXFORD
OXFORD UNIVERSITY PRESS
1986

OXFORD UNIVERSITY PRESS

Oxford   New York   Toronto
Delhi   Bombay   Calcutta   Madras   Karachi
Petaling Jaya   Singapore   Hong Kong   Tokyo
Nairobi   Dar es Salaam   Cape Town
Melbourne   Auckland

and associated companies in
Beirut   Berlin   Ibadan   Nicosia

Published by Oxford University Press, Inc.,
200 Madison Avenue, New York, New York 10016

Oxford is a registered trademark of Oxford University Press

LIBRARY OF CONGRESS CATALOGING-IN-PUBLICATION DATA
Davis, Francis.
In the moment.
Previously published essays. Includes index.
1. Jazz music—United States.
2. Jazz musicians—United States.   I. Title.
ML3508.D38   1986      785.42′092′2      86-8437
ISBN 0-19-504090-2

2 4 6 8 10 9 7 5 3 1
Printed in the United States of America

FOR DOROTHY DAVIS
AND TERRY GROSS

117221

# Contents

# Introduction

Things are tough all over in the 1980s, but especially so for jazz, a music long ago banished to the no man's land between popular culture and fine art, where it figures to remain so long as its mongrel beginnings are held against it by those in high places. It's no longer honorable to exist on the fringes, which leaves jazz musicians out in the cold, in this decade of the homeless and *Lifestyles of the Rich and Famous*. Although jazz is strictly poverty row so far as the major record companies are concerned, accounting for less than 4 percent of all disc and tape sales, certain nouveaux riches pop stars have decided that it has the potential to become a fashionable address, and they are pricing the original tenants out. This unexpected gentrification might be amusing if its visible consequences weren't so alarming: Forget *People*, forget *Rolling Stone*, jazz musicians without corporate-level backing (particularly *black* jazz musicians) are no longer welcome even on the cover of *Down Beat*. Not when Sting and Linda Ronstadt pull in a better demographic. Meanwhile, what little jazz one hears on the radio has paid too dear a cost to get there, and not enough alternative concert venues have materialized to replace the jazz nightclubs that padlocked their doors in the '60s and '70s.

If there is a ray of hope in this gloomy picture, it is the unexpected arrival of talented and dedicated young jazz instrumentalists, composers, and singers. By young, I mean under forty, which at this date means those born since the end of World War II. I realize that a good number of the musicians I am branding prodigies are already older than Charlie Parker was when he recorded "Now's the Time"; a handful are older than Parker was when he died, to say nothing of Charlie Christian and Jimmy Blanton. But the melancholy fact that jazz no longer attracts a mass following means that recognition takes longer in coming, and a bulge in the population has caused our definition of "young" to creep steadily upward—if I had begun this book a decade ago, I would probably have included a section on musicians under thirty; a similar volume ten years from now might make fifty the cut-off age.

Once considered a young man's game, jazz is now generally regarded as manna for nostalgia sufferers and trivia buffs (the re-issue boomlet has been a mixed blessing), so they are a source of much fascination, these jazz baby boomers, in part because it amazes the mass media that anyone under forty listens to jazz, much less performs it. They are a heterogeneous group, and any generalization about them is certain to smack of wishful thinking. There have been trend pieces extolling them for their hindsight, and others excoriating them for the same tendency. It all depends on whether the writer in question is looking for evidence that the jazz avant is finally dropping its guard or evidence that jazz is dead (a pronouncement that used to mean nothing more profound than that jazz was no longer on the hit parade, but in these far more pretentious times means that jazz, like modern art in general, has reached what the art critic Gary Indiana has termed "the condition of epilogue," that virtuostic deconstructions and recapitulations are all we have to look forward to from here on in).

I think that this issue of aesthetic conservatism is a red herring. If this newest jazz generation has produced its share of neo-classicists (as jazz critic Gary Giddins felicitously dubs those replenishing older styles), it has also produced its post-modernists, infidels for whom all of jazz history, up to and including the present, is grist for the mill. What I am saying, I suppose, is that unlike many of my colleagues, I do not interpret this generation's emphasis on form rather than free expression as evidence of counter revolution against what used to be called free jazz. Quite the contrary. The melodic and harmonic foundations that jazz borrowed willy nilly from European concert music and American Popular Song have served it well over the decades and will continue to do so. But for the last 25 years, if not longer, jazz has been engaged in a sometimes torturous search for its own forms. That search is continuing, with such relative newcomers as Anthony Davis, David Murray, Billy Bang, Mathias Rüegg, and Craig Harris leading the way. The past is one of the few places left for them to look. In any event, it could be argued that neo-classicism is itself one aspect of post-modernism. It is significant that the younger musicians supposedly returning to the fold are forming larger ensembles and writing extended compositions, not merely running the changes on hastily concocted "heads." They are reaching back beyond bebop for inspiration, and in a music that has always seemed to pride itself on a short memory span, that is a radical, not a reactionary, development.

I am also trying to say, albeit in a roundabout way, that I do not share the fear that some of my colleagues have expressed for the survival of jazz as an art form. The survival of individual jazz *musicians* is another matter, though. In selecting among my previously published essays for this collection, it startled me to realize that so many of them ended on a weary note of resignation. For those of us who began collecting jazz after 1960, the previous decade will always be the Golden Age we just missed. In terms of the wealth and diversity of jazz now available on record, the 1980s may one day be regarded in the same light. The difference, of course, is that in the 1950s, before the red-lining of popular culture, jazz still drew a loyal and well-informed constituency from college campuses, black neighborhoods, and those fringe areas of society where bourgeois and bohemian tastes intersected. Such is no longer the case, and while the problem facing Wynton Marsalis is coping with material success in advance of artistic maturity, the problem facing most of his contemporaries is coming to terms with the obscurity and almost certain insolvency to which their calling dooms them (for all we know, a similar fate might ultimately be in store for Marsalis too). These new faces might take heart from the perseverance of Sonny Rollins, Ornette Coleman, Don Cherry, Roscoe Mitchell, George Russell, Warne Marsh, and the other practiced hands I celebrate in another section of this book.

The down-scale economics of jazz, the surprising—and not unwelcome—emergence of the composer as the pre-eminent figure in what has traditionally been regarded as the improviser's realm, the coming of age of a new jazz generation, the lingering influence of father figures like Duke Ellington, John Coltrane, and Thelonious Monk—these are some of the themes that drift in and out of these chapters, if it is not too presumptuous to speak of recurring themes in what is essentially a series of postmarked dispatches rather than a book-length treatise. *In the Moment* is a sampling of the artist profiles and critical evaluations I have published since 1981 in a variety of newspapers and magazines, including the *Philadelphia Inquirer*, the *Boston Phoenix*, *The Atlantic*, *High Fidelity*, *Rolling Stone*, *Musician*, *Down Beat*, *Jazz Times*, and the *Village Voice*. I owe the title to pianist and composer Anthony Davis (no relation, by the way) who spoke of improvisation as playing "in the moment" when I first interviewed him five years ago. It was an offhand remark, and I'd heard many musicians say much the same thing, but for whatever reason, the phrase struck a chord of epiphany. As I thought about it, it began to acquire multiple meanings, the most obvious of which pertained to the immediacy and perishability of improvised music (and the irony that Davis is among those vanguard composers who would argue that it is time to pull in the reins on improvisers was not lost on me). Although Davis intended no such significance, the phrase also seemed to herald the advent of his generation—the 1980s are going to be remembered as their decade: Davis, Wynton Marsalis, David Murray, Bobby McFerrin, and the others (see postscript).

Finally, though, the more I thought about it, the more the phrase struck me as descriptive of my method of inquiry as of the music I was writing about. Of necessity, I think of myself as a deadline reporter, and if my record reviews represent judgment calls so do my profiles. Denied the luxury of spending as much time with my subjects as I might like (blame it on the pressure of drumming out enough copy to make a living in a marketplace that puts a low value on jazz journalism), I often have to make quick assumptions about a musician's character and motivation, and there have probably been some instances in which I have assumed too much. (Musicians presuppose that all jazz critics are frustrated musicians. That's incorrect: the good ones are frustrated novelists.) Still, I believe that the spot coverage I have provided is valuable for what it reveals of the changing methodology and mores of jazz, and for that reason I have generally refrained from second guessing myself in preparing these articles for publication between hard covers, although I have seized the opportunity to correct factual errors, to reinsert passages originally excised for reasons of space, to update where necessary, and to fine-tune my prose. Jazz journalism is a form of advocacy journalism in that it attempts to lure converts. Jazz criticism, on the other hand, means arguing fine points of scripture with the already devout. I wanted to include examples of both kinds of writing in my first book, so there is a selection of critical essays toward the back, and a good deal of critical reflection in some of the artist profiles.

You know what they say about the defendant who acts as his own attorney. What does that make the writer who thinks he can go it alone without an editor? I have been fortunate in gaining the council of some shrewd editors, including Sheldon Meyer and Leona Capeless of Oxford University Press; Milo Miles of the *Boston Phoenix* (who should really think about changing his name to Mo Joost); Georgia Christgau of *High Fidelity;* William Whitworth, Cullen Murphy, Corby Kummer, Eris Haas, and Allison Hume of *The Atlantic;* Jim Davis, Linda Hasert, Jonathon Storm, and Peter Landry of the *Philadelphia Inquirer;* Jock Baird, Vic Garbarini, and Mark Rowland of *Musician;* Jim Henke and Lisa Henriksson of *Rolling Stone;* Mike Joyce and Ira Sabin of *Jazz Times;* Art Lange and Charles Dougherty of *Down Beat;* and Bob Rusch of *Cadence.* I owe debts of gratitude to all of them, as well as to Lisa Bain of *Esquire,* who assigned the piece on Sonny Rollins and fought in vain to save it from being killed; to Gary Giddins, who assigned and prepared the piece on John Lewis for a *Village Voice* jazz supplement; and to Bob Blumenthal, Eric Bruskin, Robert Christgau, Dorothy Davis, John Ferguson, Steve Futterman, Terry Gross, James Isaacs, Dan Miller, Dan Morgenstern, Mark Moses, Robert Mugge, Kit Rachlis, Leslie Saunders, John F. Szwed, Ludwig Van Trikt, Peter Watrous, Rafi Zabor, and my agent Diana Price, for the comfort, encouragement, and insights they offered at crucial stages along the way.

*Philadelphia*                          F.D.
*February 1986*

*Postscript:* I should make it clear that I do not necessarily consider the New Faces to whom I have devoted chapters to be more "important" than those I mention in passing or neglect to mention at all. *In the Moment* is not intended as a post-1946 version of John Chilton's *Who's Who of Jazz*. If it were, there would be more about other relative newcomers whose work shows great promise, including trumpeters Terence Blanchard, Baikida Carroll, Stanton Davis, Jon Faddis, Michael Mossman, Hugh Ragin, Herb Robertson, and Claudio Roditti; trombonists Ray Anderson, Robin Eubanks, George Lewis, Steve Turre, and Gary Valente; French horn players Vincent Chancey and Tom Varner; soprano saxophonist Jane Ira Bloom; alto saxophonists Tim Berne, Steve Coleman, Paquito D'Rivera, Kenny Garrett, Donald Harrison, Ed Jackson, Jameel Moondoc, and Robert Watson; tenor saxophonists Tony Dagradi, Ricky Ford, Chico Freeman, Bill Saxton, and Benny Wallace; all-purpose reedmen Marty Ehrlich, John Purcell, and Edward Wilkerson; flutist James Newton; vibraphonists Jay Hoggard and Khan Jamal; pianists Geri Allen, Marilyn Crispell, Kenny Kirkland, Mulgrew Miller, Amina Claudine Myers, Michel Petrucciani, Michele Rosewoman, Hilton Ruiz, Eric Watson, and James Williams; guitarists Pierre Dorge, James Emery, Kevin Eubanks, Bill Frisell, Birili Lagrene, Emily Remler, Vernon Reid, and John Scofield; bassists Anthony Cox, Phil Flanagan, Mark Helias, Fred Hopkins, John Lindberg, Charnett Moffett, Lonnie Plaxico, Avery Sharpe and Harvie Swartz; bass guitarist Jamaaladeen Tacuma; cellists David Eyges, Deidre Murray, and Abdul Wadud; drummers Pheeroan Aklaff, Thurman Barker, Gerry Hemingway, Bob Moses, Cornell Rochester, Marvin "Smitty" Smith, Akira Tana, Jeff Watts, and Kenny Washington; composer and record producer Kip Hanrahan; and the members of the Microscopic Septet (saxophonists Don Davis, John Hagan, Phillip Johnston, and David Sewelson; pianist Joel Forrester; bassist David Hofstra; and drummer Richard Dworkin) and the Rova Saxophone Quartet (Bruce Ackley, Larry Ochs, Jon Raskin, and Andrew Voight).

# I
## NEW FACES

# Anthony Davis's New Music

Anthony Davis's music—as documented on the albums he has made as a leader, as well as those to which he has brought an organizing intelligence as a sideman—summarizes the last 20 years of innovation in jazz and offers an optimistic prognosis for the future. Davis is in the forefront of a new generation of musicians who can claim the hard-won advances of Ornette Coleman, Cecil Taylor, and the Art Ensemble of Chicago as their birthright, who can embrace the distant jazz past without jeopardizing their standing as modernists, and who can borrow structural devices and instrumental procedures from Europe without relinquishing their places in the Afro-American continuum.

"But I'm not really a jazz musician," Davis cautions those of us eager to hail him as the most important pianist and composer to emerge from the jazz avant-garde since Cecil Taylor. "I've never related my conception of music—or Cecil Taylor's music, either, for that matter—to the term *jazz*. To a lot of jazz audiences, the music I play is very alienating. They still come expecting to hear solos on 'I Got Rhythm' changes, and I'm not interested in that. All the labels they put on music are stupid, but so long as there are labels, if I could be associated with *new music* instead of jazz, it would give me

3

more freedom to create, and I wouldn't be tied down to pre-existing forms, the way I am with *jazz*."

That Davis voices such dissatisfaction with jazz and its audiences says something about his own biases and ambitions, but it also raises pertinent questions about where jazz is headed in the 1980s and what sort of audience it can expect to take with it.

One fluffy summer afternoon, Davis and I chatted over lunch in a French cafe across the street from the Manhattan highrise where he lives with his wife, the fantasy novelist Deborah Atherton, and their young son. As Davis spoke of his beginnings and his current prospects, several recognizable themes kept surfacing: his role as a composer in what has traditionally been considered an improvisatory music; the increasingly conservative mood of jazz audiences and many of his contemporaries; the need to locate a new, less parochial audience with whom he can communicate on his own terms; and the ambiguous position in which reawakened interest in the jazz tradition places the innovative black musician.

Davis's background and consequently his frame of reference are more cosmopolitan than those of must musicians associated with jazz. The son of a university professor, he was born in Paterson, New Jersey, in 1951, and lived in New York, "up on 138th and Madison," until he was five. Except for a year in Italy when his father was awarded a Fulbright Fellowship, Davis spent his adolescence in a succession of campus towns, including Princeton, New Jersey, and State College, Pennsylvania. "Was I an academic brat?" he winced. "A *campus* brat? I don't know. I guess so. The parents of most of the people I grew up with were also involved with academia, especially once we moved to Penn State. There are a lot of advantages to growing up in an academic environment, however insular it might be. They had a really good music department at Penn State, so I had the opportunity, while still in junior high, to study with professors from the music faculty.

"I was a music major at Yale—finally. I started out in English and Philosophy, but in my senior year I switched, so my B.A. is in Music.

Most of my instruction at Yale was in classical music, though, and it didn't really have that much of a bearing on my development, although I was exposed to some things I wouldn't have known about otherwise, like Medieval music, which still interests me, and Indian music, which I studied both at Yale and at Wesleyan with Amrad Raghaven, a fantastic South Indian drummer."

Davis remained in New Haven for a few years following his graduation from Yale, postponing the inevitable move to New York until 1977: "I came here because the music's here, the musicians are here, because I wouldn't have been able to make a living as a musician in New Haven. It was an important move. But if I had come here earlier, I think I'd have a far more conservative outlook now, especially since I started off with the same influences every pianist my age started off with—McCoy Tyner, Herbie Hancock, Andrew Hill. There are many conformist pressures that you face in New York. They go beyond commercial pressures; it has to do with winning approval from other musicians. If you come to New York with a pretty strong sense of your own identity, as I did, it's a lot easier to deal with. Being in New Haven, within a protective academic environment, I was able to develop my own ideas."

Davis has been fortunate enough to find something resembling an academic sanctuary even in the wilds of Manhattan; living in separate units within the same dormitory-like high-rise complex as he and his wife are such musicians as trombonist George Lewis, pianists Muhal Richard Abrams and Amina Claudine Myers, and tenor saxophonists Frank Lowe and Ricky Ford, as well as a number of dancers, writers, and visual artists. It recalls the creative company Davis kept at Yale. Matriculating at the university around the same time as he—or living in town—were several other young musicians with whom he was to form enduring alliances: Lewis, saxophonist Dwight Andrews, guitarist Allan Jaffe, vibraphonist Jay Hoggard, drummer Gerry Hemingway, and bassists Wes Brown, Mark Dresser, and Mark Helias. Drummer Ed Blackwell and alto saxophonist Marion Brown—older, better-established figures from the jazz avant-garde's first wave—had settled in nearby Connecticut hamlets to teach. But the most decisive influence on Davis during his stay in New Haven was the transplanted Chicago trumpeter, composer, and theorist Leo Smith.

"Leo's wife was the director of a private high school in Orange, Connecticut, so he was living just outside of New Haven. I became involved with him when I was a student and joined New Dalta Ahkri, an ensemble with Leo and Wes Brown. Leo introduced me to a different concept of playing, which involved the idea of composition, rather than improvisation, being of central importance in the ongoing development of black music. I think that Leo is one of the most important and underrated composers to emerge since Ornette Coleman. I think that Leo, along with Anthony Braxton, laid the foundation for what's happening in music now. We're in a new period, and some people are confused by what they're hearing, because the music is developing chiefly in the area of composition, not in terms of what people have been taught to listen for—new directions in improvisation.

"Most of my music is composed—written out. I think that improvisation is just one available option within the larger framework of a given piece. As a composer, the dynamic of a piece is more important to me, in a sense, than the performances of the individuals playing the piece. It's almost closer to the classical tradition of interpretation, of *realizing* a given work of music, than it is to the jazz-oriented concept of showcasing a soloist or creating a vehicle for a group of different individuals."

When Davis says that most of his music is written, he means literally that—that it is notated. He is aware that notation is anathema for Cecil Taylor, as it was for the late Charles Mingus—two of the composers he most admires. "I think they were upset with the limitations of notation, with the preconceptions it brings to a performance. They were trying to bring immediacy back into the music—that sense of creating in the moment—and they were also trying to create a collective music. I think that was important in that cycle, but what's important now is to reassert some control, because, at this point in the music, there's been too much random noise. I'm not saying that about

Mingus or Cecil Taylor. But what I am saying is that I want everything that's played to be related to what's been played before and what will happen later; when you think like that, you have to deal with compositional form and planning. I find it inadequate just to say 'play like this' or 'play like that,' because finally what you're saying, when you try to communicate your ideas that way, is 'play something I've heard you play before.' "

At the time I spoke with him, Davis was preparing to record a longer, orchestrated version of "Under the Double Moon (Wayang No. 4)" (a piece from his solo piano album *Lady of the Mirrors*)* with the octet he calls Episteme: George Lewis, trombone; Dwight Andrews, woodwinds; Shem Guibbory, violin; Jay Hoggard, vibraphone; Abdul Wadud, cello; Warren Smith and Pheeroan Aklaff, percussion. "I'm interested in scoring some of my ideas—not only my compositional ideas but my improvisational ideas too—for an ensemble of that size. The piece will involve improvisation—it would have to, because there are some wonderful improvisers in the ensemble—but there will be an organic link between what I've written and what the soloists play. What I'm trying to do, really, is to take what I've learned as an improviser, take that unified concept one has as a soloist, and communicate that to other improvisers."

Davis said he feels he has reached the stage as a composer where he can write music that doesn't call for his own participation as an instrumentalist—music for solo voice, for example, or for violin, cello, or chamber orchestra. "Eventually, I would like to write orchestral works which would involve improvisation, but *scored* improvisation, so those works could be played by improvisers and non-improvisers alike. One of my dreams is to write a ballet, and I'd like to compose more film music." (He has scored three independent films, including Carolyn Emmons's *Man Around the House,* winner of a 1980 Oscar

* Davis has recorded "Under the Double Moon (Wayang No. 4)" three times: a duet with vibraphonist Jay Hoggard on *Under the Double Moon* (Pausa 7120), the octet performance on *Episteme* (Gramavision GR-8108), and the solo version on *Lady of the Mirrors* (India Navigation IN-1047).

as best student film.) He also envisions writing a musical drama; one model for it would be Stephen Sondheim's *Sweeney Todd,* which Davis called "a revelation. It's great music and great theater."

Also on the agenda are more solo piano recitals, although his efforts in this direction will not be totally improvised, as in the manner of Keith Jarrett. "The danger with that practice is that the music can become a progression of clichés. I mean, you go from doing one style you know how to do well to another style you know how to do. I hear him playing within himself; everything's within his fingers. Composed music faces the same barriers; there's always the problem of getting beyond your own limitations, beyond what to you has already become a cliché, but I like to approach that through pre-meditation. I think it's possible to go beyond yourself when playing in the moment, but composition can set the stage for you. I've done some things with George Lewis that were hardly notated at all. But even when I'm improvising freely, I'm still thinking compositionally, in terms of the overall structure, so it amounts to the same thing. The important influences on my playing have all been composi-tional—Ellington, Monk, Mingus; there were early classical influ-ences, too—Messiaen, Chopin, and Stravinsky."

Davis's *Lady of the Mirrors* is an album of unapologetic piano music. No inaudible orchestra lies in waiting in Davis's left hand, and no invisible horn soloists line up in his right. The keyboard which bears the curve and pressure of his fingers is neither the well-tempered scale nor the skin of a drum. In the contact between pianist and piano, no graven image is permitted. Describing the programmatic content of each of the pieces in his liner insert, Davis draws analo-gies to the music of Duke Ellington and the blues, to science fiction and Balinese "shadow" (or "puppet") theater, and the arts of dance, painting, and still photography. Yet even as these performances suc-ceed in delineating their stated subjects and moods, their "content" seems wholly musical, with Davis testing his powers of concentration as an instrumentalist, an improviser, and a composer. "Under the Double Moon," for example, is a movement from a dance suite based on the Balinese Wayang, titled after one of Deborah Atherton's unpublished novels. In performance, however, "the piece really addresses itself to the technical problem of hand independence," as Davis admits in the notes; it is actually the right hand that can be said to "accompany" the left for long stretches, as Davis generates percussive suspense by jabbing repeatedly at a shell-like note at the piano's high end. The title piece gathers similar tension from bass and treble clef oppositions, and from clusters, broken rhythms, and leaping intervals that reflect Davis's fascination with modern dance. "Five Moods from an English Garden," though beginning with an evocation of trilling birds, is non-representational, as befits a piece inspired by the Russian non-objectivist painter Vasily Kandinsky. "Beyond Reason," with its swirling tremulos and ostinatos and slivers of icicle-blue dissonance, is Davis's vindication of European Romanticism, and "Man on a Turquoise Cloud" is a modernist structure erected upon another magnificent ruin—a bedrock blues tribute to Ellington that also nods in the general direction of Thelonious Monk.

Reviewers have compared Davis to Ellington, Monk, and Cecil Taylor, not so much because he sounds like any of them but because his best writing proposes, as each of theirs did in its time, a formal consolidation of recent improvisatory gains. And he has dared to use the legacy of those pianists as the raw material for bold original works.

"It's natural you should," Davis said when I told him I thought I detected the shadow of Ellington in his "Crepescule: A Suite for Monk," and traces of Monk and Taylor in his homages to Ellington, "On an Azure Plane" and "Man on a Turquoise Cloud."* "Those figures are all historically linked. There's a whole Ellington piano tradition. It extends from Ellington to Monk to Cecil Taylor, not to mention Randy Weston and Abdullah Ibrahim [Dollar Brand] and several other important pianists who are also composers. It goes back beyond Ellington, too. Historically, pianists have been the best educated of musicians—that sounds condescending, and I don't mean it

* "Crepescule: A Suite for Monk" and "On an Azure Plane" are both included on *Past Lives* (Red VPA-134).

to be. But pianists have had to deal with arranging, harmonies, comping—the whole structure of the music. That's been true from Scott Joplin on, and I think it explains the importance pianists have had as composers. The piano has a long tradition that parallels the history of the music, from the development of ragtime to the later development of stride and onward, and I'm part of that tradition."

Davis's continued application of his early classical training links him to the Ellington tradition in yet another, more ironic way. In 1939 Ellington was branded a social climber by those former admirers who thought they detected the taint of European influence on "Reminiscing in Tempo." Over the years, John Lewis and Cecil Taylor have also been censured for their assimilationist tendencies. Now Davis is becoming a target of those who fear that black music barters too much of its root energy when it conducts trade with Europe.

"Of course European music has influenced me," Davis said. "I think that Europe has influenced everything in the world at this point. But there's an African influence in my work, too, and the influences aren't mutually exclusive. After all, the early 20th-century European composers like Stravinsky and Debussy drew from ragtime, and jazz composers have borrowed in turn from them. By this point, there's an American musical tradition that includes both European and African strains, and that's all there is to it—I mean, we haven't been a colony now for some 200 years. It's ridiculous that any new development in black music is assumed to have some hidden connection to European consciousness. It advances a stereotypical image of what the Afro-American experience is all about. It's unfortunate that certain parties are subverting the Afro-American tradition—which is a strong and very positive force for change—as a means of maintaining the status quo, of limiting the connection that jazz has to other musics and to the world of ideas.

"There's suddenly a lot of pressure to do music from 'in the tradition.' But the truest homage to Charlie Parker, for example, isn't to play his tunes or play just like him, but to do what George Lewis has done, to play something *new* that wouldn't be possible *without*

Charlie Parker's example.* The most vital contribution you can make to furthering the jazz tradition is to create your own music, create a new music."

If Davis's slant on tradition is less sanctimonious than that of many of his black music contemporaries—if he is inclined to view it as a dynamic and not as a totem—perhaps it is because the idea of a tradition isn't so recent an acquisition for him as it is for many of them. He is a descendant of the Hampton Davises, the family that founded Hampton Institute, one of the country's oldest black colleges. His father was Charles T. Davis, author of an influential book on Richard Wright, co-editor of the anthology *On Being Black,* first black faculty member at Princeton University, and chairman of Afro-American Studies at Yale from the inception of the program in the early '70s until his death in March 1981. In the estimation of Dr. John F. Szwed, a former colleague of Dr. Davis's at Yale, Dr. Davis established "the strongest and only serious black studies program in the country, with the possible exception of the one at Stanford, which was copied from Yale's model, with Dr. Davis' guidance."

"My father contributed a lot," said Davis, with understandable pride, "and, of course, he was very important to me individually, not only in terms of eventually being very supportive of my career in music—which upset him at first and caused some arguments when we found ourselves on the same campus—but also in maintaining my interest in other fields, in teaching me that music is just part of the whole spectrum of the Afro-American experience. My family wasn't rich, but there was always a lot of pride in what our ancestors had accomplished, and a lot of pressure on the younger members of the family to achieve distinction, which I think is why so many of us became artists of one sort or another—my younger brother Christopher is an actor, director, and playwright; my cousin Thulani is a poet and editor; another cousin is an architect; and another is a photographer and filmmaker. With our background, we were spared the

* On *Homage to Charles Parker* (Black Saint BSR-0029), with Lewis, Davis, Richard Teitelbaum, and Dwight Andrews.

burden that artists usually face of having to scuffle to make a living early in their careers. A whole generation of Davises—including my father and my Uncle Arthur, who is chairman of the English Department at Howard—was involved with the academic world, and I suppose I let the family down on that score. But I'm sort of making amends for that now. I'm teaching Composition and History of Creative Music from 1900 two days a week at my alma mater, and I'm trying to decide whether to go on with my education and earn some degrees. The university setting offers all kinds of opportunities for a composer, and some of the excitement my students feel about music rubs off on me—I become very excited sharing what I know with them. The paycheck from teaching also allows me the independence to say no, to do only those projects I really want to do."

One of the offers to which Davis would say no is the opportunity to play commercial music. "I'm just not interested in that at all. I know there are aspects of my music that are more commercial than others—that sounds presumptuous, but it's something every musician knows about himself. I want the freedom to present the most experimental aspect of my work, as well as those that are more immediate. I don't want to feel as though I can't play music that I like. I think you have to give the audience your best. Play the best music you can. I'm interested in communicating with audiences on other levels too, through the use of words, text, dance, and visuals.

"Being a musician doesn't make me better than anyone else. I'm a human being, and I'm thinking about a lot of things that other people are also thinking about. You have your own perceptions as an artist because you're put on this planet to create mystery, but you're put here to unravel mysteries, too. So I think you have to trust that the audience will have the sophistication to understand you, and you can't afford to condescend to them. And your ultimate audience, when you think about it, is God—however you conceive it. You're not only playing for people here and now; you're playing for past generations, for the people who have died. When I'm playing or writing music now, I'm thinking about my father, about Duke Ellington, about the contributions they made, and I feel compelled to create to my fullest capacity. I'd be letting them down if I didn't. That's how I feel."

(JANUARY 1982)

# II

*Hemispheres* (Gramavision GR-8303) is a dance suite in five movements, a collaboration between pianist/composer Anthony Davis and dancer/choreographer Molissa Fenley that was premiered in 1983 as part of the Brooklyn Academy of Music's Next Wave Festival. Although Fenley's contributions were of necessity sacrificed in the recording studio, one intuits a dancer's involvement in the rippling physicality and agitated panache of the accompaniment Davis has scored for a 10-member ensemble of winds, percussion, and strings. With its undulations and repetitions, its interlocking meters and shifting, layered harmonies, the music on *Hemispheres* initially sounds like Davis's proprietary stroll through the territory he staked out for himself between the kingdoms of Duke Ellington and Philip Glass on his hypnotic 1981 release *Episteme*. But what ultimately divorces *Hemispheres* from the tough-minded mysticism of its predecessor is its theatricality, its hearty acceptance of Fenley's invitation to dance.

In the sense that *Hemispheres* is jazz dance music, it is, with its learned allusions to the Broadway stage and the European concert hall, dance music of a radically different stripe from that currently being purveyed by disparate jazz funkateers like Herbie Hancock, Ronald Shannon Jackson, and Oliver Lake. Still, some comparison is in order inasmuch as both sides (whatever their different motives) attempt to restore balance between soloist and ensemble. Jazz has always borrowed indiscriminately, from sources both high and low, and the net result of its many borrowings has always been the setting of improvisational boundaries. Jackson's Decoding Society and Davis's group Episteme are both precision units in which improvisers are called upon to relinquish some of their autonomy in the name of group order.

It is surprising, therefore, that *Hemispheres* owes much of its vigor and élan to the jabbing trumpet solos of Leo Smith—and not only because Davis usually permits his performers very little interpretive leeway. Smith has long seemed one of those problematical figures destined to register greater impact as a theorist and mentor (indeed, Davis is one of his disciples) than as a player. But on the flamboyant "Little Richard's New Wave" and the ominously tranquil "A Walk Through the Shadow," Davis manages to elicit scintillating work from his trumpeter by denying him the longuers that have marred so many of his solo LPs. Distinguishing the improvised passages in Davis's music from those passages that have been sketched out beforehand can be as tricky as telling the dancer from the dance, so insistent is he that improvised solos maintain the narrative continuity of his compositions, but the few choruses here that *sound* improvised are of a uniformly high order. Trombonist George Lewis paces Smith with fluttering, starkly drawn solos on both of the aforementioned titles. "Ifa the Oracle—Esu the Trickster" climaxes with agitated, nimble turns by J. D. Parran and Dwight Andrews (on contrabass clarinet and soprano saxophone respectively) over a treadmill rhythm rolled out by the leader's piano, David Samuels's vibraphone, and Pheeroan Aklaff's lashing drums. (It is surely no coincidence that Aklaff has been the drummer on so many of the 1980s' most provocative albums. Without the steady gallop the sensitive and sorely underrated Aklaff brings to *Hemispheres,* it might have become ponderous and top heavy, particularly the finale, "Clonetics," a piece whose lurching forward motions recall the pianistics and foot work of Thelonious Monk, as well as Leonard Bernstein's score for *Candide.*) The opening "Esu at the Crossroads" is a combination overture and miniature piano concerto, with Davis weaving gracefully around the massed strings and horns.

Still, it's the balance of instruments and the intricate musculature of Davis's writing that make *Hemispheres* so seductive. "A Walk Through the Shadows" is the most beguiling piece of all, with keening, finely sifted passages for the strings (violinist Shem Guibbory, cellist Eugene Friesen, and arco bassist Rick Rozie). "A Walk" appeared on *Episteme* as a rather cloistered piano exercise; expanded to 13 minutes here and opened up for orchestra, it acquires some of the majesty of Ellington's devotionals (and its recurring drone and pedal establish once and for all that Davis's style of minimalism is hardly a heretical, classical-music affectation, that jazz has its own history of minimalism in works like Ellington's "It Don't Mean a Thing" and "La Plus Belle Africaine" and Monk's "Skippy" and "Friday the Thirteenth").

Davis can hardly be held accountable for *Hemispheres'* one nagging flaw. Listening to this ravishing and at times robust music, one begins to wonder how Molissa Fenley described its rhythms with her body. If ever a work cried out for video preservation, this is it, but video technology now seems to be the exclusive property of rock image makers and chi-chi conceptualists like Laurie Anderson and Nam June Paik. (If the recent PBS special *Good Morning, Mr. Orwell* confirmed George Russell's observation that the avant-garde is the last refuge of the untalented, it also announced that video is quickly becoming the last refuge of the avant-garde.) Even minus its visual correlative, however, *Hemispheres* is a musical triumph, because its expansive body language demonstrates that the most provocative composer to emerge from jazz in the last decade and a half is not going to settle for the anemically modern or the fashionably recondite.

(JANUARY 1984)

# III

Anthony Davis was no more than a spectator at a rehearsal I attended for *X*, his three-act opera based on the life of Malcolm X. *X* was scheduled to premiere as a work-in-progress in Philadelphia a month later, one of five productions to be mounted by the American Music Theater Festival during its maiden season. But on this clutching hot day in SoHo, Philadelphia was still far enough in the future that Davis could be forgiven if he seemed preoccupied with more immediate concerns. He was to perform his piece "Still Waters" with the New York Philharmonic the following evening, and he owed commissioned pieces—due before the end of the summer—to the Houston Symphony and pianist Ursula Oppens. For that matter, the second and third acts of X still needed work—work that begged to be completed in solitude, at the piano bench. But the first act was already out of Davis's hands, and he looked as though he was trying to get used to the idea of being an onlooker, the role he would have to assume on opening night.

Davis watched in silence as director Rhoda Levine blocked out the terpsichore for a scene in which a character named Street (a fictional composite of the various Stagger Lee-types the young Malcolm X ran with in Boston and Harlem) entices Malcolm with a dissonant aria extolling the spoils of "the life." (Although the aria had no title, it did have a hook, and Levine and the cast referred to it as "My Side of Town.") Around and around the actors playing Street and Malcolm (Avery Brooks and Peter Lightfoot, respectively), the other cast members writhed in flailing dance steps that were half slowed-down lindy hop, half speeded-up Twyla Tharpe. Levine is a former choreographer, and anyone stumbling in on her rehearsal unaware might have assumed she was preparing her company for an avant-garde deconstruction of *Guys and Dolls*, not a night at the opera. She was making them sweat.

During a lull, Davis walked over to the rehearsal pianist whose tone clusters, pedal points, and trills—the bare bones of the score—were substituting for Davis's 10-member group Episteme, which would be in the orchestra pit on opening night. "Relax those sixteenth notes up a little bit," he advised, his bushy Afro bobbing as he illustrated the hambone rhythm he desired with fluid gyrations of his shoulders and hips.

"Rhythm is very important in this score," he remarked after taking a seat again. "There's going to be a contrabass clarinet improvisation over that figure, and a guitar riffing underneath. I want to evoke the music that Malcolm danced to when he was a shoe shine boy at the Roseland Ballroom in Boston, and I want to cue the audience right away what the character of Street represents, so I've found myself writing viper music—music vaguely reminiscent of Fats Waller and Cab Calloway.

"This will be the first time my music has been performed without me as one of the performers," said Davis, who comes from a tradition in which bridging the gap between composition and execution usually depends on the laying on of hands. "[Pianist] Marilyn Crispell will take my place with Episteme, and Peter Aaronson, the show's musical director and a much more experienced conductor than I am, will conduct. I'm just going to sit in the front row and watch, which I know will be difficult, but I want to maintain an objective eye. I'm learning to delegate responsibility—that's part of what appeals to me about collaborative works.

"X is still in the process of being written, and probably will be for years to come. When the American Music Theater Festival gave me the go ahead to write an opera, they had no idea I was planning Tristan and Isolde! We hope to present X in as complete a fashion as possible in Philadelphia, with the understanding that it will go on developing after it closes. This is my first opera, after all—my first dramatic work of any kind—and I need to gain some sense of which of the music I'm writing translates into stage action and which doesn't. I'm learning as I go along."

X is a family affair: it is also the first opera for Davis's brother Christopher, who wrote the story, and for their cousin Thulani Davis, who wrote the libretto. "It was originally Christopher's idea," says Anthony Davis. "He has experience as a stage actor and director, and he wanted to base a musical on the life of Malcolm X, which isn't as impractical a notion as it might sound, now that Stephen Sondheim has shown that it's possible to do all sorts of things in the commercial theater. I liked the idea, because I had always wanted to apply my music to a larger dramatic form, the way Sondheim had in *Sweeney Todd,* and I had always wanted to write a work around a political theme. But after thinking it over, I suggested to Christopher that Malcolm's life might play better as opera, with singing, rather than spoken dialogue, furthering the narrative. I also thought that doing it as an opera would enable us to do it on a larger scale. And as Thulani pointed out, scale was necessary if we were going to give a sense of how many millions of people were galvanized by Malcolm's message—and not just those people who converted to Islam because of him, either."

Although X draws on incidents depicted in *The Autobiography of Malcolm X,* Christopher Davis hastens to point out that he and librettist Thulani Davis also drew from countless other sources, so their opera is in no sense an adaptation of *The Autobiography* (the dramatic rights to which belong to Warner Brothers). Nevertheless, autobiography as a *concept* is one of *X*'s themes. "My father taught a course in black autobiography, which is the oldest black literary tradition, from slave narratives and Frederick Douglass on through *The Autobiography of Malcolm X, Soul on Ice,* and *Manchild in the Promised Land,*" says Christopher. "Transformation is always the key theme in those books, and the transformation always means gaining the power of the word—learning how to read and write and express yourself, so that you can define yourself on your own terms. The author always begins by telling who his parents were in the very first sentence. The writing is always powerful and direct, and there's always the use of repetition to reflect the way black people create their own version of history in the telling and retelling of certain stories."

"It's a literary tradition that stems from an oral tradition, and it was Malcolm's principal tool as a recruiter for the Nation of Islam," adds Thulani Davis. "Instead of handing of leaflets, or reading from the Quram, he would tell people his life story in order to convince them to join his mosque."

X begins with the off-stage death of Malcolm's father, the Reverend Earl Little, in East Lansing, Michigan, in 1931. Reverend Little was cut in half by a trolley; the police said he stumbled under its wheels by accident, but his family suspected he had been beaten and left on the tracks to die by the Ku Klux Klan, in retribution for his pro-Marcus Garvey sermons—the authors of X take the latter point of view. It ends with Malcolm's assassination at the Audubon Ballroom in Harlem in 1965, after his falling out with Muslim leader (and surrogate father) Elijah Muhammad. (What tacit part, if any, Elijah played in Malcolm's murder is a subject the authors leave open to conjecture.)

In the aftermath of Malcolm's assassination, several black composers associated with the free jazz movement (but unaffiliated with the Nation of Islam) embraced him as their sage and dedicated works to him; whatever their level of political involvement or spiritual attainment, they recognized in Malcolm a rage equal to their own. Anthony Davis, a representative of a later wave of avant-gardists and a product of the black bourgeoisie, views the slain Muslim leader with more detachment. "I was only 14 when he was gunned down. Growing up in a family that was active in the church and civil rights movement, I gravitated more toward Martin Luther King and the doctrine of non-violent integration. Later, after I left home and read Malcolm's speeches and autobiography, I began to understand that, by raising the issues of separatism and economic self-determination, Malcolm addressed the discontinuity of the black urban experience in a way that Dr. King, from his Southern agrarian frame of reference, could not. Dr. King was a great inspirational figure, a moralist, but Malcolm represented the more pragmatic side of the struggle, and I think you can measure his impact on history by looking at his impact on the thinking of Jesse Jackson, who is supposedly Dr. King's disciple.

"What makes Malcolm so compelling a dramatic protagonist, beyond his politics, though, are the many transformations you see him making over the course of his life—from country boy to street hustler to spiritual leader, world statesman, and political martyr. He combined violence and contemplation, the intuitive and the intellectual, mother wit and the groping for a more philosophical foundation—which is why he continues to be a force twenty years after his death, because those are the twin poles of black experience in America. His story is one of the great stories of our century, and it's also a story that I think begs to be *sung*.

"Malcolm had a link to music, and that link was probably John Coltraine, who symbolized musically what Malcolm symbolized on a social level—the intersection of the spiritual and the political. I tried to acknowledge that in the opera—the concurrence of Coltrane and Malcolm in the 1960s. For example, when Malcolm's brother Reginald, who has already joined the Nation of Islam, visits Malcolm in prison in the beginning of the second act, he sings 'Elijah is the messenger/the messenger of Allah.' It's meant to have the sweep of John Coltrane's tenor saxophone. Coltrane's phrasing was a style of preaching, and so were Malcolm's speeches. That's something else they had in common—and I tried to capture that without drawing from Baptist church music, which is antithetical to Muslim devotional music."

"Malcolm had a great sense of rhetoric, a way of using homey expressions and giving them a double-edged meaning: 'the chickens coming home to roost,' for example, which he said to reporters about the Kennedy assassination," says Thulani Davis. The author of two volumes of poetry, she has contributed texts to pieces by her cousin, Anthony Davis, and her husband, saxophonist Joseph Jarman of the Art Ensemble of Chicago. "For the libretto, I tried to echo Malcolm's phrasing without using too much of his actual phraseology. I wanted a distillation of his speech, not the actual speeches. I tried to keep the language simple and direct, without too much embellishment or metaphor. I know that some of Malcolm's followers are probably worried that we're going to declaw Malcolm in order to make him safe for opera. Those people are going to be surprised. They're going to be impressed with the amount of research we've done on the subtle differences between the Black Muslims and the orthodox Muslims in the way they worship and what they believe, with the care we've taken to ensure that the prayers are right, the pronunciations are correct."

*When I was little / They called me 'nigger,' / Called me 'nigger'
so much, / I thought it was my name,* Malcolm (who was born Malcolm Little) sings to a potential convert on the corner of 125th Street
and Seventh Avenue in the second act. "That was a joke he used to
tell," Thulani Davis explains, "and it's a very telling joke. The importance of *naming* is one of the thematic links in the libretto. Malcolm experienced several rebirths, each involving the taking of a new
name, a new way of defining who he was—Malcolm Little, Detroit
Red, Malcolm X, and finally El Hajj Malik El-Shabazz, Islamic for
'one who is reborn.' When the Muslims hit on the idea of renaming
themselves, they tapped into something very old and powerful and
almost forgotten. Naming is an Africanism—in some African religions, the belief is that a woman becomes pregnant because the man
whispers the name of their offspring in her ear while they're making
love. So names are sacred. But when we were brought to America,
our names were taken away from us. Slaves often had successions of
names not of their own choosing—they would be given another name
every time they were sold. This was something Elijah Muhammad
talked about, and it struck a responsive chord in Malcolm and untold
numbers of other black Americans—the idea that the names they
were born with said nothing about who they were or what they might
become.

Which comes first? The words or the music? "The words," Anthony
Davis said, in response to the clichéd question I was almost too embarrassed to ask. "To do it the opposite way would restrict Thulani
too much, though I might have a figure in mind that I'll play for her
to see if she can do anything with it, and, of course, we both confer
with Christopher about what he's trying to depict. But Thulani's
blank verse lends itself very readily to music, and she has a foolproof
ear for what music can and cannot be sung—and no reluctance to
tell me which is which."

"Anthony's score is a remarkable accomplishment," says Thulani
Davis. "The opera spans thirty years in Malcolm's life, which were
also thirty years during which black music was evolving at a rapid

pace. When Malcolm was wearing a zoot suit and running numbers, the big bands were still popular; by the time he was murdered, another kind of jazz was taking form with John Coltraine and Ornette Coleman, and whether or not Malcolm was aware of them is unimportant. The point is that their music reflected the black consciousness of that period, no less than Malcolm's philosophy did. Another composer might have taken the easy way out and simply recreated those different musical styles. But Anthony has filtered them through the prism of his own music to create an exciting and original work."

(JUNE 1984)

# IV

Only the first act was staged when X debuted as a work-in-progress in Philadelphia in 1984. (In addition, there was an oratorio-like presentation of choral numbers from the second act.) In my review in the following morning's *Philadelphia Inquirer*, I wrote that as an idealistic attempt to couch a story from black America in the lofty diction of the opera house, X was heir to *Treemonisha*, the Scott Joplin opera which folded after a single performance in Harlem in 1911 and was not resurrected until 1975, when Joplin was awarded a posthumous Pulitzer Prize. I wished X and its composer a kinder fate, but if you read between the lines, you could tell that I doubted that a kinder fate was in store.

Happily, I was wrong. X received its first full-length production in Philadelphia fifteen months later, on its way to its grand premiere by the New York City Opera in 1986. (What's the difference between a first full-length production and a grand premiere? Cultural politics. Beverly Sills and City Opera have more clout than the Philadelphia-based American Music Theater Festival. Regardless of who wins custody, however, X is clearly AMTF's baby, and the opera's speedy reappearance is eloquent testimony to AMTF's willingness to nurture a major work from conception to maturity—the ultimate measure of a company's stature, long after the overnight reviews have yellowed and the box office receipts have been tallied.) The full-length X offers more than operatic sound and fury. As directed by Rhoda Levine, it's kinetic drama; John Conklin's set design is more spartan than it needs to be (what a friend of mine calls Regulation Experimental Theater, with chair slats serving as cell bars, etc.), but Levin's blocking and Curt Osterman's spectral lighting fill in a lot of the blank spaces. And Christopher Davis's story, in combination with Thulani Davis's taut, fierce, declamatory libretto, passes the fundamental test of drama, in the process of underlining Malcolm's bitter and ironic twist on Horatio Alger: even though Malcolm's life and death are matters of public record, one sits waiting to see what's going to happen next, what motives and psychological consequences the authors are going to attribute to events taken from yesterday's headlines.

The most obvious level on which X succeeds, however, is as an evening of intricate and propulsive music by one of America's most gifted and adamantly uncategorizable younger composers. Major new operas are rare enough, but works of this scale by black composers are all but non-existent, because so few black composers have been given the necessary carte blanche. The staggering cost of mounting three performances of X in Philadelphia, with a 35-piece orchestra and a 40-member cast (including figurants)—estimated at $250,000 by an unofficial source close to the AMTF—perhaps provides a clue to Anthony Davis's displeasure with the word "jazz." Unlike their classical and theatrical counterparts, who enjoy the benefit of well-established institutional support systems, jazz composers must apply for funding as individuals, which effectively rules out the possibility of a jazz composer raising a quarter of a million dollars for a single project. Ironically, though—as Davis points out—if there were not separate categories for jazz, black composers might not be funded at all. (Along the way to its full-length debut at the Walnut Street Theater in October 1985, X received grants from the Ford Foundation; the National Institute for Music Theater; the Kitchen Center for Video, Music, Dance, Performance and Film; the Opera Music

Theater Program of the National Endowment for the Arts; and various other public and corporate funding programs.)

To put an unfortunate misconception to rest once and for all, X is no ersatz "jazz" opera, unlike another of 1984's AMTF offerings, Noah Ain's *Trio,* which was jazz only in the sense that its all black cast sang melismatic drivel, and opera only in the sense that it said it was. Although Davis's score for X involves some improvisation by the members of Episteme, functioning concerto-grosso style from inside the orchestra, none of the singing is in the vernacular, not even the few bars of atonal scat the character of Street unleashes in the opening act. Like Philip Glass and Steve Reich, Davis favors inner-moving harmonies and cyclical, busy-bee rhythms borrowed from Indonesia; and the calculated disparity in scale between a "minimalist" score and a larger-than-life mise-en-scène with a twentieth-century archetype at the center is bound to tempt some to compare X to *Satyagraha* and *Einstein on the Beach.* But Davis's voicings are sleeker and more cosmopolitan than Glass's, and a comparison to Duke Ellington or Charles Mingus might be more in order. Davis's score echoes Glass and Reich; Ellington, Mingus, and John Coltrane; the ballads from *West Side Story* and *Sweeney Todd.* It recycles some of Davis's own chamber and solo works, including "Clonetics," "A Walk through the Shadow," and "Middle Passage," and there are probably references to Wagner and Stravinsky that fly right over my head. But finally, the score is all Davis, and it's like nothing one has heard before, even from him. Here at last is that Third Stream, that confluence of the idiomatic and the formal, that John Lewis and Gunther Schuller prophesized in the 1960s but were never successful in achieving in their own works. Although X might not *be* jazz, it is of obvious potential importance *to* jazz, if only for the glorious passages accompanying Malcolm's conversion to Islam and his pilgrimage to Mecca, in which Davis redeems Coltrane-like glossalalia and billowing modal textures that one had come to think of as devalued through over-use.

It might not be common practice in reviewing opera to single out individual members of the orchestra for praise, but X is no ordinary opera, and Episteme is no ordinary pit orchestra. (Besides, send a jazz critic to the opera, and you see what happens.) Saxophonists Dwight Andrews and Marty Ehrlich turned in several molten, wailing improvisations; and trombonist Ray Anderson shook the walls with his tailgating during the sequences set in the Boston ghetto demimonde in the 1940s.

In its own way, of course, opera is as empirical an art form as jazz, which is to say that an opera—*any* opera—is only as good as the cast which sings it. In this respect, Davis has been lucky. X proves that there is no shortage of talented black opera singers and stage actors, even if roles created specially for them have been at a premium. (The credits under the performers' names in *Playbill* include *Evita, Jesus Christ Superstar, Sophisticated Ladies, The Cotton Club,* and even *Miami Vice,* in addition to *Porgy and Bess, Treemonisha, Faust, Cavalleria Rusticana,* and *The CIVIL warS.*) As Malcolm, Avery Brooks was magic, riveting the eye from the word go, even though he didn't get to sing a note until the final number of the first act. Brooks, who stole the show in a minor role when X was presented as a work-in-progress in 1984, was promoted to the lead for workshop performances in Harlem and Brooklyn in the summer of 1985, but left the cast when ABC tapped him to play Hawk, Robert Urich's fly, glowering alter-ego in the fall series *Spenser: For Hire,* based on the detective novels of Robert B. Parker. Following Brooks's defection, the Metropolitan Opera's Michael Smartt—a 1984 Tony nominee for the Houston Grand Opera's production of *Porgy and Bess*—signed on as Malcolm. But Smartt bowed out before opening night in Philadelphia, and Brooks stepped back in at the last minute. What a gruelling week it must have been for Brooks, who flew back and forth from Boston to Philadelphia daily, shooting his TV series in the mornings and performing a role that required him to be on stage three solid hours at night. If Brooks had found it necessary to look at a crib sheet, one would have been inclined to forgive him under the circumstances. But he didn't, at least not during the performance I attended. In Brooklyn over the summer, Brooks bore an uncanny physical resemblance to Malcolm; in Philadelphia, with his pate shaved clean for his TV role, he forfeited that advantage. Yet he conveyed so much inner turmoil and determination with his carriage, his hand gestures, and the set of his jaw that he still recalled the charisma of the real Malcolm X. It had little to do with the doo rag that Brooks affected during the prison scenes or the rimless glasses he donned later on to signal Malcolm's spiritual and intellectual awakening—these were merely props a more literal-minded performer might have used to launch an impersonation. What Brooks was doing was *acting*, and it was a treat to watch in a day and age when TV docu-dramas have persuaded actors that impersonation is good enough.

Brooks exudes such star power that one suspects he has to work overtime not to upstage other actors. In *Spenser: For Hire,* with the doughnut-hole they call Robert Urich as his only competition, Brooks chews up the scenery. X proved his ability to fit into an ensemble. As Street—the role Brooks originated in 1984—Thomas Young had a tough act to follow, but he succeeded in making the part his own. Young was also Elijah Muhammad, a daring bit of dual casting (sin and salvation as opposite sides of the same coin) intended to provide Brooks's Malcolm with a consistent antagonist, a recurring father-figure, from act to act. It worked because Young is such a versatile singer and actor, and because his tenor blended so melifluously with Brooks's bass baritone, and there was such physical chemistry between them. Priscilla Baskerville, whose boundless soprano was put to frivolous uses in the film *The Cotton Club* and the original Broadway production of *Sophisticated Ladies,* brought a restrained pathos to her role as Malcolm's mother; and there was fine singing by Kevin Maynor and Deborah Ford as Malcolm's brother and sister, Reginald and Ella. In fact, the only principal cast member whose singing left anything to be desired was Avery Brooks, an all-arounder who lacks only an opera singer's verismo—a shortcoming that was unnoticeable at the Brooklyn Academy of Workshop performances over the summer but occasionally proved telling in Philadelphia's thousand-seat Walnut Street Theater. Difficult though it might have been to imagine a more convincing Malcolm, given Brooks's countless other attributes, it would have been interesting to hear a traditional opera singer like Michael Smartt in the role (and, as Christopher Davis pointed out before Smartt's withdrawal, this is precisely what is going to have to happen if X is to enter the standard repertoire).

Apart from Brooks's lack of operatic credibility, I spotted two other flaws, both of them minor. Because Christopher Davis's story telescopes 30 years of Malcolm's life (and 30 years of American panorama) into some 3,500 bars of music and three hours of real time, some of the transitions are bumpy—for example: on the basis of what they saw depicted on stage, those members of the audience who haven't thumbed *The Autobiography of Malcolm X* lately might have assumed that the Boston police jailed the pre-Black Nationalist Malcolm for miscegenation, not burglary. And Anthony Davis's overture, although an estimable piece of music given a buoyant reading by pianist Marilyn Crispell, is just too lengthy to fulfill its intended dramatic purpose. As the overture builds to a succession of crescendos, the cast assembles on stage in groups of two and three in anticipation of the action—a beginning borrowed from *Sweeney Todd*, most likely. The only problem is that we don't yet know who any of these people are, and their dress doesn't give their identities away, the way it might in a *Sweeney*-esque period piece. Still, this static mode of introduction at least serves notice that the actors will be doubling as witnesses to history (the entire cast is on stage a good deal of the evening, with spotlights isolating the featured singers in any given scene). It also contributes to a Brechtian distancing effect which, though already something of an avant-garde cliché, is a welcome development in black musical theater, which—following the box office grosses of *Ain't Misbehavin', Dream Girls,* and even *The Gospel at Colonus*—seems in constant jeopardy of signifying nothing more than a nostalgic trip uptown with those folks who sure do love to sing and dance.

In the long run, though, it might be audiences who choose to keep a distance—white opera-goers because of the volatility of Christopher Davis's story, the resolute modernism of Anthony Davis's score, and the Muslim esoterica in Thulani Davis's libretto; blacks and jazz fans because of the air of privilege and foppish refinement surrounding opera. In my original review, I worried that X might not soon find its ideal audience. Frankly, I still worry. The opening nighters I saw it with (the usual fat cats, with a heavier black delegation than normal) grew restless as the evening went on, and I thought it churlish of them to withhold from Avery Brooks and the rest of the cast the standing ovations and endless curtain calls they so richly deserved. Despite the imprimatur of City Opera, some companies are going to see X as nothing more than an equal-opportunities write-off: Anthony Davis tells me that one prestigious West Coast company asked if he could stage his opera in inner city playgrounds next summer (his response was to ask if they would expect Philip Glass and Robert Wilson to mount a portable *Einstein on the Beach* outdoors), and Thulani Davis adds that many classical-music types have asked her why her cousin can't do the opera with just his band and a small choir. I'm not sure the world is ready for a full-fledged black opera, much less an opera about Malcolm X, but I hope that my skepticism proves unwarranted. I ended my first review by saying that X had the potential for greatness, and on that score I think the full-length version proved me right. This is a show at once so subtle and overpowering that you leave the theater whistling the chord changes. Like *Sweeney Todd*, it convinces you that, if what they say is true—that all art aspires to music—all music should aspire to opera.

(OCTOBER 1985)

# The Right Stuff

Like most other fields of endeavor these days, jazz is governed by a rigid code of attitudes embraced as just and proper by performers and onlookers alike, and Wynton Marsalis would thus seem to be cut from all the right stuff. Consider his credentials: youthful idealism enflamed by personal ambition, brassy self-assurance muted by a gentleman's decorum in dress and behavior, a genuine reverence toward the music's history equaled by a machismo drive toward furthering its propagation. And as the offspring of the neglected New Orleans pianist Ellis Marsalis, the trumpeter is a certified second-generation jazz musician, which gives him quite a boost in a period when much of what passes for jazz criticism romanticizes the bonds between figurative fathers and sons. Scornful of pop, funk, fusion, free jazz, and anything else that strikes him as compromise or sham, Marsalis is as infuriating a paradox as Tom Wolff's astronauts—a rugged individualist out to restore traditional values with little tolerance for those who play by a looser set of rules; a straight arrow who talks like a rebel, though what he's rebelling against is non-conformity. According to Marsalis, jazz went crazy in the 1960s for the same reason the rest of the world did: no one was tough enough, dedicated enough, *man* enough, to live up to responsibilities. Although it's difficult to fault Marsalis as a trumpeter or bandleader, I sometimes wonder what it says about this era in jazz that so resolutely conservative a young musician has become its cynosure.

Marsalis has two bravura new albums united by the obeisance each shows for the touchstones in its respective idiom, one a jazz album featuring his quintet, the other a program of Haydn, Mozart, and Hummel with conductor Raymond Leppard and the National Philharmonic. *Trumpet Concertos* (CBS IM-37846) is a record any trumpeter could be proud of and no jazz listener need fear. One need hardly be intimate with the classical repertoire to appreciate Marsalis's technical prowess and interpretive humility, or to recognize in the Haydn concerto (1796) the transcendent sweep of an epochal piece of music. Next to the Haydn, the playful Leopold Mozart concert in D major (1762) sounds lightweight, and the Hummel (1804) turns cheesy in its orchestral pomp. But cheesy or not, the Hummel is the showcase that invites a trumpeter to flaunt his virtuosity over the entire range of the horn, and it's fun listening to Marsalis show off. His few transgressions on these concertos (the extra spin he applies to his trills on the final movement of the Haydn piece, for example) are merely venal exuberance. *Trumpet Concertos* is a triumph for Marsalis, but what is he going to do for an encore? Of necessity, classical music must remain a diversion for him—one or two more albums would exhaust the standard literature for trumpet, and he has shown no inclination to collaborate with avant-garde classical composers.

No, for Marsalis the term "classical music" means music from the late-18th and early-19th century. And currently, jazz also risks limiting itself to a period of classicism—beginning with Charlie Parker ambling into Minton's in the early '40s and ending with Ornette Coleman boarding a plane for New York in 1959. During those two decades, bebop became synonymous with jazz, and like many of his generation, Marsalis owes strongest allegiance to this era. *Think of One* (Columbia FC-38641) finds him succeeding Miles Davis as arbiter of what the jazz mainstream can absorb and what in all good conscience it cannot. The problem is that Marsalis is reluctant to go beyond the point where Davis left off after abdicating around 1967 (polyrhythms and atonality are oh-so-tentatively broached) so that portions of *Think of One* could be retitled *Recapitulatin' with the Miles Davis Quintet.*

For all that, *Think of One* is a vivacious record, a partial fulfill-ment of the glories promised on Marsalis's eponymous 1982 debut (Columbia FC-37574), although nothing approaches the excitement of the earlier record's piano-less "Hesitation," on which the trumpeter and his brother, saxophonist Branford Marsalis, improvised simul-taneously on "I Got Rhythm" changes with enough élan to rival Ornette Coleman and Don Cherry. Not the least impressive of Wynton Marsalis's many talents in his ability to captain a tight ship. Pianist Kenny Kirkland, drummer Jeff Watts, and alternating bassists Phil Bowler and Ray Drummond make up a responsive ryhthm sec-tion that shows firm initiative in channeling the horn solos. Marsalis is in handsome form, his solos bursting with irascible growls and puckered runs; and Branford paces him with dryly engaging soprano and tenor solos. The nicely varied set includes prickly, quicksilver originals by Drummond, Kirkland, and the leader; a supernal Elling-ton ballad; the standard "My Ideal"; and an ingenuous stop-and-go treatment of the Thelonious Monk title tune.

*Think of One*'s most encouraging tactic—the emphasis on variety, pacing, and group interaction—will be taken by many for a lack of spontaneity, I'm afraid; and it is true that Marsalis projects more vividly in concert. *Jazz at the Opera House* (Columbia C2-38430), produced by the late jazz critic Conrad Silvert, offers the juiciest live Marsalis on record thus far. Silvert brought to San Francisco a dozen or so of his favorite soloists (including Marsalis, saxophonist Wayne Shorter, pianist Herbie Hancock, bassist Charlie Haden, drummer Tony Williams, and vibist Bobby Hutcherson) and deployed them in random combinations. For the most part, the predictable jam-session rodomontade ensued, but this twofer is worth hearing if only for Wayne Shorter's inky, enveloping tenor (not exactly a plentiful commodity these days) and the crackling Marsalis solos on "Hesita-tion" and "Sister Cheryl." The remaining titles indicate an overworked and listless program—let's call a moratorium on "Round Midnight," "Maiden Voyage," and "Straight, No Chaser" *right now*. Marsalis or no Marsalis, *Jazz at the Opera House* intimates that jazz too is quickly succumbing to a shortage of repertoire, and that it is going to take more than valiant efforts by steadfast keepers of the faith to replenish the supply.

(AUGUST 1983)

# II

Wynton Marsalis came to Philadelphia one day in the summer of 1983 to do advance publicity for an upcoming concert, and a tiring round of interviews and tapings had put him in a salty, contentious mood by evening, when I caught up with him. He conceded that he had been the beneficiary of the kind of build-up seldom lavished on jazz musicians anymore. "But you know why I've gotten all that publicity?" he asked. "Not just because I was so young when people first heard of me. This music has a long history of prodigies, and nobody thought it was unusual when Lee Morgan went on the road with Dizzy Gillespie when he was 17 or 18, or Paul Chambers went out with Miles Davis at around the same age. No, see, when I first came to New York in 1979, everybody was talking about fusion. Everybody was saying that jazz was dead because no young black musicians wanted to play it anymore, and because the established cats who should have been setting an example were *bull*shittin', wearing dresses* and trying to act like rock stars. So when people heard me, they knew it was time to start takin' care of business again. I wasn't playing shit no one had ever heard before, but at least I was playing some real music."

Marsalis, who was born in 1961, overdramatizes the plight of jazz

---

* It later dawned on me that by dresses, Marsalis meant the dashikis many black musicians wore in the nationalistic '70s. At least I hope that's what he meant.

before his coming, but let it pass—it is indisputable that he has had a rejuvenating effect on jazz, if only in terms of winning it more media coverage. I asked him why he had stipulated to CBS that he also be recorded as a classical artist. "Because I like that kind of music, and it's important that people know I can play it," he said. "That way, what I have to say about jazz will carry more weight. I intimidate people because I know what I'm talking about. People try to say I'm arrogant, but I never said I could play. Hell, man, I'm still learning . . . I still have astronomical amounts of shit to learn, and that's not just false modesty either. That's the attitude you have to have. When Miles Davis was my age, he wasn't shit, either. He was still imitating Fats Navarro on some of those early sides he cut with Bird in the 1940s."

Asked to name the trumpeters who most influenced him personally, Marsalis rattled off what might just as well have been a litany of Great Trumpeters recited from memory—Davis, Navarro, Louis Armstrong, Dizzy Gillespie, Freddie Hubbard, Don Cherry, and Woody Shaw. Cherry is the only surprise on the list, and Marsalis is begrudging in his praise of the former Ornette Coleman sideman. "I think Cherry brought the trumpet to its furthest point conceptually—him and Miles. But Cherry has never bothered to learn to play his instrument. He doesn't project—sometimes you can't even hear what he's playing. That's why fellow musicians don't show him the respect he deserves. Every musician who has been a jazz innovator has also been a master technician—every single one. So you can't include Cherry among the innovators. But he and Ornette Coleman did some things every other musician picked up on—with Coltrane, the debt to Ornette was publicized; all the other cats tried to pretend it was just something they thought of themselves by coincidence. Miles is a prime example of that."

I noticed that Marsalis's conversation kept drifting back to Miles Davis, which seemed fitting, since the Prince of Darkness also casts a long shadow over Marsalis's solos, particularly those at slow and medium tempos. And significantly, Marsalis happened along in jazz at a time when Davis's comeback had dashed all hopes that he would return to his style of the mid-'60s—and when many listeners for whom mid-'60s Miles was still the quintessence of jazz were desperately casting about for a new idol. "People are always coming up to me and saying, 'You hear what Miles said about you?'" Marsalis complained, "I say, 'I don't care what Miles has to say about me.' I love Miles. He's one of the greatest musicians this century has produced, but you wouldn't know that from listening to the crap he's trying to peddle to the public now. The only thing I wanna hear Miles talk about is what he thinks *he's* doing. Let him explain that."

Davis was present the night that Marsalis received his first trumpet. "I was about five or six, and Miles, Clark Terry, Al Hirt, and my father were all sitting around a table in Al's club in New Orleans—this was when my father was still working in Al's band. My father, just joking around because there were so many trumpeters sitting there, said, 'I better buy Wynton a trumpet.' And Al said 'Ellis, let me give your boy one of mine.' It's ironic looking back on it, because Miles said, 'Don't give it to him. Trumpet's too difficult an instrument for him to learn.' Ha!"

That trumpet sat in its case untouched until Marsalis was 12. In high school, he played it in funk bands "that did cover versions of Earth Wind & Fire and the Commodores—all that bullshit." At 14, he performed the demanding Haydn Trumpet Concerto with the New Orleans Philharmonic. But it wasn't until 1979, when he dropped out of Juilliard School to join Art Blakey's Jazz Messengers that Marsalis began to play jazz in earnest. "I sat in with Blakey, and he was impressed with my technique, so he hired me on the spot. But I was still pretty raw. There were things I would have had together by that age if I had been born back in another period, if I had been able to hear the giants of jazz like Coltrane and Miles and Jackie McLean and Kenny Dorham on the radio when I was coming up, the way earlier generations were able to. But I'm telling you, things will be that way again real soon."

Marsalis was implying that there are plenty more where he came from, and his words already have the ring of fulfilled prophecy. Terence Blanchard, the New Orleans trumpeter who replaced Marsalis with the Jazz Messengers, was 19 and looked about 12, but he knew his way around his horn. And young saxophonists Donald Harrison and Jean Touissaint have also followed the Marsalises up the pipeline from the Crescent City to the Big Apple, with the requisite stopover in the Jazz Messengers. According to Marsalis, still more upstarts are on the way, not all of them from New Orleans. "We're entering a period now when there are young kids 14 and 15 years old all over the country who can really play. They'll all be emerging four or five years from now, and they'll insist on being heard. I don't think people are going to try to sound like me, but you are going to see young cats getting serious about their music, and I definitely think I have something to do with that."

(JUNE 1983)

# III

Although jazz musicians have long regarded string sections as a sign of class, their notions of what constitutes "class" have changed over the years—not necessarily for the better, either. Robert Freedman's string arrangements for *Hot House Flowers* (Columbia FC-39530), Wynton Marsalis's collection of romantic ballads, are not as tatty as those Neal Hefti penned for Clifford Brown in 1955, or those Jimmy Carroll concocted for Charlie Parker in 1949. But in their busy eclecticism, their overinflated moodiness, and their coy brushes with an already outmoded concept of modernity, Freedman's charts vie with the soloist in a way that Hefti and Carroll's less ostentatious backings did not. Give Freedman credit for ingenuity, if nothing else. Can you imagine John Lewis's "Django" without its walloping bass line? Unfortunately Freedman can, and in his hands, Lewis's noble ode to the gypsy guitarist Django Reinhardt becomes a three-handkerchief tear jerker with no undercurrent of celebration.

Yet *Hot House Flowers* is a pleasant enough listening experience, thanks to Marsalis's growing maturity as a balladeer. Like many younger improvisers, he used to camouflage his discomfort at slow tempos by accelerating into double time at the earliest opportunity. (It was as though he regarded melody as so much pretty wrapping he had to rip off in order to get at the chord changes, the good stuff inside the box.) Here he resists that temptation, and his phrasing is airborn no matter how lugubrious the setting. Still, he never really cuts loose until the pace quickens a bit and the strings retreat to a moderate distance behind a choir of brass and woodwinds on the Miles-ian "When You Wish upon a Star" and the engagingly frivolous "I'm Confessin'"—and then his ardent playfulness wins one over completely. Branford Marsalis, sporting a thicker tone and a slower vibrato than usual, also turns in his liveliest work on these two numbers, by far the jauntiest on the album.

Meanwhile, Marsalis's second classical LP, which also features the soprano Edita Gruberova, is a grab bag of excerpts from Handel and Purcell and trifles from minor eighteenth-century composers.* Marsalis has just about depleted the existing literature for trumpet, and this calls into question the wisdom of the dual career he apparently envisions for himself. If he wishes to maintain a presence in classical music, perhaps CBS should think about commissioning original works for him. In any event, it would do him no harm to collaborate with composers whose definitions of jazz and classical music are less schematic than his own, and who do not regard the two disciplines as yin and yang—Anthony Davis, for example. Heaven knows, Marsalis could use the stretch.

(OCTOBER 1984)

## IV

"Nobody believes I'm a year older than Wynton," complains Branford Marsalis. "It's not just that everyone heard of Wynton before they heard of me. I just *look* young. Wynton's band is going to Japan

* Columbia Masterworks IM-39061.

again soon, so I had to have new snapshots taken for a visa. I held them up against my passport photo, which was taken four years ago, and I haven't aged a day. I still look like a baby boy.

"The older I get, though, the more I respect a decision my father made which didn't make much of an impression on me when I was growing up. He sacrificed his career in order to live up to his responsibilities as a family man, and that's something you don't expect from a musician—from anyone, really. Everybody you meet these days is so goal-oriented, so *me*-oriented. My father stayed in New Orleans and played with Al Hirt's band until around 1968, when he accepted a teaching job for some small amount of money. And if he was frustrated, he never moaned about it. He never let on to us. That's why I'm not married. When I do get married and have kids, I don't want to be on the road, away from home all the time. I want it to be right, and I want it to last—just like my parents' marriage."

More easygoing than his younger brother, Branford is no less forthcoming. But he would neither confirm nor deny rumors that he too will soon release a classical album. "*If* that happens, they'll probably have to transpose pieces originally written for oboe or violin or soprano voice, so that I can play them on soprano saxophone. Contrary to popular belief, there are at least 150 saxophone showpieces in the classical literature. The problem is they're all so dull, there's no point in performing any of them."*

One exception, he concedes, is the *Concerto for Saxophone and Orchestra* by Alexander Glazunov, a turn-of-the-century Russian composer. "That's the piece I performed when I auditioned—unsuccessfully—for the New Orleans Symphony five or six years ago. Nobody in the orchestra had even heard of it! The conductor asked me which movement I was going to play, and I had to say, " 'Er, it's all in one movement, sir, so I'm just going to play excerpts.' He said 'A concerto in

---

* Branford Marsalis's comments need updating. He and Teresa Reese were married in Paris in the spring of 1985, around the same time that he began work on a classical album. Meanwhile, according to the latest scuttlebutt, Wynton Marsalis has banished both Branford and pianist Kenny Kirkland from his band as punishment for recording *The Dream of the Blue Turtles* (A&M SP-3850) with the pop-star Sting.

one movement! That's impossible! Let me see that score . . . oh, boy, you're right!' I knew I was in trouble right then and there, because they felt like they had egg all over their faces, just like if you went to a jazz concert and requested an old tune nobody in the band knew.

"In all fairness, though, both of the saxophonists who auditioned after me played the Glazunov too, and *they* made the orchestra. They were further advanced than me—really nailed that piece down, the jerks."

Marsalis has experienced few setbacks since then. His rise to prominence has been meteoric, even if he remains somewhat overshadowed by his younger brother, with whom he currently shares a duplex in Brooklyn. Since the release of the spotty *Scenes in the City* (Columbia FC-38951) in 1984, the saxophonist has become a bandleader in his own right, "just to keep busy and to experiment during those periods when Wynton is engaged with other projects."

The saxophone was not the instrument Marsalis cut his teeth on, nor did he grow up envisioning a career in jazz. "I wanted to play drums, but my father didn't want all that racket around the house, and he didn't want a drum set falling on him every time he opened the door to the closet—he had a feeling that would be where whatever instrument he bought for me would wind up. So instead, he bought be a clarinet when I was about 8 years old, the same year that Wynton got his first trumpet.

"I *hated* the sound of the clarinet. It didn't penetrate the way a saxophone can, and my teachers wouldn't let me use any vibrato on it, either. Plus, if you play clarinet, other kids say you're a sissy—a sweet boy, you know? But I stuck with the thing, and finally I got an alto saxophone for Christmas the year I was in eighth grade, just in time to join the high school jazz band, even though I wasn't particularly interested in jazz then. My father's record collection only went up to 1960, and although that stuff was wonderful, it didn't feel like a social expression of *my* time. Wynton used to keep after me to take jazz more seriously and to practice more, but I didn't care. I just wanted to be a pop arranger and record producer—the next Quincy

Jones. I figured I'd learn just enough about jazz harmony to drop the big chord at the right moment, go to L.A. and make the big money."

What changed his plans was his exposure to the record collection of drummer Marvin "Smitty" Smith, his classmate at the Berklee School of Music in Boston. "I started off at Southern University, where I studied with [clarinetist] Alvin Batiste and roomed with [alto saxophonist] Donald Harrison. Donald and I were pretty big stuff at Southern, because there weren't that many good musicians enrolled, and we could afford to coast. But at the end of our freshman year, Alvin told us that if we came back to Southern the next semester, it was an automatic 'F' for us the minute we walked through the door. There was no motivation at Southern, and he knew that would hold us back. So we transferred to Berklee, and that's where I met Smitty.

"Smitty played me *Miles Smiles* and *Nefertiti* and all those great records Miles made in the mid '60s with Wayne Shorter, Herbie Hancock, Ron Carter, and Tony Williams; and that music just blew me away. For the first time in my life, I became immersed in music, almost to the exclusion of having a social life or remembering to eat three times a day."

That was in the fall of 1979. Just three years later, Marsalis was touring Japan with Hancock, Carter, Williams, and brother Wynton in VSOP II. "For the first three weeks, all I could think of was how I used to sit in my dorm room listening to records by these guys and staring at their photos, until finally Ron took me aside and said, 'Look, we ain't payin' you to stand there admiring us. *Play!*' After that, I was all right."

Indeed, nothing fazes him now, not even rubbing elbows with mega-celebrities at last spring's Grammys, where his brother walked off with trophies in both classical music and jazz. "It was so plastic backstage, man, with the servants to the stars running around giving orders like *they* were stars, too. This big bodyguard that worked for Irene Cara or Donna Summer—one of them chicks, I forget which— wouldn't even let us walk down the hallway past her dressing room.

We had to run and get a security guard just to prove to him that we were authorized to be there! Everybody was looking at us like 'Who are *you?*' until after we performed and Wynton made his little speech.* Then it was all 'Oh, *hello* there!' Spare me, I thought, spare me."

Marsalis says that it doesn't bother him when critics complain that he phrases too much like Wayne Shorter. "Better they should compare me to someone hip like Wayne than to Ace Cannon. Would you believe that my nickname at Southern was Ace? Which really used to piss me off." What he fails to take into account is that Cannon might have been a more inspired choice as a model, given the hoard of Shorter imitators already on the scene. The critical backlash that has been mounting against the Marsalis brothers is, I think, more an expression of dismay at their musical atavism than one of resentment at their overnight media access. After all, jazz has undergone countless stylistic permutations since those mid-'60s Miles Davis LPs that serve as Wynton and Branford's point of departure were first issued. The brothers' belated discovery of those records may have tricked them into thinking they were hearing something new; likewise, to the middlebrow audience which ignored jazz altogether before embracing Wynton Marsalis, any jazz beyond Count Basie sounds adventurous in the extreme. The Marsalis brothers may be musical reactionaries who are fooling even themselves into believing that they are radicals. And they may occasionally echo their idols Davis and Shorter a little too closely. They have accomplished so much so fast that it is sometimes shocking to realize how much they still have to learn—I once heard Branford play Johnny Mercer's "I'm an Old Cowhand," which he announced afterwards as "a tune by Sonny Rollins, called 'Way Out West'"; if he and his brother quote Tin Pan Alley less frequently than their elders, I suspect it's because they know fewer songs. But

---

* Denouncing commercialism, compromise, and (some observers believed) Herbie Hancock, whose band had just performed "Rockit," accompanied by break dancers dressed as robots.

what makes them so special—Branford no less than Wynton—is their ability to sound fresh and vibrant within the confines of a largely played-out genre, no mean feat for musicians of any generation. They are still at an age when it is fair to categorize them as promising—no less than that, but no more, either.

(OCTOBER 1984)

# The Tenor of These Times

"The music has to start swinging again," announces tenor saxophonist David Murray, whose words on such matters are worth attending, as he has been a lodestar of change upon the jazz firmament almost from the moment he first burst upon New York in 1975. "I think it reflects the sociological aspects of the times. People don't want music they have to suffer through—Ronald Reagan's got them suffering enough already, and they want some relief from that. They're in the mood to hear something snappy, and I can deliver it, because I feel the same way. The last three years or so, whenever I go out to hear music, I just get bored and slip out the door unless the players are swinging or trying to excite me in some new way. So I decided to form a band that would be exciting all the time, no low points from start to finish. There's always something happening in my octet you can pat your foot to, even when we're not swinging in 4/4 per se."

Murray has exerted so forceful and decisive an influence within the jazz avant-garde for what seems like so long now that one has to make a conscious effort to remember that he is still under thirty, especially since his stocky build and self-possessed manner also belie his youth. Wherever progress has been made in jazz this last decade, Murray has been right there in the middle of things, making steady progress himself. He proved his evangelical fervor and his demon facility, his ability to go full-tilt all night and his readiness to take on all comers, during the loft bloodlettings of the mid-'70s. Realizing by the end of the decade that this anarchic approach to improvisation was leading him down a blind alley, Murray learned to pace himself more intelligently both as a sideman with James Blood Ulmer's free-funk Music Revelation Ensemble and Jack DeJohnette's Special Edition and as a founding member (with Julius Hemphill, Hamiet Bluiett, and Oliver Lake) of the powerfully thrusting yet delicately balanced World Saxophone Quartet.

The David Murray Octet is a scaled-down, more economically feasible model of the big band Murray assembled for concerts at Howard University and New York's Public Theater in 1978. "You're more industrious with a big band," Murray sighs, "and you can shake a building faster. I'd rather be writing for a big band, but since that's not practical at the moment, the octet has become my big band. You see, at the end of the '70s, it seemed to me that there was a need for a person my age to harness all the loose energy that was floating around into a vehicle that could contain it—a big band. It was something I felt *I* had to do, because it was something I felt I *could* do. I think that's what's going to make me stand out from all the other young tenor players out there now—I want to be known for *all* I can do, and that includes writing music and leading bands as well as just playing the horn."

If Murray's declarations sound excessively self-promotional, consider the objective case to be made on his behalf. The open-ended writing and eruptive soloing on *Ming* and *Home*—the David Murray Octet's first two releases for the Italian label Black Saint*—attest that in renouncing bluster, Murray hasn't made the common mistake of sacrificing ardor, dynamism, and push in the bargain. When he speaks of wanting to present "swinging music," he is not another wounded rebel sounding a shaky retreat to hard-bop mannerism. Nor is he yet one more jazz blueblood proposing a marriage of convenience with

* Black Saint BSR-0045 and BSR-0055, respectively.

the new money of funk when he says that he wants to offer listeners "something snappy" to see them through the current economic crunch. There is a nascent movement toward consolidation afoot in jazz, and Murray's emergence as leader of the toughest, most vivacious, and most purposeful band going coincides so dramatically with the widespread reacknowledgement of such forgotten totems as versatility, formal excellence, and communicable swing as to suggest that coincidence has nothing whatsoever to do with it.

The close of a confusing decade for jazz and the beginning of the Reagan budget cuts was not the first juncture of history at which Murray deemed it imperative that he and his music rise to the occasion. "I'm a product of the '60s, I guess," he says, explaining that the day the Reverend Martin Luther King was assassinated in 1968 he was prevailed upon to address his Berkeley, California, junior high assembly "because I was student body president and popular both among the whites and the blacks, on account of being a musician and one of the better athletes in school. Everybody was talking about running outside and cracking heads, so I made this long impassioned speech about brotherhood, probably modeled after one of King's speeches, and when I finished talking, I called the Notations of Soul—this 15-piece soul revue I co-led with [pianist] Rodney Franklin—up on stage. We played for about two hours, until everybody stopped beating up on each other and began digging on each other again."

By that eventful day, the adolescent saxophonist (whose family had moved to integrated Berkeley from the Oakland ghetto while he was still in infancy) had already been playing professionally for over a year. He had first picked up a tenor saxophone at the age of nine, after learning the rudiments of harmony from his mother (a pianist in the Pentecostal church) and fingerings from his elder brother (an aspiring clarinetist). "Now that I double on bass clarinet, I almost wish in retrospect I had started off on clarinet as a kid, and I probably would have, too, if my brother hadn't beaten me to it. I wanted to be different."

While still in high school, Murray began sitting in with experimental bands in Berkeley and San Francisco. His jazz career began when he enrolled at Pomona College in Los Angeles and came under the wing of drummer, music critic, and (then) faculty member Stanley Crouch, whom he characterizes as a demanding teacher both in the classroom and on the bandstand. "I took an English course with Stanley as a pre-freshman that was tougher than any of the courses I took once school began for real. Because of Stanley's presence, there were always a lot of musicians on campus—Bobby Bradford, Butch and Wilber Morris, Charles Tyler, Arthur Blythe. Stanley was never critical of me in terms of my technique—because I had been playing pretty well before I ever met him, don't forget—but he never let up on me either. His criticisms were always more in the nature of suggestions: 'Why don't you try it this way? Why don't you check out this guy or that guy?' He'd point me in the right direction and trust me to go the rest of the way myself."

When Murray found himself pointing in the direction of New York, Crouch went to dramatic lengths to dissuade him from dropping out of school. "He wrote a surreal play called *Saxophone Man* for his Black Theater class, with me in the title role and big puppets with names like Big White City Weirdship and Nick the Goniff chasing me through the streets. It was his perception of what things would be like for me in New York. But I was determined to go, and I thought I might do pretty well there, because I was listening to all the records by the people who were supposed to be the leading young tenor players, and I thought I had something to say that was a little bit different."

Crouch must have ultimately conceded to his student's wisdom, because the two of them wound up journeying east together, renting a loft above an East Village jazz club, and producing their own concerts there when they were unable to crash established venues. It didn't take long for Murray to impress his peers or gather champions in the jazz press. Nor did it take long for a backlash to mount against him. For example: A California tenorist who arrived in New York a few years in advance of Murray, but had a harder time winning acceptance, once complained to me, "I saw David come here and get all these jobs and all these articles written about him overnight, and I got mad. I had played with him in San Francisco, and he wasn't *that* tremendous." (Of course, what this disgruntled musician failed to take into account was that the David Murray he had heard in the Bay Area was but a fledgling 15-year-old at the time.) Then, too, as Murray began touring Europe regularly, and as dozens of records were issued under his name on labels of various national origins, charges soon followed that he was spreading himself too thin.

"Actually, I never felt I was being recorded *enough*," Murray laughs, "because the records I made in Europe were all concert albums that didn't accurately pinpoint the progress I felt I was making. When I first came to New York, I think I was playing more melodically, almost the way I play now. But I was influenced by all the energy music I heard here, and started incorporating elements of that into my playing. And in Europe, if you've got a reputation as a free player, they expect you to play free. But gradually, I realized that wasn't what I wanted. If you listen to my records in chronological order, you'll notice me gradually laying off of the overblown notes. I still use energy techniques as a kind of capper to my solos. I try to use the top of my register to embellish what I've already done on the bottom. I try to put all my 'energy' into achieving pure, crystal-clear notes."

Visually, Murray is still a ball of fire when he solos, bucking from his knees in time to rhythms stated and implied and celebrating his high notes with small, swift leaps off the floor. But there is little wasted motion in the solos themselves. A thematic and sequential improviser who exhausts the possibilities inherent in one motif before moving on to the next, Murray likes to gnaw away at a line by sliding in and out of key and will often gradually ascend to the tenor's higher elevations to triumphantly sustain a high, needling squeal over his last few bars. Certain aspects of Murray's style—his sometimes braying, always exacerbated vibrato; his love of hill-and-valley intervals; his penchant for writing anthematic heads and advancing his solos through linear, melodic means—have led some writers (myself included) to proclaim him a scion of Albert Ayler. Murray himself claims greater familial bond with Coleman Hawkins, Ben Webster, and Paul Gonsalves—and one immediately thinks of the way he will sometimes widen his vibrato to a croon and cross his phrases with trills in apparent homage to those romantic old masters.

"Ayler was influential in making me wary of the dangers that can befall a jazz musician," Murray says. "After all, his body was found floating in the river.* That's what I was thinking of when I wrote 'Flowers for Albert,' but everyone heard the tune and all of a sudden decided I sounded just like Albert Ayler. But I never turned Albert's solos back to 16-RPM so I could transcribe them and play them note-for-note the way I did with Paul [Gonsalves]'s 27 choruses on Duke's 'Diminuendo and Crescendo in Blue' or Coleman Hawkins's 'Body and Soul,' or lots of other things. I've always liked Ornette Coleman's conception on tenor, from the first time I heard that a capella tenor solo he plays on the *Ornette on Tenor* LP. It's funny—everytime Ornette sees me, he tells me I should be playing alto, because I've got an unusual tenor embouchere, more like an alto player's. So I just tell him that as far as I'm concerned he should forget about alto and play tenor all the time."

Murray points out that not all his influences were saxophonists: "Duke Ellington has always been an inspiration for me, especially now that I'm writing for a larger instrumentation. I only wish I had that luxury Duke had of working all the time and keeping people on payroll so he could write specially for them. Right now, I have to think more in terms of the instrumentation itself, because the individuals in my octet change as different people become available."

The first two David Murray Octet records benefit from stable personnel drawn from the cream of New York's most advanced players: Butch Morris and Olu Dara, trumpets; George Lewis, trombone; Murray and Henry Threadgill, reeds; Anthony Davis, piano; Wilber Morris, bass; Steve McCall, drums. (Trombonist Craig Harris,

* Ayler's corpse was fished out of the East River in 1970; whether his death was the result of suicide or foul play has never been officially determined.

alto saxophonist Jimmy Lyons, pianist John Hicks, bassist Art Davis, and drummer Ed Blackwell have passed through the band since the records were made.) On *Ming*, in particular, Murray demonstrates ingenuity in revamping older material to suit new impulses and the individual characteristics of the men on hand, most notably in transforming "Dewey's Circle"—a breakneck tribute to tenor saxophonist Dewey Redman in its original quartet manifestation—into a sauntering New Orleans street parade, with the sassy Olu Dara serving as Grand Marshall. "I wanted to express my admiration for all the things the earliest black trumpeters accomplished with that instrument, and Olu, being the great cornetist that he is, naturally got the call and interpreted the piece beautifully." In performance by the octet, "Flowers for Albert" has tossed off its wreath of mourning to become a juking, devil-may-care Rollins-like near-calypso—it's as though the opportunity to score for a pride of horns awoke the optimist in Murray. "I'm learning there are more ways than one to play a composition," Murray says. "For instance, I just made 'Murray's Steps'—one of my older pieces that I still like to play—into a ballad just by changing the bridge. I sent Wynton Marsalis a chart of it, because I think it's something he and Branford could have a lot of fun with, if they decide to play it. I think a lot of my pieces have lasting qualities that could make them jazz standards, but since nobody else is playing them—people just want to play their own compositions these days—I guess I'll have to go on playing them different ways myself until I pass."

Murray lives with his second wife, the photographer Ming Smith (an earlier marriage to poet/playwright Ntozake Shange lasted but three stormy months) in a second-floor walk-up a few doors west of the corner where dreary Varick Street is welcomed into shimmering Seventh Avenue South, within walking distance of the Village Vanguard, Sweet Basil, and the other top drawer Greenwich Village clubs. Only recently has anyone been willing to pay Murray to take that walk. His octet made its club debut at Sweet Basil last fall and has been invited back for two weeks this summer.

The day I spoke with Murray, he was preparing to take his quartet—John Hicks, piano; Art Davis, bass; Ed Blackwell, drums—on a six-week tour of Europe. "I'm very excited about that. Art tells me that this is the most challenging group he's been part of since he played with Coltrane, and I'm very flattered. I've always been searching for the right chemistry in a quartet, and I think I've found it at last."

There are also special projects, such as the concert Murray played with strings at the Public Theater last December, and a confrontation with clarinetists Jimmy Hamilton, Alvin Batiste, and John Carter at the same site a few weeks later. And, of course, Murray is still involved with the World Saxophone Quartet. "I think we've really proved with that group that four saxophonists can now coexist, whereas 10 or 20 years ago, it would've become a cutting contest, a real bloodbath. Maybe 20 percent of what we do is written. The rest is collectively improvised once we agree on things like voicings and solo lengths and so on. If the mix of people was any different, it wouldn't work. But Oliver [Lake], Julius [Hemphill], and Hamiet [Bluiett] are old friends from St. Louis who have played together long enough to know what one another will do in any given situation, and I pick up on that."

So even if work isn't yet as plentiful as he might like, Murray suffers no shortage of creative outlets. A full-time big band remains an unfulfilled ambition,* but in the meantime, he is glad to settle for a configuration which combines a big band's sonic horsepower with the greater improvisational maneuverability of a small group. "I try to keep that standing-up excitement you get in a small band. You know what I mean? I've seen guys in big bands sitting down, reading their parts, and looking bored. I want my cats to pay attention to the charts, because I don't want them just blowing anything that comes into their heads all at the same time—I don't like that kind of thing

---

* Since this was written, the David Murray Big Band has made its recording debut (*Live at Sweet Basil, Volume 1*, Black Saint BSR-0085) and become a semi-regular attraction in New York clubs. Nonetheless, "full-time" remains the operative phrase.

anymore. But I also want them to watch me and follow what I do, because I conduct with my horn.* We're constantly inventing riffs behind the solos, and not all of them are going to be written down there on that piece of paper on the music stand."

Keeping an eye on David Murray might be a good idea, not only for the musicians in his groups, but for all of us hoping to gain an inkling of what's in store for jazz in the immediate future. Murray is no longer just another talented young man with a horn caught up in the tenor of his times, but a mature composer, bandleader, and soloist who should have a large say in determining what the tenor of these times will be. And Reaganomics or no, things are definitely looking up.

(JUNE 1983)

* Although Murray continues to conduct the Octet with his horn, Butch Morris is now the non-playing conductor of the David Murray Big Band.

# Heeding Inner Voices

Bobby McFerrin can sing like a frog and he can sing like a girl, and if he were a rock 'n' roll revivalist instead of the most astonishing jazz singer to come along since Betty Carter, he could probably cut a dynamite a cappella "You've Lost That Lovin' Feelin'" that would put those tuna hoagies Hall and Oates to shame, somehow conveying the tumult and grandeur of Phil Spector's wall-of-sound production in the process of matching both Righteous Brothers' voices to a T. He is that phenomenal. While jazz history offers a number of precedents for him, beginning with Louis Armstrong and the sadly overlooked Mills Brothers, it's impossible to listen to him (for me, anyway) without flashing back to street corner harmony groups and the mouth sounds with which wise guys in the back row harassed substitute teachers in junior high. That's the great thing about him—he is blessed with such a native and likeably goofy pop sensibility that any attempt at selling out would probably narrow rather than broaden his appeal; too quirky for mass consumption (let's be realistic), he nonetheless has all the makings of an across-the-board cult figure, given any meaningful exposure at all. But this is a lesson it's probably going to take record companies some time to learn.

McFerrin's second album, *The Voice* (Elektra Musician El-60366), recorded live *sans* instrumental accompaniment at European summer jazz festivals, was one of 1984's most delightful jazz releases. It was also something of a surprise, following McFerrin's eponymous 1982 debut (Elektra Musician El-60023), which caused many jazz critics to dismiss him as yet another entrant in the crowded name-the-next-Al Jarreau sweepstakes: a bland, affable, rubber-mouthed pop singer dabbling in improvisation to humdrum fusion accompaniment. "I never wanted to climb on that merry-go-round to begin with," says McFerrin, his speaking voice surprisingly thick and nasal for a singer's. "Basically, I made that first album just to have a record out. It was a calling card I hoped would land me some live gigs and get my career rolling along. All along, it was the *second* album I was looking forward to. I knew that once I made a solo voice album, people would sit up and pay notice. *I knew it, I knew it, I knew it!* And I was right, wasn't I?"

He was. When *The Voice* was released in the summer of 1984, McFerrin and the rest of Elektra's jazz roster were in limbo, following the defection of company president (and jazz fan) Bruce Lundvall to EMI. Yet with only token promotion, *The Voice* sold over 50,000 copies in six months, a negligible figure by pop standards but comparatively enough to make McFerrin a hot item in jazz. Even under Lundvall's enlightened regime, Elektra was reluctant to permit McFerrin to record solo, much less thump the drums on behalf of the finished product. Lundvall says that he gave McFerrin the go ahead, despite objections from higher ups at WEA International, when McFerrin invoked an even higher authority: "He told me that God wanted him to record a solo voice album."

"The general reaction was, 'you mean there won't be any *music* on it? You're not going to be singing real songs?'" remembers McFerrin, who has since rejoined Lundvall at EMI. "Even now, I still get some flak about singing solo, and I probably lose some gigs because of it. Because I'm a vocalist, I'm expected to perform the standard repertoire and travel around with a little three-piece back-up group. So long as there are instrumentalists who respect what I do, it's inevitable that I'll perform with some of them. [McFerrin frequently teams up with guitarist John Scofield and bassist Will Lee for New York club engagements, and he has brought badly needed levity to albums by Chico Freeman and Weather Report.] But I intend to go performing all by my lonesome, too. Some people say that what I do isn't really singing, it's just a gimmick, and I can't possibly be serious about it. But I am."

Seen in another light, gimmickry is no temptation for McFerrin, because his art is all gimmickry to begin with, and he revels in that. *The Voice* is an ironic title—McFerrin, whose range is three-and-a-half octaves, possesses many voices. Or do they possess him? In particular, his airborne falsetto sounds oddly disembodied, almost as if he were doing its bidding rather than the other way around. Conflicting personalities rise from his subconscious as breath makes its way up from his diaphragm. On the menacing "I'm Alone," for example, he is every chesty B-movie chain gang prisoner lamenting imposed celibacy, but he soon also becomes the compliant woman of his own erotic conjuring. On "I'm My Own Walkman," he is both the truculent inner-city teenager bopping down the streets to a private soundtrack (*"say what?"*) and the pious older brother spouting words of wisdom above the din; and on "Take the A Train," he is both speeding subway and its slightly crazed passengers. The character he evokes on "I Feel Good" is not James Brown but someone singing a James Brown hit to himself who gets carried away (as we all have) and starts *doing* James Brown in his mind, splits and leaps and all, finally convinced he *is* James Brown as he looses a ferocious approximation of J.B.'s tomcat growl. It recalls Andy Kaufman's nerdy Elvis impersonator, whose awkwardness magically vanishes the instant he dons the King's vestments and curls his lower lip into a snarl. Like Kaufman, McFerrin plays both ventriloquist and dummy, and his "I Feel Good" is not so much a James Brown cover as an electrifying first-person demonstration of a pop deity's power to effect transformation in his listeners.

Singing unaccompanied, save for when he invites the West German audience to hum or clap along, McFerrin coaxes up a daffy assortment of sonics and characterizations on *The Voice*. His circular breathing technique enables him to sing while inhaling and exhaling, thus allowing him to be his own background choir on "Blackbird" and "T.J." He mumbles like a wino and uncorks trumpet-like riffing one might think was being produced by tissue paper on comb on "Big Top" and "A Train," and creates the sound of static between frequencies on "Walkman," as well as coming up with airy calliope sounds and illusionary Bach-like counterpoint on "Blackbird," "Music Box," and "El Brujo." And on "I Feel Good," he slaps himself silly. "I like to *move* when I sing," he says. "I'll punch the air or jump or stand on my toes—anything to help that note trapped inside of me come out. Sometimes I thump my chest because it helps to *feel* the rhythm on my body."

McFerrin is in a category all by himself as a jazz singer: he doesn't embellish pop melodies, yet despite the hipster onomatopoeia he has fun with on "A Train," "Big Top," and "Donna Lee," scatting is the least of his abilities. (Even so, his syllabification is infinitely more sophisticated than that of the legion of dutiful modern singers who glide their fingers up and down invisible horns as they bip and beep, as though scat were another form of mime. Which it might as well be, considering how precious it's becoming.) Believing that "the voice is a supreme instrument in itself," he generally disdains horn impersonation of the sort favored by the singers some people will tell you are the only "genuine" jazz vocalists. Oddly enough, it was Jon Hendricks—one of the fathers of horn-like vocalese—who gave McFerrin his first break. "I moved to San Francisco in 1980," explains McFerrin, who still lives there, "and I was playing these real tinseltown, paper-maché piano bar kinds of gigs, when Jon called me early one Friday morning and asked if I could jump on the next flight and join his group for their opening night at Fat Tuesday's in New York the following Monday. Which meant I had the weekend to learn his arrangements, all those intricate lyrics he sets to improvised solos that are plenty complicated to begin with. But naturally I said yes, because I had been looking to do something more challenging and more productive to my career."

McFerrin stayed with Jon Hendricks and Company only a few months. "Jon and I worked very well together all in all. We argued a lot, though never in a malicious sort of way, and I usually wound up giving in out of admiration for him and a desire to please him and keep my job. I remember once we were planning a tribute to Eddie Jefferson at Carnegie Hall, and we argued *for days* about the solo I was supposed to take on my featured number with Jon's daughter Michelle. Jon wanted me to sing the solo note for note the way Eddie had recorded it, and I could see his point in a way, because that's what Jon Hendricks is all about: not adding anything to a solo and not taking anything away from it, either, but respecting it for what it is and trying to be absolutely faithful as you add words or sounds to it. Maybe because I'm from a later generation of singers, my position was that you take the material you're working with and use it as the springboard for the creation of something completely new."

McFerrin was born in New York City in 1950, the son of Metropolitan Opera baritone Robert McFerrin (who dubbed Sidney Poitier's singing voice in the 1959 film of *Porgy and Bess*) and operatic soprano Sara McFerrin, who presently chairs the voice department at Fullerton Community College in Southern California. Despite his vocal pedigree, McFerrin never took formal singing lessons as a child and gave no thought to becoming a singer until he was in his late twenties. "It's funny. I used to dread having to sing background vocals in the funk and fusion bands I played keyboards in as a kid." In 1977, he was earning his living playing piano for dance workshops at the University of Utah "and feeling pretty burned out and wondering what my direction in life was going to be, when a voice told me I should *sing*. My life has been wonderful ever since. It wasn't a voice from heaven or anything like that. Not the voice of God, like in the movies, with echo and delay," jokes McFerrin, a devout Christian who carries a miniature New Testament in his back pants pocket and will quote from it if you let him. "It was just the sound of one of my own thoughts, like everybody hears from time to time. The difference was I acted on it immediately."

He lists what seems like an odd trio of influences for a singer, until one realizes that self-reliance—his own stock in trade—is the quality he admires in each: Keith Jarrett ("His solo piano concerts convinced that one person could go up there on stage and make music all by himself"), Fred Astaire ("For his dancing more so than his singing, and for his solo steps more so than his duets with Ginger Rogers. I used to pretend to be sick so I could stay home from school whenever one of his movies was on television in the afternoon. His joyfulness and rhythmic abandon is something I try to capture in my singing.") and Charles Ives ("The biggest influence of all, because he let his imagination have full reign. He composed because he loved music, not because he expected to make a living from it.") Clearly a virtuoso at what he does, McFerrin likes to begin performances with no idea of what order the set will follow and let inspiration take him where it may. Like many virtuosos, he is something of a showoff, a master at playing on the expectations of his audiences. "In a way, I think of myself as a manipulator and an illusionist," he admits. "It might seem to audiences that I'm doing a thousand things at once up there, but I'm not. I'm just singing. So that's one illusion. Another is that I'm putting on a show all by myself, when really it's me and the audience. They're part of the performance, too."

Audiences encountering McFerrin for the first time tend to adopt him as their own—not just jazz audiences, either. When he sang "I Feel Good" and Bach's "Air on the G String" on the American Public Radio folk music series A Prairie Home Companion in February 1984, "the people in our live audience just about jumped out of their seats and onto the stage," according to Margaret Moos, the show's producer, who booked McFerrin, even though she worried how a jazz singer might go over. "On our show, a performer has approximately eight minutes, then something else comes on. It's not like doing a concert where you have the whole evening to win everybody over. You have to get them—*bang*—right away, and Bobby was able to do that." Adds Garrison Keillor, the show's host: "I thought the people were going to rush the stage and carry Bobby on their shoulders through the streets of downtown St. Paul. He is an incredible performer."

(OCTOBER 1984/MARCH 1985)

# If It Sounds Good, It Is Good

"I have to be careful of what I say in interviews," explains Craig Harris, "because I was once misinterpreted as saying that there were no interesting trombonists in the late '60s and early '70s, and that simply isn't true. That's an insult to many people I admire, including J. J. Johnson, Curtis Fuller, Jimmy Knepper, Grachan Moncur, and Roswell Rudd, not to mention the pioneers from the swing era who were still going strong. There were a lot of great trombonists; the problem was that, with the exception of Duke Ellington and Charles Mingus, nobody was spotlighting them—that's how I should have put it. There were two or three in each of the big bands in the old days, but after that you hardly ever saw a trombonist in a quartet or quintet unless it was led by one. A lot of it probably had to do with economic factors. But these things move in cycles, and now you have people like Henry Threadgill, David Murray, Muhal Richard Abrams, George Russell, Anthony Braxton, Charlie Haden, Carla Bley, and Abdullah Ibrahim [a/k/a Dollar Brand] all forming larger groups and featuring the instrument again—which is why it seems like dozens of young trombonists like myself, George Lewis, Ray Anderson, Steve Turre, Joseph Bowie, Gary Valente, and Robin Eubanks are arriving on the scene all at once."

Harris makes it sound as though his growing reputation is no more than the result of being in the right place at the right time. In reality, it is difficult to separate cause from effect; it could just as logically be argued that the current bumper crop of versatile young trombonists is encouraging bandleaders to make room for the horn in their ensembles. However one chooses to explain it, the old sackbut is suddenly on the upswing, and Harris's sense of historical connections— together with his penchant for harmonic layerings, polymetric long division, and rubato tone poems—makes him the trombonist most suited to a period in which traditionalism and experimentation regularly intersect, and in which the most forward-looking jazz composers are also those most blessed with hindsight. He has been a dues-paying member of practically every important mid-to-king-size band to convene in this decade, including the Henry Threadgill Sextet, the David Murray Octet and Big Band, Olu Dara's Okra Orchestra, Lester Bowie's Brass Fantasy, Jaki Byard's Apollo Stompers, Charlie Haden's New Liberation Orchestra, and short-lived leviathans led by Abrams, Ibrahim, Sam Rivers, and Cecil Taylor. Watching Harris cavort with any of these outfits (rather shy in person, he is quite the showboat once the music starts, given to fiery red jumpsuits, floor-length scarves, and pop-eyed expressions of exertion à la Louis Armstrong), it is easy to imagine him breezing into Harlem 50 years ago and throwing a scare into any of the 'bone triumvirate in the Duke Ellington Orchestra. As the mood seizes him, he can evoke Juan Tizol's cosmopolitan exotica, Lawrence Brown's romantic tumescence, or Tricky Sam Nanton's gutbucket ribaldry and winking sleight of hand. He delights in mouthing the off-color notes that two generations of tight-lipped bop trombonists almost succeeded in expunging from the horn's vocabulary over the audible objections of recalcitrant plunger specialists like Al Grey, latter-day tailgaters like Knepper and Bill Watrous, and avant-garde rabble-rousers like Rudd. With their moans, shrieks, horse laughs, war whoops, comic epithets, and good-natured raspberries, Harris's solos are like casebook illustrations of one of Ellington's favorite maxims: If it sounds good, it is good.

"I wasn't around in the '20s or '30s, when jazz was still new," says Harris, who was born in Hempstead, Long Island, in 1953. "But from the records I've heard and the stories that older musicians have shared with me, I get the impression that back in that era, horn players prided themselves on developing their own unique sounds, whereas today everybody strives for the same sound. I started fooling around with the plunger in 1976, the year I graduated from college. The plunger had been out of fashion for a long time because trombonists coming after J. J. Johnson wanted that fast, clean sound he was famous for. I wasn't trying to revive the past or anything like that. I just liked the contrast between the sound of the open horn and the different sounds that plungers and mutes made it possible for me to achieve. I was probably motivated by the same restlessness a tenor saxophonist feels when he reaches for a flute or a soprano sax. It gives him a wider range of colors to explore, and as a brass player, I wanted the same advantage."

"Violin, trumpet, and drums—those are the instruments everyone wants to play in the sixth grade. Then the funny-looking instruments are passed out. I had long arms, so I got the trombone," Harris recalls. As a teenager, he played in his high-school marching band and worked weekends in a local rhythm 'n' blues cover band. "Jazz was the furthest thing from my mind. The only jazz record my parents owned was *Bitches Brew,* which I used to play all the time because I liked its psychedelic jacket. But I had no idea who Miles Davis was or even what instrument he played. I learned all the arrangements for my weekend gigs off records, which I guess was good preparation for improvisation, in a way. Fred Wesley, the great trombonist with James Brown, was my favorite. But I was never really good enough to copy his solos note for note like I wanted to, which used to frustrate me."

After a year on a lacrosse scholarship at the State University of New York at Farmingdale—where he intended to major in social sciences—Harris transferred to the branch campus at Old Westbury, at the urging of bass guitarist Alonzo Gardner, a boyhood chum. "Alonzo kept telling me what a fantastic Afro-American Music Department they had there, with faculty members like [percussionist] Warren Smith and [saxophonists] Ken McIntyre and Pat Patrick. I studied composition, improvisation, and theory, and the three years I spent there were an endless series of revelations for me. I started listening to everything I could get my hands on—John Coltrane's *Om* and *Meditations*, Cecil Taylor, J. J. Johnson. My favorite cut by J.J. was "That Old Devil Moon," from *The Eminent J. J. Johnson* on Blue Note. His playing was so graceful—I had never heard anything like it."

Aside from Johnson, Harris made no special effort to listen to trombonists. "I was more interested in figuring out how the horn fit into the overall scheme of things than I was in copying specific players. But I got to hear all the great ones anyway, and they all made lasting impressions on me. Listening to Archie Shepp, I heard Grachan [Moncur] and Roswell [Rudd]; listening to Max Roach, I heard Julian Priester; listening to Duke, I heard that fabulous section he had. And I heard Jimmy Knepper with Mingus—that was my big ambition, to play with Mingus like Jimmy had, and I bet that's what I'd be doing right now, too, if Mingus were still alive. I also listened to a lot of Latin music, where the trombone is usually very prominent; and I haunted all the New York jazz clubs, nursing the one beer I was able to afford until the bartender gave me a look that said it was time to order another drink or make room for someone else who would."

The summer following Harris's graduation, his former instructor Pat Patrick, who was at that time still a member of the Sun Ra Arkestra, invited him to sit in with Ra at The Bottom Line in New York. Ra must have liked what he heard, because Harris wound up touring with the Arkestra for close to three years, though he never took the final step of moving to Philadelphia and becoming a full-fledged member of the cultlike Sun Ra "family." "People say that Ra must cast spells on his musicians to make them stay with him so long. But it's the music he writes that accounts for their loyalty—nothing more mysterious than that. We were constantly on the go, mostly in Europe, and it was a great learning experience for me. Sometimes none of his music would be written down, then the next piece would be notated in its entirety—you never knew what was coming next. Ra could draw from three decades' worth of music that he had written for that band. If he called a number I didn't know yet, he'd tell me to lay out, and that would be my lesson for the next afternoon. We'd practice the piece in his hotel room. Working with him, I got free lessons in orchestration, leadership, and showmanship." Free jazz-history lessons, too, it turns out. "One series of concerts we did was a tribute to Fletcher Henderson. Ra made me learn parts off Henderson's original recordings from the '20s and '30s. A lot of that experience has stayed with me."

Like many contemporary musicians, Harris is something of an amateur ethnomusicologist, collecting instruments and field recordings from around the globe. A trip to Nigeria with Ra for FESTEC '77 piqued his interest in Pan-African culture. "Like most people, when I thought of African music, I thought of drums. But on that trip, I saw Yoruba vocal choirs and string orchestras from Algeria and Senegal with instruments I still haven't learned all the names of." Since 1980, he has doubled on the *didjeridoo,* a hollowed-out wooden tube four feet long and three inches in diameter that he discovered on a mission to Australia with the expatriate South African pianist Ibrahim. "It's the instrument of the Aborigines, who wait for a thick branch to fall off a tree, then soak it in a riverbed and wait for the white ants to come along and eat away the inside. That's not how I got mine, though—I bought mine in an Australian instrument shop. It caught my fancy, because it's an ancient forerunner of the brass family in a way. You blow into it using a brass embouchere, buzzing with your lips to produce a vibration. Buzzing and circular breathing—a technique I was already using on trombone—and using different tonguings, you can produce as many as three different frequencies, one on top of the other, so that it sounds almost like a synthesizer, which is pretty ironic when you think about it. At the same time, you can also use it percussively, because it's hollow and resonates just like a gourd when you bang on it."

Lately, Harris has been turning up in some unexpected places. He played in the pit band that accompanied Lena Horne on Boardway in 1981–82, a job he says which "might not have been the most creative in the world, but it taught me the discipline of having to show up on time every night and knowing that I had to hit all the notes exactly as they were written—no two ways about it." Last winter, with funding from the Carnegie Foundation, he played a series of concerts for the homeless in Manhattan shelters. This summer, he collaborated with the dance troupe Urban Bushwomen on a piece called *Points*. Last year, he made his film debut in Francis Ford Coppola's *The Cotton Club*, though if you blinked you probably missed him and all the other black New York musicians hired to impersonate the men in Duke Ellington's "Jungle" Orchestra. It wasn't them you heard playing Ellington's music, either. Ironically, leading man (and amateur cornetist) Richard Gere was allowed to do his own playing (as was reportedly stipulated in his contract), although a racially mixed studio orchestra under the direction of Bob Wilber was called in to ghost for the professional musicians appearing on screen. "We didn't play at all, though we were initially given the impression that we would, and we certainly rehearsed enough Ellington and Cab Calloway," explains Harris, who lives with his wife Diane in an enormous three-story brownstone they are in the process of restoring, across the street from Harlem's Mt. Morris Park, a few blocks south from where the actual Cotton Club used to be. "All the filmmakers really wanted was for 14 black musicians in tuxedos to be on stage pantomiming their instruments whenever the cameras were rolling. We were blackfacin'—that's what we called it. But that's Hollywood for you."

Harris's best work as a sideman can be found on records by Ibrahim (*African Marketplace*), Henry Threadgill (*When Was That?* and *Just the Facts and Pass the Bucket*), David Murray (*Murray's Steps* and *David Murray Big Band Live at Sweet Basil, Volume 1*) and Muhal Richard Abrams (*Blues Forever* and *Rejoicing with the Light*). His first two dates as a leader were disappointing. 1983's *Aboriginal Affairs* (India Navigation IN-1060) was a tone parallel to the outback, ambitiously conceived but rather carelessly executed by a sextet that included Harris's former mentor, alto saxophonist McIntyre; last year's *Black Bone* (Soul Note SN-1055) was a blowing date that never came to life despite what promised to be an exciting match-up between Harris and tenor saxophonist George Adams.

The new *Tributes* (OTC 804) is the first record to capture Harris's full measure as a soloist, bandleader, and composer. The *didjeridoo's* eerie blues cry isn't enough to sustain interest over the length of the one track on which Harris forsakes trombone, but everything else is so fabulous, it's easy to overlook this minor self-indulgence. The choice items are a brace of pungent sweet-and-sour ballads that reveal Harris's unexpected flair for legato embellishment. And there is plenty of variety, too, with an elongated bop line, an African high life delivered in march formation (it could be titled "Henry Threadgill Meets Abdullah Ibrahim," in homage to Harris's former employers), and in inspired bit of chanting tomfoolery dubbed "24 Days an Hour," which shows that Harris indeed learned a thing or two from Sun Ra. The supporting cast is superb, with bassist Dave Holland and drummers Billy Higgins and Famoudou Don Moye underlining the rhythmic acuity of Harris's writing, and with Vincent Chancey's French horn adding just the right amount of mustard to an all-brass front line that also includes trumpeter Junior Vega and cornetist Olu Dara.

The trombone's return to prominence is part of a larger brass renaissance in jazz: tubas are throwing off the shackles of Dixieland, French horns are renouncing the artifice of Third Stream, and trumpets are remembering how to growl. Harris, who obviously feels a bond with his fellow brassmen, originally hoped to add another trombonist (preferably a greybeard) to the line-up on *Tributes*. But Lawrence Brown, who retired from the Ellington Orchestra a decade ago, declined Harris's offer, joking that he now uses his horn as a flower pot. And Trummy Young, the former Jimmie Lunceford star who looked forward to playing Harris's music, died a few months before the recording session.

Harris would like to see the septet he assembled for *Tributes* become a permanent band, but since neither he nor any of his contemporaries works frequently enough to keep sidemen on salary, "working bands are a fantasy in this day and age. That's why you see composition making a comeback, which is another example of how things move in cycles. The approach to improvisation hasn't really changed all that much in the last few years. The change has been in what surrounds it, the move away from conventional 12- and 32-bar forms to test new ideas—not that anything you can do is ever really new. Some of the Fletcher Henderson material I played with Sun Ra was pretty unusual in structure, even by today's standards. Now everything has to be written down, because bands don't play together often enough to develop that kind of telepathic communication that went on between Duke Ellington and his men, or between Sun Ra and the guys who have been with him practically all their adult lives, like John Gilmore and Marshall Allen. We try, but we have to start all over again from scratch every time out."

Fortunately, Harris has been able to draw from a nucleus of musicians who have formed alliances in a number of transient bands. For example, he and Dara, who played alongside each other in the Threadgill Sextet for four years, now team up in Murray's Big Band as well as in Harris's own septet and Dara's Okra Orchestra. Both Harris and Chancey are in Brass Fantasy, and Higgins is currently both Murray's drummer and Harris's. "Sure, we all know one another's moves. But it's just not the same as playing together all the time," complains the trombonist. As our afternoon together drew to a close, it became increasingly apparent that Harris would have to line up several substitutions for his septet's premiere engagements the following week; Dara, Vega, Holland, and Higgins all begged off due to prior commitments, and although the men who would replace them (saxophonists Oliver Lake and Chico Freeman, bassist Lonnie Plaxico, and drummer Marvin "Smitty" Smith) were their equals in blowing ability, the instrumentation would be different, and there was no guarantee the same rapport would be there.

"We live in the era of the free agent, just like baseball," Harris sighs. "But just imagine what my bands or any of the bands I've played in—David's, Muhal's, Threadgill's—might sound like if we could play together every single night for six months, the way I once did on a tour of Europe with Sun Ra." It is indeed something to be imagined, for it seems unlikely to come to pass, given the limited market for jazz. Still, any band with Craig Harris as a member has quite a bit going for it right there.

(OCTOBER 1985)

# Violin Madness

Although violinist John Blake already had ten years of classical study under his belt when he first became infatuated with jazz as a college freshman, learning to improvise and learning to swing were like beginning all over again. "I never blamed the instrument itself, though," says Blake, who has since brought both a concert violinist's dash and a fiddler's ribaldry to the McCoy Tyner Quintet. "I would hear records by other jazz violinists and realize the problem was with me. Most of them were older, self-taught players whose sensibility was far removed from mine. So I began listening to Coltrane and McCoy, to Wayne Shorter and Herbie Hancock—to the way saxophonists and the pianists influenced by saxophonists articulated their phrases, the way they'd bend notes or slide around them and accent off the beat. I wanted to capture that vocal quality Coltrane had when he played the blues. I wanted the violin to cry and sing."

Blake was bucking pretty heavy odds. Despite the violin's family resemblance to African string instruments, and despite the ingenious uses to which it has been put by disenfranchised people (both black and white) at hoedowns and country dances, it carries echoes of class distinction and racial oppression that make it suspect within jazz. When Billy Bang started playing the instrument in junior high school, he was embarrassed to be seen going to class through the streets of Harlem. "The violin wasn't from my neighborhood," he says, "and it wasn't welcome there."

At some point, every violinist who plays jazz on that most venerable and patrician of instruments must imagine he is the first to dare such folly, and there is an element of logic to that delusion. Throughout the brief history of jazz, violinists have tended to emulate reigning trumpet or saxophone idols, and the Louis Armstrong-based attack of a Stuff Smith or a Joe Venuti isn't likely to provide much guidance if your goal is to graft Coltrane multiphonics onto your strings. Although jazz has produced upwards of half a dozen great violinists (including Smith, Venuti, Eddie South, Ray Nance, Stephane Grappelli, Leroy Jenkins, and—before overexposure to amplification induced cosmic vibrations—the young Jean-Luc Ponty), jazz violin has produced no cynosures on the order of Charlie Christian, Django Reinhardt, and Wes Montgomery, the trinity of patron saints guitarists can return to for counsel, even guitarists for whom fostering the illusion of breath-length cadences is more crucial than leaning proper plectrum techniques.

Apart from talent, dedication, their relative youth (each is in his late thirties), and the instrument they play, the classically trained John Blake and the largely self-taught Billy Bang share little in common. Their paths have never crossed, although at one time or another each has graced the string orchestra that tenor saxophonist David Murray leads around New York on sabbaticals from his Octet. Yet the fact that two such gifted and individualistic violinists should emerge in jazz at roughly the same moment links them together in a way. For in carving out reputations for themselves, they are also carving out a jazz tradition for their instrument.

Bang—who was born Billy Walker in Mobile, Alabama, and moved to Harlem with his unwed mother while still an infant—began playing jazz 15 years ago at the relatively advanced age of twenty-one. The violin was forced on him by a junior-high teacher at about the same time schoolmates began calling him "Billy Bang" after a popu-

lar cartoon character. The nickname he accepted good-naturedly, but
the violin troubled him: "I thought it had girlish associations, and
I was particularly sensitive to that sort of thing because I was very
slight and liked doing things boys weren't supposed to do, like reading and writing poetry."

The violin stayed in its case while Bang attended a radical prep
school in Stockbridge, Massachusetts, as a hardship student. One of
his classmates there was Arlo Guthrie, son of the most famous of
folk troubadours and subsequently a popular folk-rocker in his own
right. "Once in a while, I played drums with Arlo, who would sing
and play guitar. Every weekend, friends of his father—like Pete
Seeger and Peter, Paul, and Mary—would be up at the school visiting Arlo or singing at some demonstration, so for three years, folk was
the only music I heard." That may account both for the presence in
Bang's repertoire of such unlikely ditties as "Alouette" and "Skip to
My Lou," and for the sing-around-the-campfire lyricism that brightens
even his most opaque, discontinuous improvisations. "I still love those
old songs for their simplicity; simplicity is something I strive for in
everything I play, although it might not always sound that way. I
remember one time [tenor saxophonist] Frank Lowe was playing in
my band, and he nearly fell down laughing when he saw that I had
put the sheet music to 'Red River Valley' on his stand. He was reluctant to play it because he thought of it as a kids' song. But the great
thing about tunes like that is you can improvise on them every which
way and they still sound familiar. Frank wound up loving it."

Ironically, around the same time that Guthrie's "Alice's Restaurant" was becoming an anti-war anthem, Bang was fighting in Viet-
nam, an ordeal that politicized him and indirectly led him to jazz.
"I probably would have been a war resister, but in my neighborhood
you were considered chicken if you didn't go when they drafted you.
Nam forced me to confront myself as a black man in a racist society.
Sometimes it seemed like there was more open hostility between
black and white GIs than between us and our so-called enemy, who
were just people struggling for the same freedoms my own people
were fighting for back home. When the Army sent me to Hong

Kong for R and R, I met a Chinese woman I wound up staying with, and I remember one day she looked at me and said, 'Why were you in Asia killing yellow people when black people are being gunned down in the streets where *you* live?' I couldn't answer her. Believe me, I came home full of anger and bitterness."

Returning to civilian life, Bang became obsessed with the music of John Coltrane. "His solos were strong enough to focus the feelings I had inside of me and channel them into something positive. It was very anti-establishment music, somehow analogous to the books I was reading by Eldridge Cleaver and Malcolm X. I wanted to play saxophone the way Coltrane did, as a political statement, but it was too late to learn. So I figured the violin was at least an instrument I already knew a little bit about." He emulated Coltrane and Ornette Coleman before coming under the wing of Leroy Jenkins, the doyen of free jazz violinists. "Every Tuesday and Thursday afternoon for four years, I'd go over to Leroy's place, and he would show me correct methods of fingering the strings and sweeping the bow. But mostly we just played together, and he was important to me as an example of someone older who had successfully dealt with the same sorts of problems I was dealing with—granted, he had been dealing with them at a much more advanced level. We both were attempting to prove there was a role for violin in modern improvised music."

Bang describes his style as a synthesis of Jenkins's classicism and Coleman's more intuitive approach to violin—as accurate an assessment of his role as any, though it seriously downplays his startling originality both as leader of his own bands and as a member (along with bassist John Lindberg and guitarist James Emery) of the delightful String Trio of New York. Like Air, the Revolutionary Ensemble, and the Modern Jazz Quartet, the String Trio is one of those cooperatives in which the whole exceeds the sum of its parts, impressive though the parts may be to begin with. Even at their most fragmented, convoluted, and scratchingly contrapuntal, the three-part inventions of the String Trio's four releases on Black Saint maintain a lift and tang that recall the Hot Club of Paris and the scherzo movements of the world's best-loved symphonies. On his own Bang has recorded prolifically in a variety of contexts, ranging from the unaccompanied *Distinction Without a Difference* (hat Hut IR 04) to the unusual assembly of four strings, three reeds, and three percussion that play his ambitious charts on 1983's *Outline No. 12* (Celluloid/OAO CEL-5004)—a record that conveys the thrilling news that his writing is gradually acquiring some of the grit and pluck of his playing. He is one of the wittiest soloists to surface on any instrument in recent years, and perhaps the first since Dexter Gordon to justify the questionable practice of interpolation both musically and dramatically: on *Bangception* (hat MUSICS 3512), an album of duets with drummer Dennis Charles, he underscores Coleman's rootsiness, as well as his own harmonic acuity, when he asks Ornette's "Lonely Woman," what did she do to be so black and blue?

Although John Blake is as diminutive as Bang, and although he too grew up in a black neighborhood, the violin did not have to be forced on him. "I raised my hand when they asked us in third grade who wanted to learn to play. Little did I know what I was getting into. It's a difficult instrument to master, and it feels so unnatural holding it under your chin with your arm outstretched. I probably would have given it up if my mother hadn't persuaded me to stick with it. The kind of stigma Billy talks about didn't begin to bother me until high school, and by that time it was too late. I was hooked."

As a student, he idolized such classical violinists as Jascha Heifetz, David Oistrakh, and Nathan Milstein. Although he fumbled when he first began to improvise, Blake disagrees with Wynton Marsalis's oft-quoted contention that it's a thousand times harder to become a good improviser than to become a good classical musician: "I think Wynton makes statements like that to get people to take jazz seriously, and bless him for that. But it's not that simple. Granted, in classical music you have the notes in front of you, and all you have to do is interpret them. But on the other hand, when you're improvising, you can plot your solos so as to stay safely within your technical limitations, whereas in playing the classical literature, you're constantly running into technical challenges, and there's no way to side-step them. It's just hard to be *good*, period."

Slowly but surely, there is a branch of jazz taking root wherein skill at interpreting complex notated passages is as paramount as improvisational resourcefulness, and Blake's background in the classics has served him well in illuminating the music of such ambitious composers as James Newton, David Murray, Anthony Davis, and Cecil McBee. Similarly, he chose the sidemen for *Maiden Dance* (Gramavision GR-8309), his debut as a leader, on the basis of "their sensitivity to texture and their ability to maintain a sense of structure throughout a piece, improvised solos and all." Blake has also studied the Carnatic violin style of southern India, and he feels that his use of Indian sliding techniques has enabled him to achieve his early goal of capturing the tenor of the human voice.

Blake served as musical director for pop-jazz saxophonist Grover Washington, Jr., for five years in the mid '70s, a lucrative gig that still provides steady income in the form of composer's royalties. But it was during his four-and-a-half years with McCoy Tyner that Blake began to find his improvisational wings and gain the attention of critics and other musicians. Last spring, Tyner and Blake parted ways amicably: "McCoy was going through a period of adjustment following the death of Jack Whittemore, who had been his agent for many years. He decided to cut down to a trio, and we both felt it was about time for me to go out on my own anyway." Tyner's esteem for Blake is reflected in the pianist's cameo on *Maiden Dance;* his clinging duet with Blake on his own Dvořákian blues "For Tomorrow" is among the album's biggest treats, not least for the rare pleasure of hearing Tyner in a deferential accompanist's role.

The pianist on all other cuts is the infallible Kenny Barron, whose touch is lighter than Tyner's but who also proves capable of precipitating Tyner-like storms (his solo on the title track is a series of devastating, evenly timed explosions over the polyrhythmic crossfire of Wilby Fletcher's traps and cowbell and Leonard "Dr." Gibbs' hand drums), and the bassist is the worthy Cecil McBee, who anchors the rhythm section and crafts adroit solos that are anything but facile in design. As a soloist, Blake sometimes falls prey to self-induced rapture, and as a writer (all the material on *Maiden Dance* is his, save for the Tyner contribution and the standard "Beautiful Love"), he sometimes confuses the sticky for the sweet: only his swashbuckling abandon rescues the baroque/Latino "Todos Mas Niños" from preciosity, and when cooing voices enter "The Other Side of a World," you half expect credits to roll over the final freeze of our hero riding off into the sunset. But even in a jazz era that rewards romantic self-indulgence, romantics who take chances are rare, and Blake at his best sweeps you away with his lyric ardor.

Blake and Bang are both at a stage where they are asking themselves who's out there listening, and wondering how they can swell the ranks. Although Blake is in constant demand as a sideman, he still lives in his native Philadelphia, commuting to New York whenever the call goes out for him. His second LP for Gramavision, which he began recording in January, features his working band: pianist Sid Simmons, percussionist Gibbs, and two former Tyner compatriots, drummer Fletcher and bassist Avery Sharpe. Last year he entered the studio in another capacity, producing a frankly commercial album for West Virginia pianist Bob Thompson.

For his part, Bang has resolved to meet the masses halfway via Forbidden Planet, whose lineup includes a bass guitarist, a synthesizer player, and a fast-tongued rapper. According to Bang, much more than commercial acceptance is at stake in his decision to play funk: "I have to resolve certain contradictions within myself. I went through a period when I felt that dance music with no redeeming educational value was decadent. But now I'm going back to the old neighborhood, so to speak. I want to close the gap between myself and the people who say they can't follow the kind of music I generally play—the people I grew up with in Harlem and the South Bronx. The music I heard on the streets all during my childhood was soul music—nobody called it 'funk' back then—and I've always had an affection for it. Jazz was something my mother's boyfriend and my uncles listened to, that I had to learn to appreciate later on." To judge from a rough-mix cassette of Forbidden Planet currently making the rounds, Bang still has a long way to go before reconciling his improvisational daring with his desire to make music with grass-roots appeal. And since the band is playing mostly for sedentary listeners on college campuses rather than for the hip hop crowd, his reunification with the peoples of Harlem and the South Bronx will remain symbolic for the time being, a fact he ruefully concedes.

The uncertain economic future of jazz makes it difficult to predict what lies ahead. One thing is certain, however: the violin will play a major role in jazz from here on in, and so will John Blake and Billy Bang.

(MAY 1985)

# Variations on a Big Band Theme

"Jazz has become an international language, I think," says Mathias Rüegg, the 32-year-old Swiss-born leader of the Vienna Art Orchestra, referring to the fact that it is becoming increasingly difficult (and increasingly unnecessary, some would say) to categorize music by national origin. "In a sense, the written music that the String Trio of New York or Anthony Braxton's groups are playing sounds more 'European' than the improvising of some of the cats in my band, like [saxophonists] Roman Schwaller and Harry Sokal, both of whom are well-versed in the European classical literature but have also gained a lot from working with black American improvisers like Mal Waldron and Art Farmer."

Perhaps because government subsidies make it far easier to keep a large ensemble affoat in Europe—or perhaps because the very *concept* of a large jazz ensemble is so rooted in the European symphonic tradition—Europe has recently become a spawning ground for postmodernist big bands of a kind that basically no longer exist in the United States (or exist precariously at best). In the last few years Rüegg's 14-member Vienna Art Orchestra has taken its place alongside Alexander von Schlippenbach's Globe Unity Orchestra, the Willem Breuker Kollektief, the George Gruntz Concert Jazz Band, Pierre Dørge's New Jungle Orchestra, and the Mike Westbrook

Orchestra as one of the most intriguing of these contemporary European juggernauts. Internationalist in both outlook and personnel, the VAO offers far more than a pale European echo of American jazz in full cry. Yet "American jazz with—I hope—American timing and idiomatic American phrasing, but from a European point of view," is the way Rüegg characterizes *Live at the Dead Sea,* the program of new Rüegg compositions the VAO premiered on its maiden tour of North America in the fall of 1984. "The *style* as well as the philosophy of composition is the European part—certain of the sound combinations derive from the European classical tradition. But it's American jazz in the sense that the writing is basically a vehicle to encourage individual expression from the soloists. I wanted to give the players a chance to blow as a reward for the good job they did on our last project, *The Minimalism of Erik Satie,* where there was little room for individual interpretation."

The grueling North American tour—sponsored in part by the Austrian government—got rolling in Washington, D.C., the last weekend of September and climaxed with a recording session at Rudy Van Gelder's studio three weeks later, after swings through Canada, the East Coast, the Sun Belt, Texas, and the Pacific Northwest. For the two American-born members of Rüegg's troop (tuba player John Sass is originally from Boston and scat singer-cum-vocal colorist Lauren Newton is from Portland, Oregon) the tour represented a homecoming. For their leader it was something else. Rüegg had been to the United States once before, visiting New York only a year ago, but this time around he was seeing more of the U.S. than most Americans will ever get to see, and that he was seeing it all from much the same European vantage point from which he perceives jazz was underlined by his impressions of Texas. "It's like Italy or Spain," he declared, "not just the climate and the landscape, but the people as well. In the evening there is so much life—people strolling the streets singing, music coming from the open windows."

*Homo sapiens* demonstrates a remarkable ability to translate new experience back into the familiar, and perhaps only a European would think of comparing Armadillo Headquarters to the Mediterranean. But the series of hat ART double albums that preceded Rüegg to America reveal that the ability to imagine what already exists is perhaps his greatest asset as a European-based jazz composer/arranger. *Concerto Piccolo* (hat ART 1980/1), the record that introduced American listeners to the VAO in 1981, and the *Suite for the Green Eighties* (hat ART 1991/2), released the following year, were dominated by Rüegg's cheeky extended compositions, the most attractive of which utilized pastiche to wring modernist changes on traditional forms—"Tango from Obango," for instance, which was whimsically dedicated to the people and the sea of Obango, or the captivating "Em Hermineli Z'lieb," which Rüegg describes as his "compositional mastering" of an authentic Swiss *landler*. "The *ländler* is the music of the farmers, a folk dance that originated in Switzerland and the Austrian mountains and is usually played by two clarinets, contrabass, and bandoneon [a squeeze-box keyboard similar to the accordion]," Rüegg explains. "People compare the *ländler* to the polka, but it reminds me of ragtime or dixieland in its happy-go-lucky feel. So it seemed only natural to use it as a setting for contrapuntal improvisation."

The VAO's most recent albums have featured Rüegg's arrangements of material by other composers—though his variations on these borrowed themes frequently entail such massive overhaul that they too perhaps qualify as "compositional remasterings." *From No Time to Ragtime* (hat ART 1999/2000) weighed in as a kind of impudent, inverted chronology of jazz evolution, commencing in the present with Anthony Braxton's thorny, arrhythmic "N 508-10(4G)" and culminating with an orchestral enlargement of a Scott Joplin rag. "I like to have a unified concept, a completely new program, for each tour we do," Rüegg says, "and the concept that time was to perform 'Unknown Jazz Tunes'—that was the title I originally chose for pieces that had previously been played only by their composers but seemed to offer endless possibilities for expansion, like Roswell Rudd's 'Keep Your Heart Right' or Charles Mingus's 'Jelly Roll' [itself Mingus's variation on Jelly Roll Morton], or Ornette Coleman's

'Silence,' which is almost like Ornette's arrangement of John Cage's '4'33",' with all the gaps in Ornette's melody throwing the audience into confusion about how they're supposed to react. In concert, we also performed other pieces not on the album, including pieces by Booker Little and Blood Ulmer. I also wanted to call attention to the writing being done by Austrian jazz composers, so I included on the record new pieces by Fritz Pauer and Hans Koller."

In its backtracking survey of jazz history, *From No Time to Ragtime* in a sense paralleled Rüegg's own belated discovery of the jazz past. "I grew up playing classical music, and for three years I played Hammond organ in a rock band in Switzerland, as well as playing piano in a jazz trio modeled pretty much after Erroll Garner's, but for the most part my interest was in free jazz and the classical avant-garde of the 20th century. Then gradually I worked my way backwards through bop and swing, until now I know quite a bit about early jazz and ragtime." Indeed, although his heady eclecticism marks him as an unrepentant modernist, as a listener Rüegg now prefers jazz of the 1920s and '30s because of the greater symbiotic relationship between composition and improvisation he hears in older styles.

*From No Time to Ragtime* was marred here and there by excess and superficiality—some of the older pieces seemed overextended, and Rüegg proved unable to penetrate to the rhythmic marrow of Coleman and Mingus. No such problems afflicted last year's *The Minimalism of Erik Satie* (hat ART 2005), Rüegg's boldest venture so far—a crafty yet straightfaced series of transformations upon the scores of the flintiest of the French impressionist composers, involving vibist Woody Schabata, singer Lauren Newton, and the horns of the VAO. "There were several inspirations for that," Rüegg says. "First, I wanted to do a program without rhythm section. Second, I wanted to prove that musicians can express themselves even without improvising. And third, I have always admired Erik Satie, who reminds me of Thelonious Monk, in a way—they were both cranky humorists, lovers of nonsense. Satie was the forerunner of Cage and the minimalists, but he also influenced jazz musicians, indirectly through Bill Evans and Chick Corea. He was not writing jazz, of course, but he absorbed the rhythms of ragtime, just as Stravinsky did, and he anticipated much of modern jazz in his use of ancient modes and his impressionistic view of music. His compositions were predestined to be played by jazz musicians."

In wanting to obliterate the essentially bourgeois distinction between "serious" and "light" musics, Satie anticipated the efforts of contemporary jazz composers like Rüegg in another sense as well. As Polish critic Jorge Solothurnmann once observed (and Rüegg heartily concurs), the Vienna Art Orchestra does not play "serious" music, but it plays music seriously—a nice distinction equally applicable to any number of contemporary American jazz composers like Anthony Davis and Henry Threadgill, not to mention such classical avant-gardists as Robert Ashley, Philip Glass, Laurie Anderson, and Glenn Branca.

Rüegg, who was born in Zurich and came to Austria as a teenager to study composition, says "nothing was happening in jazz in Vienna when I arrived there 10 years ago, but it was a good place to make a beginning, because there was a lot of money allocated for culture, and the government officials were very favorably disposed toward jazz. In Austria now, we are accepted the way a symphonic orchestra would be. We are considered worthy of being sent out as ambassadors on cultural missions." (Wouldn't George Russell or Muhal Richard Abrams love to be able to say that?)

The VAO evolved out of alliances Rüegg formed while playing solo piano in a Viennese night club for two years in the mid-'70s. Each month or so, he would invite another musician to join him (beginning with alto saxophonist Wolfgang Puschnig) until eventually he had what amounted to a big band on his hands. For the last six years the VAO has enjoyed more or less stable personnel—a crucial factor in the band's excellence, given Rüegg's admission that he writes for specific instrumentalists (much as Mingus and Ellington did) rather than for specific combinations of instruments. "The different soloists in the band and I have known each other for so long now that when they improvise, I can almost predict beforehand what they will play," he says, "and that is something I take into consideration as I write our music."

The VAO concert I attended in Haverford, Pennsylvania (if Texas reminded Rüegg of Italy, what images of the Black Forest did Philadelphia's leafy suburban Main Line trigger?), threw the spotlight on the band's improvisers, just as Rüegg had promised, and they exercised their options with such cohesion and such a feel for thematic exposition as to make Rüegg's charts seem prescient in divining composition and improvisation as all of a piece. As conductor, Rüegg gets to stand with his back to the audience without risking being accused of rudeness. Tall and slender, wearing a hip-length black leather jacket and wrinkled black cords, his long scraggly hair tucked behind his ears, he hardly presents the authoritarian figure one expects of a conductor. He walked off-stage several times during the set, and frequently knelt passively with head bowed to sheet music in the semicircle formed by the standing horns. Yet if it appeared as though he had nothing to do, it was because his work had been done beforehand—and done beautifully, for the most part. His hand was clearly evident in the sequencing of soloists and the complementary backdrops he provided for them, like cushioning an airy Lauren Newton vocal with tuba and topping it with flute; turning percussionists Joris Dudli and Wolfgang Reisinger loose to splash behind a ducky Wolfgang Puschnig soprano chorus; stockpiling riffs behind a boisterous, heated Roman Schwaller/Harry Sokal tenor exchange that recalled similar confrontations between Johnny Griffin and Eddie "Lockjaw" Davis in the Kenny Clarke–Francy Boland Big Band.

In concert no less than on record, Rüegg's most valuable accomplice was Lauren Newton, who lines up with the horns and whose timbre and vocal catches are equal parts Cathy Berberian and Anita O'Day. "I had always wanted to write for voice, and when I met Lauren, I thought she was the best singer I had ever heard," says Rüegg of the American singer who gives his music its delicious garnish, and who has also collaborated with Rüegg on the Vienna Art Choir's album *From No Art to Mo-(Z)-Art* (Moers Music 2002).

The Vienna Art Choir is just one of the AVO's offshoots. With their leader's blessing, Puschnig, Reisinger, trumpeter Herbert Joos, and pianist Uri Scherer moonlight as Part of Art (with bassist Jurgen Wochner). "An orchestra presents inhibitions to a creative player, no matter how one tries to make improvisation part of the overall structure. In the quintet they get to blow more, and that is good for them," says Rüegg, who describes himself as the band's patron as well as its maestro. All of Rüegg's composer's royalties go back into the VAO's upkeep "because it is important for me to hear my compositions realized—otherwise they remain abstractions on paper. I constantly have offers to write for other bands—to become a kind of free-lance arranger, in effect—but I turn them down because I like to be able to collaborate with the musicians who will eventually play the music that I write, and the only way I can be sure of accomplishing that is to write only for my own orchestra." (One request that piqued his interest, which he did not reject, came from the king of Thailand, who commissioned three pieces that the VAO premiered in Bangkok and reprised on their American tour.)

Although it puts him at some distance from his music in performance, Rüegg no longer plays piano with the VAO. "I'm so busy composing all our music, copying all the individual parts, securing funding for our concerts, and arranging our itinerary that I no longer have time to practice," he jokingly complains. "Why bother anyway, you know? Uri is a fantastic pianist—a much better improviser than me. There is only so much one person can do, and I had to decide what my role in this band was going to be. I chose the role of bandleader." As was so often said of Ellington, Rüegg's instrument is the orchestra. And it is an instrument to which he brings both facility and imagination.

(FEBRUARY 1985)

# *Swing Redux*

Scott Hamilton's tenor saxophone—a reconditioned Selmer, manufactured in 1949—is five years older than he is. "I walked off with it for $500 about seven or eight years ago, when horns of that vintage weren't in much demand," explains Hamilton, whose tenor style aims for a middle ground between Coleman Hawkin's forthright stomp and Lester Young's more standoff-ish relationship to the beat. "The problem with newer saxes is that they tend to go sharp when you blow hard in the upper register, and they don't have that subtone growl I like. It's probably a question of design features the manufacturers have changed in order to accommodate the harder mouthpieces and embouchere styles most of the guys buying horns these days tend to prefer. They probably sound great if you want to play like John Coltrane, but they don't do anything for me."

Hamilton talks about a *growl*. His frequent sidekick Warren Vaché, Jr., talks about a *buzz*, his name for the glorious legato rip that has all but vanished from jazz brass. "I actually played cornet first, before trumpet, and a few years ago, I picked it up again, just for fun," Vaché says. "I haven't touched a trumpet since. I don't like the sharp, nasal edge a trumpet has when you try to play softly. I prefer a mellower sound, but I still want to cut through—I still want that buzz that guys like Louis [Armstrong] and Roy [Eldridge] and Bobby Hackett had. The cornet covers both of those angles for me."

Satirist Mort Sahl used to complain that since World War II the Presidency had passed from Roosevelt to Ford, the movies from John Garfield to Burt Reynolds, the mood of the nation from purpose to indifference. Sahl's punch line: Darwin was wrong. I know some critics who would add that small-group swing has passed from Coleman Hawkins and Roy Eldridge to Scott Hamilton and Warren Vaché: Darwin was wrong, and so was Hughes Panassié. I wish I could juice up what follows by presenting them as subjects of heated controversy, these baby boomers who have rejected contemporary developments in favor of a style that was considered passé before they were born. But controversy, which presupposes that enough people give a damn one way or the other, is conspicuously lacking in jazz these days. Like all minority groups, jazz fans feel compelled to put up a unified front whenever the public at large happens to be glancing. Meanwhile, jazz critics with categorical aversions are no longer thought derelict in their duty now that jazz has become so rich and varied (so diffuse, some would say). So while the derrière guard— who haven't had much else to cheer about lately—hail Hamilton and Vaché as trendsetters (a neat bit of wishful thinking that assumes that bop, free form, and fusion were momentary aberrations), the dernier cri crowd maintains a code of silence on the duo, as though they are unworthy even of derision. Is it possible to take a middle line on Hamilton and Vaché? I'm going to try. But first, let them speak on their own behalf:

Hamilton: "What people sometimes overlook about Warren and me is that we're not repertory players. We're not involved in trying to recreate anything, the way that Bob Wilber does with his Bechet Legacy or the guys in Widespread Depression do with big band music—to name just two groups I admire in that vein. Warren and I might incorporate the principles of another era, but we're improvisers. We're making it up as we go along, the way jazz musicians have always done."

Vaché: "When a sound is new, there's an urgency that reflects the tempo of the age. But that washes away with the passage of time, until all that remains is the music, pure and simple. Coleman Hawkins's version of 'Body and Soul' is as alive right now as when he first played it into the microphone in 1939. There are always going to be people hearing it for the first time, and it's going to sound as magnificent to them as it did to the people who heard it on the day it was released. Music transcends its original social and political implications. That's how it survives its period."

One Saturday last October, Vaché was sitting in on a job that Hamilton lined up for his quintet at a wedding reception in a swank Central Park hotel. "Isn't that always the way?" Vaché asked no one in particular after he and Hamilton were sent back to the wings in favor of John Bunch, their pianist, who was requested to play something sweet and quiet until the bride and groom arrived. "They say they want a hot jazz band for their affair, then they expect you to do the Meyer Ferguson bit anyway."

"I don't usually accept gigs like this," Hamilton assured me, explaining that like all freelance musicians, he had to file quarterly income tax returns. "It's due next week, and I was wondering how I was going to come up with the dough, when out of the blue I get offered this gig that pays a lot of money, and all I had to do was rent a tuxedo and play music all afternoon."

*He even looks like a character out of the* 1930s, cliché-per-sentence journalists too wet behind the ears to remember much about the 1950s, never mind the 1930s, say in describing Hamilton, with his slicked back hair, pencil moustache, and baggy trousers. The implication is clear: his preference for Johnny Hodges over Charlie Parker, for Coleman Hawkins over John Coltrane, is symptomatic of a more general yearning for the speakeasy ethos associated with musicians before jazz began taking itself too seriously.

More likely, Hamilton is just a careless dresser who has never given much thought to matters tonsorial. "Maybe when I was younger, I used to fantasize about what it would have been like to come up in the old days," he said. "But that's just an ego trip. If I regret any-

thing, it's that there were so many great players back then who are
gone now, and I never had the chance to hear them live."

"Don't ask *me* if I was drawn into jazz by impressions I might have
been given about the lifestyle," laughed Vaché, a chunky, well-
groomed fellow who still lives in Rahway, New Jersey, where he was
born in 1951. "When I was growing up, I had no idea there was
such a thing. My father sold electrical appliances five days a week,
ate dinner every night at six o'clock just like everybody else's dad,
and played dixieland in country clubs on the weekends—something
he continues to do to this day. He used to take me along to carry his
bass, and as I got older, he would let me play my cornet with the
band toward the end of the evening. I listened to the radio quite a
bit as a kid, but compared to my father's record collection, the Beach
Boys and the Beatles and the rest of that stuff sounded pretty incon-
sequential. My liking jazz put me out of step with my schoolmates,
but I was proud of that. It gave me an identity. It was my badge."

Vaché's taste in jazz was broader than the rest of his family's (his
brother is a clarinetist in Jim Cullum's Happy Time Jazz Band, a
San Antonio-based trad outfit). Hamilton, too, made discoveries on
his own after inheriting a love for jazz from his father. "Unlike Warren's dad, my father didn't play," explained Hamilton, who grew up
in Providence, Rhode Island. "But he was an avid record collector,
with a lot of sides from the '20s and early '30s. I loved that stuff, but
I also began listening to things that were 'modern' only in so far as
someone like my father was concerned—Ellington, Basie, Goodman,
even some Charlie Parker and Lester Young."

Hamilton forgot all about jazz when he took up harmonica and
joined a rock and blues band. "I went along with the crowd for a
while. But listening to Paul Butterfield, B. B. King, Muddy Waters,
Little Walter, and Sonny Boy Williamson naturally led me back to
jazz, because the foundations of their music was so similar." Hamilton's reawakened interest was also spurred by his friendship with
Duke Robillard, a former member of Roomful of Blues and current
leader of the Pleasure Kings. "Duke was the ace blues guitarist in
New England around that time, and we all followed his lead when

he began including Ellington and Basie tunes in his sets. I wasn't the only one inspired by him. You'd never know it to hear them now, but the guys in Widespread Depression [a nine-member ensemble that revives forgotten treasures from the big band era, along with some of the mere pleasantries] were rock 'n' rollers when they began hanging out with Duke."

Hamilton switched to tenor when he switched his allegiance from the blues. "The first tenor player to make a big impression on me was Lester Young, followed by Coleman Hawkins and Ben Webster. But the biggest influence of all was Illinois Jacquet, because I got to hear him live, not just on record, and he was doing everything I dreamed of doing—pretty ballads, jump tunes, everything."

Warren Vaché made his acting debut in *The Gig*, a 1985 film starring Wayne Rogers and Cleavon Little, about six businessmen who play in a Dixieland band on weekends (shades of Warren Vaché, Sr.). "One night when I was standing at the bar between sets at Eddie Condon's, a very pleasant fellow who turned out to be the writer and director Frank Gilroy tapped me on the shoulder and asked if I had done any acting. I was just loaded enough to say, 'No, but I'll give it a try.'"

Condon's was Vaché's old stomping ground. "When I first came to New York in the early '70s, I played there six nights a week, not 25 feet from Roy Eldridge at Jimmy Ryan's. Roy took me under his wing. It used to amaze me how approachable my heroes were, how eager they were to pass along advice. All you had to do was show an interest." Vaché and Hamilton have shared bandstands with the Eldridges and Benny Goodmans and Benny Carters and Buddy Tates, the father figures that thoroughly modern millies like David Murray and Wynton Marsalis can only admire from afar. It was inevitable that these two throwbacks would eventually cross paths, and fitting that their first encounter was at Condon's. For decades, that club and Ryan's stood as midtown fortresses against Greenwich Village jazz progressivism, until both fell to the wrecking ball in 1985. (What bebop could not undo was no match for urban renewal.)

One Sunday night in the mid-'70s (nobody remembers exactly when), the manager of Condon's threw the tyros together in a band that also included John Bunch, who became their Goodman connection. "John's a great talker, and once he's sold on you, he can sell you to anyone, even Benny," says Vaché, who worked with Goodman off and on for seven years beginning in 1975. Did Goodman ever shoot Vaché that deadly glare of disapproval that former BG-sidemen call "the ray?" "Oh, I don't know," Vaché laughs. "Benny's a very complex man, and he has more than one way of making you feel uncomfortable if he's dissatisfied with you."

"Ah, the ray doesn't mean anything," interjects Hamilton, who twice worked briefly with Goodman, in 1977 and '82. "It's just Benny's natural expression. I had no bad experiences with Benny. It was an honor to play with him."

Unlike Vaché, who holds a degree in Music Education from Montclair State College (N.J.), Hamilton is basically self-taught and cannot read music. "It doesn't handicap me as a bandleader. I know enough terminology to tell the guys what I want from them, and if that doesn't work, I can demonstrate, because I play piano well enough to pick out chords. In one way, not reading is an advantage: I'm not tempted to accept studio work." What did handicap Hamilton when he first arrived in New York was a malady common to jazzmen of his generation. "Not knowing any songs! I thought I knew plenty, but because I had learned them off jazz records, what I actually knew were their chord changes, not their melodies. John Bunch set me straight on that pretty fast." Now, when Hamilton wants to learn an old song, he listens to a vocal recording—and as Lester Young used to, he pays careful attention to the lyrics "not for poetic or sentimental reasons but just for help in phrasing the melody properly."

Both Hamilton and Vaché record as leaders for Concord Jazz (Pics: *Scott Hamilton and Warren Vaché with Scott's Band in New York City* [CJ-70]; *Skyscrapers* [CJ-111], with a Hamilton-Vaché Octet playing Buck Clayton arrangements; Vaché's *Midtown Jazz* [CJ-203]; and Hamilton's *A First* [CJ-274], with salty dog cornetist Ruby Braff), and as members in good standing of the label's floating stock company, they are helping to revive a glorious old tradition with their work behind singer Rosemary Clooney. In the 1930s, it wasn't uncommon to hear top-notch improvisers like Lester Young, Ben Webster, and Teddy Wilson handling the obbligatos and tossing off pithy solos on records by all manner of vocalists. "But because jazz is no longer a popular music, and specifically no longer a vocal-oriented music, that tradition has passed," Hamilton points out. "And that's a shame. Ironically, the only guys who know how to play something nice behind a singer now are rock musicians—they're the only ones who have had any practice."

As I understand it, the biggest gripe against Hamilton and Vaché is that their solos lack that historical primacy, that urgency to make it new, that Vaché hears in Coleman Hawkins's "Body and Soul." Fair enough. But shouldn't the same charge be lodged against Wynton and Branford Marsalis in relationship to Miles Davis and Wayne Shorter? What about the multitude of callow tenor saxophonists recycling old Coltrane licks, too obsessed with scales and passing chords to realize they're acting out a second-hand obsession. It's difficult to avoid the conclusion that Hamilton and Vaché invite skepticism not because they're old-fashioned, but because they don't play hard bop. One of the curiosities of jazz mythology is that the further Birdland and Minton's recede into history, the more they are discussed as belonging to the day just before yesterday. By contrast, Storyville and the Savoy Ballroom might as well belong to antiquity.

Much as I hate to bring this up, it's also difficult to avoid the conclusion that Hamilton and Vaché might be regarded very differently if they were black. They discovered their fathers' trad and swing collections around the same time that many of their black contemporaries were purchasing their first Coltrane and Miles albums, a period in which jazz innovation was trumpeted as compensatory black protest and the preservation of older styles was jeered as the white man's burden. Since then, the rhetoric has taken an unexpected turn: Young black musicians are now applauded for their fealty to the old

masters. A small group swing revival would seem a logical development in such a climate, and a look through the new release bins con-
firms that we might be in the middle of one. Look at the covers of
these albums, though, and the only faces not pocketed with age belong to white men. Remember when the burning question in rock
used to be could young white men sing the blues? (I bet Hamilton
does.) The only pertinent answer was: Maybe not, but with notable
exceptions, young black men sure weren't about to. They're not about
to swing anymore, either—at least not in the grand old manner of
four beats to the measure.

The blues will never really die, of course, and neither will swing.
Both continue to manifest themselves in many different guises. Still,
who would want to say goodbye to the original article? Warren
Vaché is right when he says that the music of Coleman Hawkins
(and by implication, that of Louis Armstrong, Lester Young, Ben
Webster, Earl Hines, Jo Jones, Cootie Williams, and Vic Dickenson)
will survive forever in this age of mechanical reproduction. But jazz
fans know better than anyone that records are sepulchral even when
brand new; the moment of inspiration they document is an echo that
grows ever distant. The few surviving heroes from the glory days of
swing aren't going to live forever. So, as long as the worst that one
can accuse Scott Hamilton and Warren Vaché of is atavism, not
mimickry, it's good to have them around as living proof that the jazz
tradition didn't begin with *Kind of Blue*.

(FEBRUARY 1986)

# Introducing Sumi Tonooka

Weeknight business isn't what it used to be at The Frog—at least not in the downstairs piano bar, where Sumi Tonooka has treated talkative young professionals (most of whom seem to prefer the sound of their own conversation) to aromatic interpretations of Duke Ellington, Charlie Parker, Wayne Shorter, and Bud Powell every Monday and Tuesday evening for the last three years. Even though fewer elbows around the piano mean fewer tips, Tonooka isn't complaining. "When it's quiet like this, I think of coming to work here as getting paid to practice," she says, scanning the near-empty room as the bartender issues last call. "Only it's better than practicing, because the tune I'm playing might be somebody's favorite—you never know—and I've got to play it all the way through, which forces me to integrate the technical things I'm working on into a meaningful melodic setting, instead of just getting hung up on them and running through them over and over. It's good discipline. I have absolute freedom here, so long as I don't play anything too startling during the cocktail hour. Toward the end of the evening, I can even pull out some of my own compositions, and I've been here long enough now that some of the regulars request my pieces, though they might not know them by name."

In other words, Tonooka's job isn't as thankless as it looks. Still, this French restaurant in center-city Philadelphia is hardly the ideal place to hear her. Even on a slow night, the gossip about money market funds and relationships drowns out the piano, which is there strictly for ambience. For Tonooka, The Frog is what musicians call a "bread" gig, but she's holding on to it, even though it means commuting from Brooklyn once a week, because steady work is difficult to find.

Everything could change for her, though, if only she could persuade the record companies to audition the tape she's been shopping around: a professionally engineered 1984 New York studio date that features her playing seven of her own bristling compositions in the fast company of bassist Rufus Reid and drummer Akira Tana. "It's been an education," sighs Tonooka, an attractive young raven-haired woman with dark, glittering eyes and Asian features and coloring. "Some record companies say they won't put anything out unless they've produced it themselves. Others are so overbooked that they send my tape back to me unopened. The most frustrating reaction of all was from an executive at one of the majors who said that although he preferred my music to Tania Maria's, he thought Tania had more commercial potential because of her vibrant personality. Why compare me to Tania Maria? I'm not Brazilian, and I don't sing. It shows the sort of marketing I can look forward to when somebody does sign me. I'm half black and half Japanese, which makes me what? Afro-Asian-American? That makes me exotic to some people, especially since I'm also a woman, and women instrumentalists are still looked upon as novelty acts. I know I could exploit all of that, but it would backfire on me in the long run."

Eventually, one of the smaller jazz labels will add Tonooka's self-produced session to its catalog; if not, she will do what countless other disgruntled musicians have done, and market the album herself. Either way, there's going to be excited talk about her, because she has all the tools. The pieces that show her off to best advantage are those which catch fire from her fulgurous phrasing—horn-like in its linearity and melodic signification, percussive in its density and spring. "Piano is a percussion instrument," she says, and not surprisingly, she lists among her influences a number of pianists of likemind, including Thelonious Monk, McCoy Tyner, Ahmad Jamal, and Nina Simone. "But I've also been influenced by horn players, and when I studied with Margaret Chaloff in Boston, she had me pretend that I had holes on the tips of my fingers and that I was *blowing* on the keys. She was trying to impress upon me the importance of thinking in breath-length phrases, which horn players do automatically, and drummers do, too, in a way, because drumming is such a physical activity, involving the whole body, that the respiratory system becomes involved in it as well. On piano, if you develop enough technique, it's possible to play long lines without ever pausing for breath, which is why so many pianists sound cluttered and have trouble fitting in with horns. I went through a period of listening to nothing but Dexter Gordon, admiring the way he swings so hard without overstatement, the way he tells his story with so few notes. He's been an influence, too, even though a lot of what he does isn't possible on the keyboard. I mean, as a tenor saxophonist, he can blow one note with vibrato and hold it, and it'll knock your socks off. You can try to duplicate that with tremolo and the sustain pedal, but it's never going to have the same impact."

The composer Tonooka most admires is Duke Ellington, and writing music often becomes a synesthetic experience for her, as it was for him. "I almost went into sculpture instead of music, and the visual arts still influence my thinking. 'Phantom Carousel,' for example, started off as an assignment from Dennis Sandole, whom I've been studying with for the last six months," she explains the genesis of the most overtly lyrical and impressionistic composition on her tape. "The idea was to write something utilizing a six-tone symmetric scale from the Far East that Dennis had given me to work with—just those six notes in various combinations. But I started seeing a carousel going round and round as the notes recurred. It was on a mountain shrouded in mist, and it was crying out for children to come play on it, but there were no children to be found. It began to haunt me, and the image gradually became the sound."

"I'm engaged to be married, and someday I want children," Tonooka says. "I'm approaching an age where time is running out on me. Some women are pressured to have children by their mothers, who want to be grandmothers. But my mother, who's quite the feminist and a grandmother already, asks why I'd want to interrupt my career to raise kids. I know all the arguments against motherhood, but it's something I want to experience. I make it a point to talk about this with other women musicians. [Pianist] JoAnne Brackeen will show you pictures of her grandchildren when you bring up this subject—she's proof that you can have both: a family and a career in jazz. I know one thing—I don't want to give birth until I'm in a good enough position financially to support a child on my own if necessary. I don't want to have to depend on a man to be the breadwinner."

Tonooka was born in the Powelton Village section of Philadelphia on October 3, 1956. Powelton, a haven for urban ecologists and unrepentant '60s radicals in the shadow of the University of Pennsylvania, is one of Philadelphia's more tolerant neighborhoods, to say the least. (It was, until a bloody 1978 police siege, the main headquarters of the suicidal, quasi-Rastafarian group MOVE.) In another community, the Tonooka family might have raised eyebrows, but in Powelton they must have seemed as average as the Nelsons or the Cleavers. Sumi's parents met and fell in love while working together on a pamphlet for a Socialist organization. Her father, who is black, is a former factory worker and reformed alcoholic who has spent the last twenty years writing a history of the universe. "None of us has ever figured out if he's brilliant or just insane," Tonooka quips affectionately. Her mother, who was born and raised on a farm in the Pacific Islands near Seattle and now teaches writing at the Philadelphia branch of Antioch College, is also writing a book about her experiences at Manzinar, the camp where she was detained behind barbed wire with thousands of other Japanese-Americans for the duration of World War II. "She reaches the point in her narrative where the gates slam behind her, and then she has to stop," Tonooka says. "The memory is just too devastating.

"My legal name is Sumi Morris, but I'm using my mother's maiden name. It was a feminist, matriarchal decision. She has only one brother, and he has only one son. I like the name Tonooka, which is unusual even in Japan, and I wanted to perpetuate it. When she was growing up, my mother used to fantasize about learning piano, but my grandparents were too poor to buy her lessons. She vowed that her children would learn music. My older sister, who's a pediatrician now, rebelled when my mother tried to force piano lessons on her. With me she took a softer approach, and it worked. She was a big jazz fan, with lots of records around the house—Monk, Fats Waller, Billie Holiday, Nina Simone. I remember liking the album where Nina sings 'I Want a Little Sugar in My Bowl.' I used to go around the house singing that all day long when I was very little, and my parents would laugh because I had no idea it was a sexual metaphor.

"My parents must have sent me to practically every kind of school that existed—public, private, parochial, and alternative. I didn't go to school at all for a year when I was 13, because they were so disgusted with the educational system that they decided I could learn more from a home tutor. I graduated from high school when I was 15, and I left home with $50 in my pocket, swearing never to return because of all the crazy things that were happening. My father, who had been sober for seven years, began drinking again, and my mother couldn't live with him. She was going through some pretty heavy changes herself, quitting her job as a secretary at Penn and taking courses to get her teaching degree. She left home, and since my older sister was already gone, I became surrogate mother to my two younger brothers. There's an old saying that goes 'it's easier to rule a kingdom than a family,' and my father wasn't a responsible parent with the liquor in him. My brothers were out roaming the streets every night, and it was a wild time in Powelton, with kids freaking out and experimenting with drugs. The house we slept in at night was the only thing holding us together as a family, and when my father failed to meet the mortgage payments, we were served with an eviction notice. I raised the money to save our home all by myself, by fund-raising among our neighbors. I flung it at him very dramatically and said, 'Here! Goodbye! I'm going away and never coming back again."

She wound up in Boston, where she intended to enter Berklee or the New England Conservatory. "But from the classes I sat in on, the regimentation turned me off, and I figured there was always time for college later on." Supporting herself as a janitor at Harvard and a grill girl at Sears, she studied privately with Charlie Banacus, a Lennie Tristano disciple, and with the aforementioned Margaret Chaloff, a retired New England Conservatory faculty member and the mother of the late Serge Chaloff, the baritone saxophonist in the great Woody Herman Orchestra of the 1940s.

During her two years in Boston, Tonooka became romantically involved with a pianist in a jazz-rock fusion band and moved with him to the band's farm in Connecticut. "David and I used to practice piano in shifts, and though I can't explain exactly what I learned from him, I think he loosened me up a lot. He was completely self-taught, and he approached music from a different perspective than I did. I remember he would put a lead sheet in front of me and say, 'Improvise on that,' and for all my piano lessons I was still uncertain how to improvise around a major chord. I would freeze and wind up in tears."

From Connecticut, Tonooka drifted to Detroit, where she worked what she refers to as "the chittlin circuit" with trumpeter Marcus Belgrave. Finally, three years after swearing that she was gone for good, she returned to her parents' home in Philadelphia. "Everything had changed, myself included. My father had started treatment, my mother had come back home, and one of my brothers had suffered a breakdown that brought us all back together."

Tonooka enrolled at the Philadelphia College of Performing Arts, where she came under the tutelage of classical pianist Susan Starr, and studied privately with the transplanted Parisian jazz virtuoso Bernard Peiffer. Once a week, she commuted to New York to take lessons from Mary Lou Williams. "Mary Lou would sit me down at her piano and say, 'Just think. Thelonious Monk and Bud Powell use to come up here and play that instrument. There's a lot of history there.' She'd continually tell me that I didn't have to come to her any-more—that I was good enough to go out there and play. That was very flattering, but I suspected that she told all of her students that, because that was her philosophy: you learn by doing. It turned out to be good advice."

Even before her graduation from PCPA, Tonooka started gigging around Philadelphia with tenor saxophonist Odean Pope and drum-mer Philly Joe Jones. Because feminism was late arriving in the macho world of jazz, she met with a good deal of resistance at first: "No one took me seriously until they heard me play, and some musi-cians refused to take me seriously even then. I was very reluctant to assert myself, and that was sometimes misinterpreted as a lack of deep commitment to jazz as a profession. Some musicians assumed I was a groupie, that playing piano was just my way of attracting men."

Nevertheless, she gradually succeeded in winning an avid local fol-lowing. "But it was like being a big fish in a little pond. You don't even have to be that wonderful—what counts is being on the scene long enough so that everybody around town who books concerts knows your name. I saw a lot of musicians I admired becoming com-placent, becoming impressed with their local renown." In 1983, de-termined to make a name for herself in New York, she moved to Brooklyn. "It was something I put off for a long time out of fear that I wasn't good enough to compete. Frankly, I still feel that way some-times. But I realized I was probably always going to feel that way, and that I was just going around in circles in Philadelphia, playing the same clubs year after year and not growing. I needed to stretch."

Much to her surprise, she has found more camaraderie among musicians in New York than in her hometown: "Because it's so dog-eat-dog in New York, players look out for each other. People who are out of work call each other and organize sessions, and if somebody who already has a gig is offered another one, he'll suggest somebody else. New York is a hell of a place to try to make a living, but at least there are plenty of fellow musicians to give you reinforcement."

Earlier this year, she was awarded a grant by the Japanese American Cultural Organization to compose a triptych based on her mother's experience in Manzinar: "I don't have a title for it yet, but I know that the individual parts will be called *Issei, Nisei,* and *Sansei*—Japanese for first, second, and third generations. The first section will use traditional Japanese instruments like *kyoto* and the *shakuhachi* flute. It will employ a traditional Japanese poem as text, and it will be very formal, very simple in structure, to represent my grandparents' generation. They lived with us when I was younger, and I got a sense of my mother's lineage from them. They behaved so differently, keeping their place and preparing their own food, the vegetables that my grandfather grew on our front lawn, right there in the middle of the city! Dr. Ricardo D. Trimillos, a West Coast ethnomusicologist, has agreed to help me with the instrumentation. The second part will be a combination of East and West, and will reflect the horror my mother's generation felt at being rounded up and incarcerated in their native land. I'm thinking of using my mother's prose about the camps and portions of her testimony before the Senate Committee on Redress and Reparation as the text. The last section will be jazzy, upbeat, totally modern in instrumentation, to represent my generation. For the text, the Sansei poet Russell Endo has agreed to let me use his poem 'Susumu,' which means progress in Japanese."

With no albums to her credti, Tonooka has yet to crack the major New York clubs, though she has found work at Greene Street, a pricy SoHo supper club where she often experiences a sensation of déjà vu. "I look around and think 'My God, I'm back at The Frog!' New York is no different from Philadelphia in some ways. You can go to the Village piano bars to hear great pianists like Hank Jones, Tommy Flanagan, and Roland Hanna, and no one's listening to them, either. Those bars might not be the best place to hear them, but I go anyway, because for the price of a beer I can peer over the lid of the piano and get a free lesson from one of the masters. That's something Mary Lou used to emphasize, that you can learn an awful lot just by watching a great pianist's hands." Sometimes it must seem to Tonooka that she is on the same treadmill that she was on in Philadelphia—that by virtue of being in New York, she is now courting obscurity on a national, rather than a local, level. "A lot of well-known musicians are hurting for work, and everybody is telling them that jazz is dead," she reports. "Maybe it is." Maybe so, if commercial viability is the only sign you'll accept as vital. But with dedicated young musicians like Tonooka arriving on the scene, the condition of the deceased is definitely improving.

(NOVEMBER 1985)

# The Instrument Gets in the Way

Not too long ago, Stanley Jordan was busking on Manhattan street corners, plugging his chrome-plated, aluminum-neck Travis Bean into a tiny, battery-operated amp and collecting loose change in his open guitar case. Now, as one of the first batch of performers signed to EMI's reactivated Blue Note label, the photogenic guitarist is receiving The Big Push—EMI-generated puff pieces in the music and lifestyle magazines, concert tours as opening act for Wynton Marsalis, and two luxuries unheard of for a jazz instrumentalist: a video and a promotional budget allowing for visits to disc jockeys and record distributors in key markets.

In all fairness, it should be pointed out that, although EMI's publicity department is bringing the hype to a crescendo, it was musicians and critics who started the drums rolling. Even before the release of Jordan's first Blue Note album *Magic Touch,* insiders who heard him at the 1984 Kool Jazz Festival or on his 1983 self-produced and -distributed debut *Touch Sensitive* were buzzing about the ingenuous method that Jordan calls the "touch technique." Instead of plucking or strumming the strings of his guitar with his right hand and positioning his left up and down the neck, Jordan taps (or "hammers," in guitarist's lingo) the strings against the frets with the balls of his fingers, both hands roaming freely in a manner that is at once percussive and pianistic and enables him to voice chords, bass vamps, and linear melody simultaneously.* This orchestra-in-miniature approach to guitar was initially inspired by childhood piano lessons and an adolescent fascination with the solo piano recordings of Art Tatum. But Jordan has honed the technique to a point of complexity where it now seems indigenous to amplified guitar. No one is likely to attempt it on an acoustic guitar, he says, "because just tapping the strings, you're never going to produce as much volume as you would plucking or strumming or using a pick. You give up some dynamic range with this method, and that's where amplification has to compensate." In order to facilitate the technique, Jordan lowers the action on his strings: "Moving them closer to the fretboard, it's easier to get a tone by tapping lightly, and the tones come out much clearer that way." He has also altered his tuning: "The standard tuning is E-A-D-G-B-E ascending—all adjacent strings a perfect fourth apart, except for that major third from G to B. What I did was to eliminate that major third and make it perfect fourths all the way up. The symmetry helps me to visualize the fingerboard as transparent. I don't have to search for the notes as I improvise—they're right there."

Without a guitar in his embrace, Jordan—who is in his middle twenties but looks younger and speaks in a teenager's breaking, singsong voice—seems bashful and uncertain, as though the chord that attaches him to his amplifier were umbilical as well as electric; the exaggerated knee-buckling and torso bending he goes through on stage are clearly a performer's mock courage, unconscious mannerisms picked up from watching concert footage of Jimi Hendrix, another of his boyhood heroes. Jordan was born in Chicago in 1959 and raised in Palo Alto, California, where his father worked for an electrical engineering firm. Even as a teenager, Jordan approached music ana-

---

* Rock guitarists Eddie Van Halen and Adrian Belew have also experimented with two-hand "hammer-on" technique, and so have British avant-gardist Derek Bailey, West Coast studio musician Emmett Chapman (inventor of the "stick"), and numerous folk and blues guitarists. But only as a stylistic adjunct, not a cornerstone.

lytically. "I'd listen to blues guitarists, and I'd think, 'well, maybe I don't know anything about the emotions they're expressing because I haven't lived that much yet, but it'll help if I can understand the mechanics of what they're doing.' In the rock 'n' roll bands I played with, I was always saying, 'hey, let's try that tune again, from a different angle this time.' The other guys would groan and say, 'No, man, we played it already.'" In junior high, he bought a two-record album of jam sessions from the 1972 Newport Jazz Festival and noticed that "there were certain stock phrases that recurred in all the solos. I thought 'if I can just learn all of them, I'm on my way.' Coming to jazz from acid rock and the blues, I was very lick-oriented. It wasn't until I heard Charlie Parker that I realized there was a lot more to jazz than knowing all the right licks."

By the time he enrolled as a music major at Princeton University, Jordan had evolved his own notational system based on mathematical group theory. He was surprised to learn that Princeton faculty member and classical composer Milton Babbitt had been employing a similar method of notation for years. Student and teacher naturally gravitated toward each other, even though their music had little in common beyond its shared mathematical bias. "Basically, I compose using a concept called Modular Twelve as a way of mapping relationships between pitch classes, to use Milton's phrase for it. For example, all the Gs are in one pitch class, and all the C-sharps are in another. The advantage of the system is that it allows you to name unusual intervals, and that takes some of the stigma off them. You take the notes C, D-flat, F-sharp, and G—that's a very beautiful combination, but because it's difficult to name under conventional notional systems, that gives the illusion that it's this weird sound from out in left field somewhere that's not going to strike anyone's ear as pleasant. Whereas, if you call it L-zero, the progression is zero, one, six, seven; and once you think of it that way, all sorts of transpositions come to mind. Of course, I try not to think of any of this when I'm improvising—it would just slow me down. Just like I never compose on the guitar for fear that I'll think too much in terms of what my fingers can do. I might use ideas I've gotten from playing the instrument, but sitting down to compose music, the instrument gets in the way."

Braving Manhattan after a few years in Madison, Wisconsin, following his graduation from Princeton, Jordan resisted the temptation to go knocking on record company doors. "I needed time to develop. I knew that whatever field I wound up expressing myself in, first and foremost I wanted to be treated as a serious artist. And even though I didn't really think of myself as a jazz player, jazz seemed like the best place for me. It's the music that's most alive right now, because it has the potential to connect with other kinds of music in so many ways—it gives you a solid footing for whatever you might decide to do next. I shied away from pop, which I love, because everything about the pop scene was counter to my values: all that really seemed to matter was how cute you were, not how well you played. I was extremely wary of the record business. I had read so many stories about musicians who signed with the wrong labels and were forced to make quicky records that came back to haunt them later. So I decided to take my music directly to the people by playing in the streets, producing my own record, and sitting in whenever anyone let me.

"I don't know about anywhere else, but you can always make a living playing in the streets in New York," says Jordan, who has since relocated to Orange, New Jersey, with his wife Sandy and their two-year-old daughter. "There are so many people passing by any given corner in New York that even if only one person in a hundred pays any attention to you, you have quite an audience right there. One of my favorite spots used to be on West 48th Street, near all the music stores. It's the most crowded part of town in the daytime, and you can hook up with other musicians there."

Jordan signed with Blue Note following a long courtship by the label's president Bruce Lundvall, who made his initial overtures while still at Elektra Musician. In the spring of 1984, music critic and guitar buff Bill Milkowski, who had heard Jordan playing on the street, set up an audition for him in Lundvall's office. Lundvall offered Jordan a contract on the spot, which Jordan declined, not certain he was ready for the big time.

On the evidence of *Magic Touch* (Blue Note BST-85101), which reached number one on Billboard's jazz chart, it's debatable whether he's ready now. As a composer, he puts Modular Twelve to mundane use, favoring the baroque, the sentimental, and the overripe. As an interpreter, his taste is conventional in the extreme, whether he is drawing from jazz—Thelonious Monk's "Round Midnight," Miles Davis's "Freddie Freeloader," and Thad Jones's "A Child Is Born"—or pop—Lennon and McCartney's "Eleanor Rigby," Jimi Hendrix's "Angel," and Michael Jackson's "The Lady in My Life." And as a solo improviser, he too often succumbs to the masturbatory impulse that seems to overtake many virtuoso stylists (guitarists in particular, for some reason) when they find themselves playing alone. (The '70s craze for unaccompanied jazz recitals, which is unfortunately still with us, is something of a mystery to begin with. Remember when becoming good enough to play with other musicians used to be the object of learning an instrument? And for those of us who wouldn't know a Travis Bean from a Travis Bickle, this rampant guitar worship is also puzzling: the video for the Montgomeryesque "The Lady in My Life" leaves no doubt that the lady in question is Jordan's guitar.) Worst of all, Jordan doesn't swing, except on those tracks on which bassist Charnett Moffett and drummer Peter Erskine are on hand to show him the way.

It's tempting to blame all of *Magic Touch*'s excesses on producer Al DiMeola, whose own albums demonstrate that even unaccompanied guitar recitals with no double tracking can sound overproduced if you add enough reverb ("The pristine becomes the lush and the point is quickly lost," as critic Steve Futterman once observed.) But Jordan's homemade *Touch Sensitive* (Targent 1000) suffered from many of the same problems, and his concerts crush hopes that his records misrepresent him. To his credit, he has perfected a sound uniquely his own, but so far it is *just* a sound, not a full-bodied conception. Still, if this were 1957 or even 1965, and the words "Blue Note" meant what they used to, one would have ample opportunity to hear Jordan as a sideman before passing judgment. It's entirely possible that the very traits that seem like too much of a good thing on *Magic Touch* would seem captivating in a setting in which Jordan's solos merely had to pull their own weight, not justify the existence of an LP. So the jury is still out and might be for a long time to come. Meanwhile, Jordan's dedication to music and instinctive distrust of the star-making machinery are persuasive arguments on his behalf.

(APRIL 1985)

# Maslak on the Hudson

Of the many beliefs that jazz listeners hold in common, one of the most cherished is the supposed persistence of a jazz underground. Not everyone locates that underground in the same place, of course. The more adventurous keep an ear cocked for rumblings that forecast sudden and dramatic shifts in the structure of jazz; the more conservative watch the shadows for the emergence of musicians' favorites ignored by everybody else. A cynic might observe that fans of both persuasions now find the underground burgeoning as never before, what with the mainstream's failure to absorb a quarter-century of Ornette Coleman and Cecil Taylor's linear descendants, and the record industry's blanket decision that all jazz is marginal. In an era in which jazz performers finish out of the money in both album sales and media adoration, calling any jazz musician overrated amounts to wishful thinking. It would be more accurate to say that the shrinking jazz audience, unable to participate in the star-making process, has settled for working out a pecking order among the underrated.

Yet if it seems as though jazz has burrowed underground, one sure index of the music's continued vitality is the accelerated activity *beneath* the underground. Some of the most rewarding music I've heard lately has come from submerged figures who lack the sideman credentials needed to impress established performers and who remain un-affiliated with any of the factions of the jazz avant-garde. As New Yorkers without national reputations, players like pianist and drum-mer Errol Parker and the members of the Microscopic Septet (and scores of others, most—though by no means all—of them white, in-cluding saxophonists Tim Berne, Patrick Brennan, Jameel Moondoc, and Mark Whitecage; pianists Borah Bergman and Armen Donelian; trumpeter Ahmad Abdullah; clarinetist Peter Kuhn; vibist Gunter Hampel; guitarist Rory Stuart; cellist David Eyges; bassist Shihib Sarbib; drummer William Hooker; and French horn player Tom Varner) must function as local musicians in the least hospitable of all localities. They're denied even the fantasy that succors journeymen in cities like Boston and Philadelphia, the fantasy that their lack of recognition is wholly a matter of geographical circumstance. Neither is it likely that these New Yorkers can expect greater visibility in the near future; the very eccentricities that make their music so attractive also mark them off as minor in the long run. But that hardly dimin-ishes the appeal of what these mavericks have been able to accom-plish in the face of some pretty heavy odds.

Perhaps the most intriguing of these subterranean dwellers is Keshavan Maslak, a saxophonist in his late thirties whose biography reads like the outline for the great twentieth-century American pica-resque novel. Because his name rings foreign and all his records have been imports, the few listeners who have heard of Maslak generally assume that he is European, perhaps even a Soviet defector. He is in fact a second-generation American who grew up speaking Ukrainian in an enclave of Detroit heavily populated by Slavic immigrants who fled Communist dictatorships only to wind up in the clutches of Henry Ford. "My grandfather, who was from the Ukraine, used to say that there were something like ten children in his family and only one pair of shoes—they were so poor," remembers Maslak. "So the idea was for the whole family to sacrifice and save every penny they could, so that the eldest son could put those shoes on and go to America someday. They really believed that the streets here were paved with gold. They were just peasants, what did they know? My grandparents finally came here around the time of the Russian Revolution, when life started getting even tougher for them than it had been under the rule of the Catholic Church. They settled in Detroit because they heard that Henry Ford was hiring anybody to work on his assembly lines, even people who couldn't understand a word of English.

"Ukrainians are stubborn people, and they have a lot of pride—they cling to the old ways. My grandmother lived in Detroit forty years, but I don't think she knew ten words of English when she died. My grandfather knew a little more from being out in the working world every day. My parents spoke English very well, but we mostly spoke Ukrainian to one another around the house in deference to my grandparents, and Ukrainian, Russian, or Polish to the neighbors. When I started school, I had a lot of fistfights because English was strange to me and I spoke it with an accent. The other kids could tell that my family was just off the boat, and when they made fun of me my instinct was to stand up and slug it out. But part of me was embarrassed by my people, and in my own way I rebelled against them because of all the peer pressure to 'be American' and all of that. I wanted to be accepted, the same as anybody does. It wasn't until I became an adult that I realized how important it is to know your roots. It was funny, too, because by that time I hardly knew any Ukrainian anymore, from not having spoken the language for such a long time."

Maslak's first professional experience was playing polkas and mazurkas at neighborhood revelries as a teenager. "My grandfather was a singer and mandolin player who would travel around to all the various Slavic organizations in Detroit and perform folk songs in all the native tongues. He knew them all. When I was around seven or eight, he bought me a beat-up old alto saxophone that a friend of his was selling for fifty dollars, and I just started playing it by ear. My grandfather was self-taught, but he knew quite a bit about harmony and he would write out songs for me to play. Of course, being a singer he thought like one. If the way I play now is vocal in conception, it's because of his influence. He was my first teacher, the one I inherited a lot of my values from. I made money in polka bands playing the songs he had taught me every weekend until I was 18."

As Maslak's technical proficiency increased and his musical taste broadened, his family enrolled him with professional instructors, including Larry Tiel, a classical saxophonist who had earlier tutored Yusef Lateef, Joe Henderson, and Benny Maupin. In high school, black classmates indoctrinated him into the joys of Motown and the mysteries of Coltrane, and like many alienated white adolescents in the 1960s, he began to identify with black music and black struggle almost to the point, he admits now, of wanting to *be* black: "My best friend was a black student named Al Crawford, who was also studying to be a classical saxophonist but who knew a lot more about jazz than I did. He'd play me Coltrane, Sonny Stitt, Cannonball Adderley . . . it was Coltrane who really got to me. The first jazz album I ever bought was *Blue Trane,* and I used to practice by trying to play Coltrane's solo on the title track note for note. It was very technical and very emotional at the same time, and that's a combination that appeals to you when you're very young. Plus it was a blues, and it was in a minor key like all the Eastern European songs I already knew by heart, so I could really relate to it on that level. I was just obsessed with it."

Before reaching thirty, Maslak drifted in and out of numerous guises characteristic of his generation: chaffing against the enforced discipline of the Kentonesque lab band at North Texas State University, all the while jamming the blues after hours in Dallas jukejoints; barnstorming the U.S. behind the Temptations and the Supremes in a late-'60s Motown revue; studying yoga in a San Francisco monastery in the wilting days of soft drugs and flowers; performing with minimalist composer Philip Glass and conceptualist Laurie Anderson in SoHo in the early '70s after meeting with failure in his bid to crack lower Manhattan's predominantly black jazz inner circle. Frustrated with his lot in New York, Maslak put on his shoes and went looking for a fairer shake, much as his grandfather had done a half-century before, but going the reverse route: in 1978, he made a pilgrimage to Europe, as much in quest of ancestral roots as of a larger, more appreciative audience.

Among his many attributes, Maslak is one of those horn players who heeds the call of drums—his lines convey the splash and heat and rumble of percussion even when he is playing a cappella. "I've always gravitated toward strong drummers," he says, "and I've always owned a trap set in addition to my horns, going back to the days when I used to fill in for my brother—who was the drummer in our little neighborhood polka band—when he wanted to dance with his girlfriend or go have a beer. I *hear* drums, is what it is." He has had the good fortune to form alliances with several of the drummers who were catalysts in the free jazz movement of which he is a child: innovator and former Cecil Taylor and Albert Ayler sideman Sunny Murray, European wildman Han Bennink, AACM colorist Phillip Wilson, and the jaunty Ornette Coleman alumnus Charles Moffett.

Moffett, in particular, was instrumental in Maslak's development: "Charles was running a workshop called Studio 7 in Oakland when I was living in Northern California, and he was a source of inspiration and encouragement to all the young players in the area around that time—me, Ray Anderson, David Murray, Butch Morris, Steve Turre, Curtis Clark, Arthur Blythe." It was Moffett who first brought Maslak east (to play the 1972 Newport Jazz Festival) and introduced him to Ornette Coleman, whose praise convinced Maslak to try his luck in New York instead of returning to the West Coast with Moffett. Sam Rivers hired Maslak to work at Studio Rivbea with some regularity, and there were jobs at The Kitchen with Glass, Anderson, Peter Gordon, and Rhys Chatham. But in general work was scarce, and Maslak had to take a variety of low paying day jobs—"painting apartments, driving cabs, working in the mailroom at the *Village Voice,* a little bit of this and a little bit of that" just to keep a roof over his head "on 11st Street and Avenue C, which was even more like skid row then than it is now, if you can imagine that.

"I went to Europe to play a week's worth of concerts and wound up staying three and a half years. There was a lot of work for me there—for the first time in my life, I was turning work down! I started making lots of money, at least in comparison to what I was making before. I lived in Amsterdam, but I was constantly traveling to other countries. I even did a solo tour of Poland just before the government started cracking down there. I'm a star in Eastern Europe, the prodigal son. I'm like Mick Jagger over there, I'm telling you."

Of the many records Maslak made during his European sojourn, the best are two which reunite him with Moffett. Recorded in the Netherlands in 1981, *Big Time* (Daybreak D-005) predates Maslak's current infatuation with rock and funk (about which more later), but there are numerous reminders of his other stops along the way. His voluminous sound projection and the swelling lyricism of his lines on a piece dedicated to Moffett confirm his lingering affection for Coltrane, just as the crunch of his accents on Herbie Nichols's "2300 Skidoo" testifies to his abiding love for the blues. Best of all, the high stepping Old World gaiety of the repeated triplets that prance lightly even through his most brutal rampages seems a nostalgic, if slightly wry, glance back at the weekends he spent performing behind Ukrainian singers and accordionists. Maslak's love of the tenor saxophone's freak register often makes it difficult to tell which of his horns is which, but on the two tracks featuring his tenor, his tone is dark and umber; his alto is buttery and more buoyant, sounding positively courtly on "Big Money Cha, Cha, Cha." On either horn, he is a dynamic, searing improviser, at his best when unencumbered by meter or chord structure, spanning his cries over bassist John Lindberg's prodigious two-chord ostinato on "You'll Love It," for example, or floating freely over Moffett's sentient pulse on "Big Heart." The rhythm section eggs Maslak on nicely, with Dutch pianist Misha Mengelberg abstracting solos that match the leader's quirk for quirk. The only track that fails is the pranky two-beat "You Left Your Big Shoe at My House," which begins uproariously enough with pumping stride figures from Mengelberg and droll trombone antics from guest Ray Anderson, but quickly disintegrates into a joke without a punch line.

Most of the themes on *Blaster Master* (Black Saint BSR-0079)— an album of Maslak/Moffett duets recorded in concert in Australia in 1981—will sound familiar to those who have heard Maslak's other records. "Jizz and Cocktails" (the flip title hardly does this ardent ballad, so reminiscent of "The Blue Danube," justice; but Maslak, a Charles Bukowski fan, points out that his titles "refer to themselves and not to the music and should be read as poetry." Come again?) appears as "Big Heart" on the above-mentioned Daybreak LP. "On *Big Time*, it was in 4/4," Maslak says. "Here it's in 6/8, which gives way to a blues shuffle feel. And of course my solo is freer and more extended." That last comment also applies to the itchy minor blues riff "Blaster Master" (rechristened "Mr. Moffett" for the Daybreak album a month later, perhaps in celebration of the drummer's dashing cymbal work on this performance). If you think you hear a bassist girding Maslak's tenor climb on "Jim Jizzbo," don't be embarrassed to say so—according to Maslak, the engineer who mastered the tape swore he heard a bassist too. It's actually Moffett filling up space, employing much the same strategy he used in the mid-'60s Ornette Coleman Trio, where his bass drum ruptures freed bassist David Izenzon to indulge in fanciful counterpoint with the leader. The tambourine adding bounce to the title track is further evidence of Moffett's resourcefulness, but it is not imaginary: Moffett had a tambourine mounted on a stand like an extra snare. "The tambourine is part of that down home, blues based, Southern Baptist feel Charles likes to get going behind a soloist," Maslak observes, "which I can relate to from having lived in Texas for four years when I was in college." "Jim Jizzbo" (a.k.a. "Bukowski in Love") is the vehicle for a Maslak solo at once as exploratory and shrewdly paced as any he has recorded thus far; and "Blast Yo Mama" an ejaculatory free improvisation of a kind Maslak has since disavowed. The forceful "July Jizzbo" Maslak describes as "a free, ten-minute introduction to a one-minute piece I had recorded earlier as 'Serious Fun.' This record marked the culmination of a very intense free jazz, free bop period I went through in Europe. I haven't closed the door on any of that, but I'm trying to add other things to the picture."

"When I landed in Europe, I was coming from six years of frustration in New York, and I was denying my American roots," Maslak says. "I wanted to identify with finally coming back home and all that bullshit, and the reception I got made it easy. But after a while, I realized that it *was* bullshit, because I'm not European, except by heritage. I was born in America, and my experience is just as valid as any other American's."

Maslak, who left for Europe with a beard and lank shoulder-length blond hair, returned from his odyssey clean-shaven, with his hair cropped short on the sides and swept back in a tall, spikey pompador—whether he looked more like a punk rock peacock (the desired effect) or an exchange student from some country where the 1960s never happened was difficult to say. ("Now there's a clean cut young man," my mother once remarked approvingly, pointing to a publicity photo of Maslak with his new look.) He began billing himself by his first name only "like Liberace or Dion. It's a whole marketing philosophy that works."

"I want to emphasize this new rock 'n' roll direction," he repeated several times during our first conversation in 1982. "What I listen to now is Talking Heads, Brian Eno, and new wave. There are some innovative things going on in pop music, yet at the same time it's accessible to the masses, which music really ought to be if it's going to have any contemporary relevance. So I'm playing electronic music now for a variety of different reasons—I mean, I still play acoustic instruments, but when I perform now, it's got to be in an electronic context, and I want people to hear it as rock 'n' roll."

In December 1981, Maslak formed Loved by Millions, a clamorous rhythm 'n' dissonance band with Moffett on drums, Moffett's teenage son Charnett on electric bass, Maslak's wife Pamela Lyons as vocalist, and his old SoHo associate Rhys Chatham on guitar. Although comparisons to Ornette Coleman's electric band seemed inevitable, the night I heard Loved by Millions (the first time they played together in public, it turned out) they were not ready for Prime Time. But a studio quality rehearsal tape that Maslak later played for me revealed the band's lusty promise. At its best, Loved by Millions not only tied together the disparate threads of Maslak's life to that point; in its happy minglings of black and white, young and old, families and friends, old traditions and new technologies, jazz and funk and new music and rock 'n' roll, it united the conflicting shrieks and whispers of American music and American life into one joyous roar, one barbaric yawp.*

But the original edition of Loved by Millions was short-lived. Following several personnel shuffles, the current lineup includes Maslak, Lyons, a keyboard synthesizer, and a drum computer. "I simply push the button that says START; Pamela sings, and I play free improvisations over my pre-programmed arrangements," Maslak says. He concedes that some human interaction is lost by this method, but also points out that he retains his affinity for drums. "I have to program the rhythm beat by beat. So I guess I've finally become my own drummer after all these years."

Whether the name Loved by Millions is intended optimistically or ironically must sometimes be difficult even for Maslak to say. Commercially, the band is still at that nebulous stage where it might be the opening act for a rock group one month and play to a gathering

---

* Although the tape that Maslak played for me in 1982 was never released, in 1983 he put out a single by a later edition of Loved by Millions, without Chatham and the Moffetts. That single might disappoint those wishing to hear more of Maslak (he's relegated to trading background riffs with an unidentified Fabulous Flame-*cum*-minimalist guitarist), but otherwise it's a winner. When I heard Loved by Millions in concert, Lyons's caterwauling only reminded me that even as a grieving widow Yoko Ono was pretty hard to take; now Lyons makes me think how much I like Lydia Lunch and how much I miss Patti Smith. Which is to say that Lyons has stopped thinking of herself as a performance artist and begun thinking of herself as a performer, and that her inspired amateurism gives both "Nosferatu" and "Why Why" some of the tough, sensual insistence of 1977 punk. Added to radio playlists (fat chance), either side would sound anachronistic, and I mean that as a compliment. (The single is available from 2350 Broadway, Suite 1134, New York, N.Y. 10024.)

of jazz technophobes the next, bemusing one audience and alienating the other, with no jobs in between. Despite what the immigrant in each of us wants to believe, the streets of America aren't really paved with gold, not even for an artist willing to meet the public halfway. Which doesn't prove there's no America, to paraphrase Saul Bellow's Augie March, himself a down-to-earth epic hero much like Maslak. Music as fervent and lyrical and fiercely comic as Maslak figures to go on making in one context or another come thick or thin is enough to make hope spring eternal in even the most disillusioned of hearts.

(1982–84)

# II

## PRACTICED

## HANDS

# An Improviser Prepares

After a summer tour of Japan with guitarist Pat Metheny and a string of West Coast concerts in early autumn, tenor saxophonist Sonny Rollins accepted no more work the rest of 1983. Something of a homebody anyway, he needed time to brace himself for a January record date, and time to reflect on a close call.

In April, Rollins had played New York's Town Hall, with the cocky young trumpeter Wynton Marsalis on the bill as his special guest. Rollins says that he was so preoccupied with rehearsals the afternoon of the concert that he had forgotten to eat: he had recently made several personnel changes in his band, and he wanted to give the new recruits ample opportunity to familiarize themselves with one another, their leader, and added starter Marsalis. Rollins may have been edgy for another reason that he is understandably reluctant to express: many male jazz fans invest as much ego in rooting for their favorite soloists as other men invest in prizefighters, and a segment of the audience that night wanted a clear-cut victor to emerge from what was being talked about as a fight to the finish between Rollins and Marsalis, the reigning heavyweight champion and the newest pretender to his throne.

Lucille Rollins, who has been married to Sonny Rollins for over 20 years and managed him for the last 11, says she knew something was wrong when, from her post backstage, she heard the rhythm section slam to a halt following a curious pause in her husband's solo on Charlie Parker's "Big Foot," the third number of the evening. Sonny Rollins had landed on his back, his head about three inches from Tommy Campbell's bass drum. "I whispered, *'Get up, man,'* thinking he was spoofing, before realizing that he was out cold," Campbell remembers. "I looked over at Wynton, who was shaking uncontrollably. We were all so petrified it was easier to go on playing for a few seconds than it was to stop."

Upon regaining consciousness in his dressing room, Rollins's first thought was fear his horn might be stolen, what with so many strangers milling around. An ambulance rushed him to the cardiovascular wing of Bellvue Hospital; *Bellvue,* a name that shrieks bedlam within the jazz community, the hospital to which Rollins's friend Charles Mingus had gone to seek psychiatric counseling and been locked away for weeks until a lawyer intervened. Asked to remain overnight for tests, a shaken and superstitious Rollins refused and checked himself out. His private physician subsequently ruled out heart attack or stroke—everyone's unspoken fear. But Rollins was found to be suffering from hypertension aggravated by nervous exhaustion.

When I caught up with Rollins before his concert in Boston six months later, his memory of the evening in question was hazy. He speculated that his heel must have caught on a wire, causing him to topple over backwards and bump his head—but Lucille Rollins reminded him that no one, her least of all, was buying that fanciful scenario. Still radiating youthful power and vitality in his mid fifties, Rollins perhaps finds it difficult to admit to physical infirmity (his wife reveals that, like many victims of hypertension surprise attacks, he has to be reminded to take his daily medication now that his blood pressure has returned to normal). Even so, he was only too happy to follow doctor's orders to lighten up on travel, since that meant spending more time at home in Germantown, New York, a few miles north

of Woodstock, where he and Lucille (his second wife), who have no
children, enjoy a quiet, bucolic existence.

One could work up a lather about how the scarcity of jazz nightclubs everywhere but New York City has made the presentation of
jazz a catch-as-catch-can proposition, citing as evidence Sonny Rollins's
itinerary in the waning months of 1983 (he played a Greenwich Village rock showcase, two Southern universities, and a pink-and-white
wedding cake of a room in the Copley Plaza, one of Back Bay Boston's most patrician hotels). But Rollins is no typical jazz musician, be
the yardstick creative temperament or earning capacity. His inactivity
was strictly a matter of choice, the few dates he accepted one-nighters
designed not to keep him away from home too long.

"There are certain things to be said in favor of the old days, when
you played a club for an entire week before moving on," Rollins told
me as he fit a mouthpiece over his horn before going on stage in Boston. "After a few nights, you knew the audiences you could expect,
you knew where to find whatever you needed around town, and you
built up a special kind of rapport with your musicians from being
away from home together so long. But as you get older, you miss
sleeping in your own bed every night, and you miss the mundane
activities that constitute your daily routine. And frankly, I just don't
*want* to spend a week of the time I've got left in Cleveland or Detroit or wherever."

The road has traditionally symbolized freedom for professional
musicians, an opportunity to carouse in the company of one's fellows;
and bad habits born of the road have claimed scores of casualties
from rock 'n' roll as well as jazz. Though he makes his living from
it, nightlife is not Rollins's style, and one doubts it ever was: the road
is an experience to be endured, not relished, so far as he is concerned. He spent most of his 36 hours in Boston in his hotel room,
looking forward to the flight out. Not even the lure of hearing Sammy
Price and Dave McKenna, the Copley's resident pianists, both of
whom Rollins admires, was sufficient enticement for him to stay up
late.

What he seems to resent most about performances on the road is not being able to practice his instrument (an odd thought, when one considers that performance is supposed to be the end result of practice—and that few musicians his age who perform as often as he does bother to practice at all). "At home, I usually get up around 4:00 a.m. to feed our two dogs and three cats—Lucille has them so spoiled they won't let us sleep later than that—the visiting cats, the visiting chickens, the visiting whatever else comes around, because a lot of the area around us is farmland, and you see a lot of animals. Then I go back to sleep for an hour or so and spend the rest of the day practicing. You can't practice in hotel rooms, though, for fear of annoying someone who might be trying to sleep in the next room. All you can do is watch soap operas and try to relax, and I can take only so much of that." His voice was losing some of its viscosity, becoming weightless in abstraction, and I thought it better to take leave of him, realizing that he was itching to get in a few minutes of practice now that he had the chance.

Rollins's list of associates over the last 35 years reads like a modern jazz who's who: Charlie Parker, Thelonious Monk, Bud Powell, Dizzy Gillespie, Miles Davis, Max Roach, Clifford Brown. But simple cross-referencing of this sort fails to convey Rollins's true significance. Unlike Parker, Louis Armstrong, or Ornette Coleman, Rollins did not alter the rhythmic syntax of jazz. Unlike Davis, he has never been a reliable bellwether of new trends. Although a number of his compositions (the calypso "St. Thomas" and the blues derivatives "Oleo," "Doxie," and "Airegin") have become jam-session standbys, he has not set a standard other jazz writers have sought to emulate (unlike Monk, Duke Ellington, and Charles Mingus). He has never succeeded in forming a band in his own image, and although countless saxophonists have aped his stylistic mannerisms, his influence has never been as all-pervasive as John Coltrane's was in the mid-1960s. Yet when conjuring up an image of the quintessential jazzman—heroic, inspired, mystical, obsessed—as often as not, it is Rollins we picture, because no other jazz instrumentalist better epitomizes the lonely tightrope walk between spontaneity and organization implicit in taking an improvised solo. Everyone who listens to jazz can tell a story of a night when Rollins could do no wrong, when ideas poured out of him so effortlessly that a comparison to Leopold Bloom seemed in order, until one realized that it was James Joyce one was thinking of—that Rollins was blessed with an angbite of inwit far more ruthless and sophisticated and formal than the quaint phrase "stream of consciousness" could hope to convey. The irony is that the nights when Rollins is at wit's end can be just as thrilling for illuminating the perils endemic to improvisation. The great thing about Rollins—as critic Gary Giddins once put it—is that even when he's off, he's on.

Rollins is the greatest living jazz improviser (no arguments please), and if we redefine virtuosity to include improvisational cunning as well as instrumental finesse (as we probably should when discussing jazz), he may be the greatest virtuoso that jazz has ever produced. But listening to him is rarely the unequivocal pleasure it ought to be, for not only is he the least predictable of jazz artists, he is in one way the most perverse: the ecstasy his playing arouses in others he seems stubbornly unwilling to partake of himself. He is a notorious perfectionist, and the pressure he creates for himself sometimes pulls him up short. Most jazz musicians, including some of the great ones, simply turn on the charm and let technique take over when inspiration fails to visit them, confident that few in their audiences will be able to tell the difference between manual dexterity and divine intercession. Not Rollins, bless him and curse him. He will bring a solo to a halt if the grand design he has been tracing eludes him even momentarily.

On such occasions, Rollins's default shifts the burden of giving the customers their money's worth to his sidemen, which can lead to comic scenes like one I witnessed in Philadelphia a decade ago. Rollins led an unrealistic round of applause each time his pianist climaxed a solo and began comping for the Rollins solo he thought would ensue. Looking over and noticing Rollins's saxophone dangling from its strap, the harried pianist had no choice but to nod graciously to the audience and launch another chorus, as if by popular demand.

"I don't remember that particular incident, but I have to plead guilty anyway," Rollins said when I asked him about it. "People have admonished me for pulling stunts like that, so I try not to anymore. Around the time you're talking about, I was playing two or three sets a night in clubs, and I always hoped that people would hang around for the next set, and that the next set would be better. Now I'm usually in town for one show only, and knowing that people have come out to hear *me* play, I play for them, even when I'm displeased with what I hear myself playing. But you know, there are times when things aren't clicking and I play *extended* solos out of sheer frustration, but nobody ever complains about *that*. Which makes me wonder, because it's like I'm forcing the music instead of letting it flow, and that's no good. But maybe that's what people like—they sense the tension I'm feeling and it excites them."

If Rollins's self-doubt makes him seem the stereotypical modern artist, his music betrays thankfully little of the anomie associated with modern art. He can be the jolliest of improvisers. His best solos are full of jeering subterranean moans, cheeky falsetto whistles, and pecking staccato phrases that recall the bar-walking rhythm 'n' blues saxophonists popular in black neighborhoods 30 years ago. Although he may be the most abstract thinker in jazz, he has never turned his back on blues and popular song forms, not even during his brief flirtation with free form in the early '60s; and one of the dizziest thrills jazz has to offer is following the lines of a familiar melody as they expand and contract in the funhouse mirror of a Rollins improvisation. In recent years, his populism has led him to such unlikely but felicitous vehicles as Stevie Wonder's "Isn't She Lovely" and the jouncy Dolly Parton hit "Here You Come Again." From the outset of his career, he has delighted in pop confections of the sort many of his more priggish jazz colleagues would think beneath their dignity.

"Songs like 'Toot, Toot, Tootsie,' 'Wagon Wheels,' 'There's No Business Like Show Business,' . . . songs hardly anyone had recorded before. Or *since,* for that matter," he cracked the afternoon I visited him and Lucille in the Tribeca penthouse efficiency they lease as a combination business office and home away from home when he plays New York. "Those are the songs that first made me love music, and I guess I heard most of them in the movies on Saturday afternoons when I was a kid. I tend to enjoy humorous, light-hearted things," he said, gesturing to the coffee table and sofa, which were piled high with books on genre films of every description. A hardback copy of Diane Johnson's biography of Dashiell Hammett lay open, spine up, on the daybed. "Old movies, Mad magazine, Bob and Ray—pure escapism, I know. But I guess it's okay, since I work hard at my music and have no real hobbies."

Rollins, who looks wary even when smiling, has a reputation as an unapproachable loner, an image he has done little to cultivate but nothing to dispel. Still, he and Lucille seemed genuinely pleased to be entertaining company, as we sat gazing down at gridlocked traffic. "It's so difficult readjusting to the pace of the city, even though I was born here and lived here most of my life," Rollins said. He had spent his week in New York taking care of errands—buying reeds, having his horn repaired, running clothes to the tailor. He hadn't looked up any old musician friends, and he hadn't been out to hear any live music. Next door, a teenage heavy metal band ran down their Led Zepplin and Van Halen, occasionally eclipsing our conversation. "My protégés," Rollins winced. "They keep at it all day long."

He was born Theodore Walter Rollins in 1929 (no one has called him that in years), to a Harlem family he describes as "middle class, with a piano in the living room and everything." His childhood ambition was to become a professional illustrator, but by the time he was graduated from high school, he was already earning money as a musician, playing in "kid bands with the other young guys from the neighborhood" (some of whom have also achieved adult renown, including alto saxophonist Jackie McLean, pianist Kenny Drew, and drummer Art Taylor) "and sitting in with the older guys who were kind enough to let me, like Bud Powell and Thelonious Monk." His role model was tenor patriarch Coleman Hawkins, "a forceful player with a big ripe sound, but a thoughtful player, too, very sophisticated in his knowledge of alternate chords—that was a good combination.

He was a very classy fellow, always impeccably dressed and very patient with everyone, and that was something else I tried to emulate." I asked Rollins if he ever worried that his country isolation deprives today's young musicians of similar access to *him*. "Oh, you're making me feel guilty now," he complained, rubbing his goatee and fooling with the shapeless woolen cap he always seems to be wearing, even indoors. "But you see, Coleman Hawkins and Lockjaw Davis and those guys didn't just make themselves available to me. I practically camped out on their doorsteps until they took pity on me and invited me in."

Critic/composer Gunther Schuller once praised Rollins for knowing that "well-timed silence can become part of a musical phrase"; as a corollary, one might add that Rollins's frequent sabbaticals have played as large a part as his improvised solos in defining his mystique. The first hiatus came in 1954, and no one much noticed. "There was a scourge of drugs around that time," Rollins told me, "and like everybody else, I was part of it." It was a dressing down from Charlie Parker, of all people, that persuaded Rollins to enroll in an experimental methadone program at the federal prison in Lexington, Kentucky. Rollins and Parker were together in a New Jersey recording studio as sidemen on a Miles Davis date, and Parker—who knew that Rollins revered him—asked him if he was clean. Rollins lied and said yes, but Parker learned the truth from a hushed conversation he overheard between Rollins and another musician on the date. Ironically, it had been Parker's example that had induced many musicians of Rollins's generation to shoot up in the first place. "But you have to realize Charlie Parker wasn't just a great musician. He was a very sick man who was dying from self-abuse and feeling guilty about the example he had set for others," Rollins explained. He decided that the best way to show his love for Parker was to do as he said, not as he did.

In 1959, dissatisfaction with the jazz business and his own playing prompted Rollins to interrupt his career just as it was taking off. (Speculation had it that the acutely self-conscious Rollins had become too inhibited to play after reading Schuller's close structural analysis of one of his solos in the *Jazz Review*. Rollins admits only that he resolved to stop reading his notices soon after coming across Schuller's "Sonny Rollins and the Art of Thematic Improvisation." He still carries clippings of his reviews for the purpose of identification: not so much to prove that he is Sonny Rollins as to prove that Sonny Rollins is *somebody*—a nice distinction that might occur only to a black musician idolized in jazz but scarcely recognized outside of it, and traveling with a white wife.) Although unintended as such, his second vanishing act amounted to a major publicity coup. In abandoning his audience, he had not abandoned his instrument, and not wishing to subject the neighbors in his Brooklyn apartment house to the torture of his marathon practice sessions, he would practice in the dead of night on the pedestrian level of the Williamsburg Bridge, as private a rehearsal hall as he could ever hope to find. But one night jazz critic Ralph Berton wandered by, and the anonymity that Rollins had hoped for was gone forever. Soon, the TV networks were sending camera crews to the bridge and portraying Rollins as a lofty and mystical idealist, a man who had turned his back on worldly riches to pursue self-knowledge. When he returned to the jazz scene in 1961, he was able to parlay his status as a media curiosity into a lucrative recording contract with RCA Victor.

By the end of the '6os, he had again turned away from public performance, though he continued to practice every day. He attended to chronic dental problems caused by a hard embouchere and journeyed to India to study yoga "not so much for the betterment of my music as for greater peace of mind, but my playing has benefited as a side effect, I think, in terms of greater wind capacity and greater mental concentration," he told me; and I noticed that his legs were folded up beneath him on the sofa, in the classic lotus position, even as we talked.

When Rollins began recording and accepting engagements again in 1972, his wife became his manager strictly by default: there was no one else he trusted to do the job. "I know of countless instances in which a musician's wife has taken an active role in her husband's career, usually with disastrous results to both the career and the marriage," says Orrin Keepnews, Rollins's close friend and his record producer from 1972 until 1980. "Lucille is one of the shining exceptions."

Many of the jazz wives who represent their husbands do so because their husbands have seduced them into thinking it's part of their wifely obligation, "or because they think it'll be fun, working so closely with their husbands, but they wind up hating it," explained Lucille Rollins as Sonny stared straight ahead. "You've got to know what you're doing, or you'll do more harm than good. At first, I felt like such an amateur dealing with club-owners and record producers that I used the pseudonym Janice Jesta for a while—Jesta was one of our cats. But I became more self-confident once I realized how much I love this business."

In addition to retaining veto power over her husband's bookings (he signed with an agency in 1979), Lucille Rollins, who worked as an office administrator before their marriage, handles the payroll and travel arrangements for his band. (Rollins prefers staying at whatever hotel is closest to the airport and taking a limousine to the concert— that way he can make a faster getaway and he doesn't have to wander around a strange city.) Since the incident at Town Hall, she has traveled with him to most of his jobs; backstage in Boston, she made it a point to remind him to eat before going on stage.

The couple were co-producers of Rollins's last three albums, and even before that, Lucille had become Sonny's proxy at playbacks and mixdowns, because he cannot bear to listen to his own recordings—a point that emerged from our conversation when Lucille told me that the best performance she had ever heard her husband give was at the June 1983 makeup for the aborted Town Hall concert with Marsalis. Even Rollins had to admit that he played "okay." Lucille rolled her eyes and gasped *"Okay? It was fantastic!"* Too bad it wasn't recorded, I said, and a look of resignation settled on Rollins's face: "If it had been recorded, it might not have been okay."

"Sonny will admit that recording has always been a traumatic experience for him, and as the years have passed and he feels that he has more of a reputation to uphold, it's become even more traumatic, to use his own word," says Orrin Keepnews. "To some extent, every musician I've ever worked with has felt that he never put anything of value on a record. But Sonny is the supreme example. If the essence of jazz is improvisation, then the whole concept of recording—freezing a particular moment and calling it definitive—violates that essence. And Sonny, who is the most intuitive musician I've ever met as well as the most intellectual, is the musician most acutely aware of that contradiction."

Rollins's phobia hasn't prevented him from recording a goodly number of albums commonly regarded as classics, including *Saxophone Colossus, Worktime, A Night at the Village Vanguard, The Freedom Suite,* and *Way Out West,* all dating from a fertile period in the mid- to late '50s, when he was also in the studio regularly as a sideman with Miles Davis, Thelonious Monk, and Clifford Brown and Max Roach. From the 1960s, there are such still disputed masterpieces as *Our Man in Jazz,* with sidemen enlisted from Ornette Coleman's group, and *Sonny Meets Hawk,* a Mexican standoff with father figure Coleman Hawkins.

Toward the mid-'70s, Rollins began to employ younger musicians whose first allegiance was to amplified jazz-rock fusion, and one listened to his new records with enthusiastic ambivalence and exasperated awe, much the way earlier jazz listeners must have greeted the mature work of Louis Armstrong, who also embraced the most dubious musical conventions of his day. (This comparison is relevant in another way: as Armstrong had, Rollins began overindulging his technique at the cost of continuity, climaxing too many of his solos with gratuitous high notes sustained beyond purpose.) "I've always been a very rhythmic player," Rollins pointed out when I asked him about this change in direction, "and I want the rhythms beneath me to be rhythms you can feel throughout your entire system, not just something you can tap your foot to. I know that some people think I should be using a '50s kind of rhythm section, with upright bass walking a straight four beats to the measure, the piano blocking out chords, and the drummer going 'ta-da, ta-da,' or whatever, very discreetly on his cymbals. But that's tired, and it just doesn't appeal to me anymore. I want energy and constant propulsion, and I find only young players can give that to me. And rock rhythms or funk rhythms or whatever you want to call them are what the young guys are interested in today, along with electric instruments. So it's all been a natural progression for me, if you look at it that way."

Even if one looks at it Rollins's way, his logic is riddled with holes. He talks as though there are no options beyond bop and fusion, which is simply not the case. His present drummer's beat is chunky and metronomic compared with the drummers he recorded with in the '50s and '60s (you won't catch Max Roach or Billy Higgins or Elvin Jones going "ta-da, ta da"). The bass guitarists he has been using tend to favor disruptive, guitar-like filigree rather than earthy, locomotive bass lines. Contrary to what Rollins believes, there *are* younger musicians playing hard bop who could follow him better and give him a higher lift than the fusioneers he insists on hiring, but it's doubtful if he has heard them. Talking to him, one gets the impression that he no longer monitors developments in jazz the way he did when he was younger—or the way Coleman Hawkins did throughout his career. In this, Rollins is no guiltier than most of his contemporaries, and in all fairness, it's as much lack of opportunity as lack of curiosity that's to blame. There's no 52nd Street anymore—no golden strip where musicians cross paths and trade secrets—and no one predominant jazz style. In its maturity, jazz has become both a bewilderingly pluralistic form of expression and a commercially marginal enterprise, a combination that effectively rules against an apprentice system or a chain of command. It's not surprising that outside of their own cliques, most veteran musicians have no better idea than the casual listener of who the hot young players are.

If Rollins's secret motive is to woo rock audiences, he has overestimated his capacity for the ordinary—his records have not been "commercial" in the simplest, most accurate sense: they haven't sold in enormous quantities. Yet with *No Problem* (Milestone M-9014) and *Reel Life* (Milestone M-9018), both released in 1982, Rollins's advocacy of a modified back beat began to pay unexpected artistic dividends. He was swinging more ferociously than ever, and he had escaped the sham democracy of modern jazz, which entitles each band member to solo to his heart's content on every single number. Rollins was now the star; his sidemen were relegated to back-up positions; and that was the way it should have been all along. Long portions of the 1984 release *Sunny Days and Starry Nights* (Milestone M-9122) are given over to exuberant, jabbing exchanges between Rollins and drummer Tommy Campbell, with the rest of the band laying low or laying out. It's such a pleasure to hear Rollins duking it out with a drummer this way again that one is willing to ignore the fact that Campbell doesn't pack very much punch. The record also demonstrates Rollins's increased mastery of pop recording techniques. Multi-tracking enables him to be his own duet partner on Noel Coward's "I'll See You Again," and to weave a luxurious improvisation around his own held notes on an original ballad dedicated to Wynton Marsalis. (Pianist Mark Sloskin's overdubbed celeste is an especially nice touch on "Wynton," recalling Thelonious Monk's use of the delicate instrument on his 1957 recording of "Pannonica" with Rollins.) Also boasting a wickedly inventive chromatic orbit on Jerome Kern's "I'm Old Fashioned," and three snorting "St. Thomas"-like calypsos, *Sunny Days and Starry Nights* is the first Rollins LP in ages that one can enjoy from start to finish without first scaling down one's expectations. But like all of his records, it captures only the echo of his genius. To catch him in full cry, one must hear him live. And even then, there are no guarantees.

On an overhanging wall opposite the bar at the Bottom Line are framed color glossies of Elvis Costello, Van Morrison, Philip Glass, and Phoebe Snow. A large, dark, characterless room near Washington Square, the Bottom Line is not a jazz club, but it is Rollins's club of preference in New York, because he can attract as many people there in one night as he would over several nights in a smaller jazz venue like Sweet Basil or the Village Vanguard. When I heard him at the Bottom Line in November 1983, all the tables were full an hour before showtime, the crowd was three deep in front of the bar, and SRO tickets were all that were available for the late show. It was at the Bottom Line that Mick Jagger heard Rollins and asked him to add saxophone tracks to the Rolling Stones' *Tattoo You*. Jagger was nowhere to be seen the night I was there, and whatever musicians were in the crowd respected Rollins's desire for privacy. In his dressing room between sets, he greeted only relatives and two close friends, a journalist and a physician, both there socially rather than professionally.

Rollins began playing well before the audience was admitted, hunching his shoulders and pacing the short runway between his dressing room and the stage, part fullback and part expectant father, as he worried over a long aching phrase that eventually blossomed into the old chestnut "Where Are You?" His sidemen ordered cold sandwiches and fried chicken dishes from the club's dinner menu, and the sound and lighting crews ran around shouting instructions to one another . . . "He doesn't like much follow coverage, not much saturation. Just create an environment and let it happen . . ." "The sax on top with everything else below it, right? . . ." Rollins was oblivious to all of them.

Without breaking stride, he played "Where Are You?" at the soundcheck, too, chipping away at the melody until nothing was left but a luminous, abstract, imperishable paraphrase, a point of departure for the stupendous choruses that seemed ready to come brimming out of his horn as the band began chording for him and he began tugging at their beat. But when Rollins surged into double time, he left the others clutching at air, and everything broke down. It was painfully obvious that his sidemen were not conversant enough with "Where Are You?" (which Rollins recorded in 1961 and perhaps heard Gertrude Niessen sing in the 1937 film *Top of the Town* at a Saturday matinee when he was in grade school) to take liberties with it.

After their leader left the stage, guitarist Bobby Broom jumped into Tommy Campbell's vacated drum chair; and together, he and bass guitarist Russell Blake hammered out a funk riff that brought a smile to both their faces. The whole bizzare scene portrayed with a vengeance the difference in age between Rollins and his charges, all of whom are in their mid- to late twenties. The camaraderie one listens for in a good band was missing from this unit, perhaps as a result of their not having spent much off time together on the road. ("I just *practiced* with Coleman Hawkins," Rollins had told me. "I never hung out with him or anything, because I was just a kid and he was a grown man. What could we possibly have had in common?") Frequently, Rollins and his sidemen even take separate flights, because he prefers arriving in town a day early so that he won't have to battle travel fatigue when it comes time to play—quite a departure from the days when a whole band would travel together on a bus. Trombonist Clifton Anderson—Rollins's nephew, sometimes practice partner, and newest member of his band—told me that there had not been a full group rehearsal in the four months he had been with Rollins. "Everyone in the band realizes that Sonny is a master, and the people turn out mainly to hear him, not us," Anderson said. "So as long as he's in a good mood and really feels like playing, we just try to keep up with him. But it can be hard. He can throw you, seguing from number to number the way he does and trying out tunes in different keys."

Once the show started, Rollins continued to pace, the shadow cast by the brim of his floppy red velvet hat forming a hood over his eyes. On some numbers, he played an aural game of hide and seek with the crowd, offering nothing that could be considered an improvised chorus. Yet his sweet and sour theme recapitulations were so delicious, his movements which cheered on the rhythm section so disarming, and his habit of cradling his horn in his arms and announcing song titles directly into the lipstick mike mounted in the bell at once so distancing and so benign (talk about star presence!) that the audience rewarded him with rapturous ovations for these pieces anyway, shouting their approval of solos they had only imagined hearing.

But on "Cabin in the Sky," "I'll Be Seeing You," and "I'm Old Fashioned," Rollins unloosed solos beyond anyone's power of imagining save his own. His band gave him all the energy and propulsion he could have wished for, creating grooves that had this jazz audi-

ence dancing in its seats and might have had a rock audience dancing in the aisles. But Rollins's barking crescendos carried such vehe-
ment rhythmic impact and shone with such harmonic iridescence as
to render all accompaniment superfluous. And indeed, the most satisfying moments of the evening came when he dispensed with the band
altogether for twisting out-of-tempo intros and lapidary cadenzas which
he tossed off with an astonishing and somehow reassuring what–
me-worry? nonchalance. He was in such high spirits that as he bit
into the roguish "Alfie's Theme," he motioned Anderson to weave a
counterpoint behind him, and what had served as a brief and per-
functory sign-off riff in Boston just a week before stretched out over
15 minutes with bubbling solos all around. The set fell short of per-
fection (there was nothing as magnificent as those few tentative measures of "Where Are You?"), but Sonny Rollins accomplished two
things only he could have: he convinced you that the next set might
be the best live jazz concert you'd ever hear; and more important, he
convinced you that, coming from an improviser, that's a promise as
thrilling for the making as for the keeping.

(APRIL 1984)

# There's No Success Like Failure, and Failure's No Success at All: Ornette Coleman's Permanent Revolution

When Ornette Coleman made his East Coast nightclub debut opposite the Art Farmer–Benny Golson Jazztet at the Five Spot Cafe in Greenwich Village on November 18, 1959, "all hell broke loose," in Coleman's apt phrase. "Everybody in New York was saying you've got to go down to the Five Spot and hear this crazy alto player from Texas. It was like I was E.T. or something, just dropped in from the moon, and everybody had to come take a look at me."

The 29-year-old alto saxophonist arrived in New York having already won the approval of some of the period's most influential jazz opinion-makers. "Ornette Coleman is doing the only really new thing in jazz since the innovations in the mid '40s of Dizzy Gillespie and Charlie Parker, and those of Thelonious Monk," John Lewis, the pianist and musical director of the Modern Jazz Quartet, told an interviewer after hearing Coleman in Los Angeles. (Lewis later helped Coleman secure a contract with Atlantic Records.) Coleman's other champions included critics Nat Hentoff and Martin Williams and composer Gunther Schuller, all of whom wrote for the magazine *Jazz Review*. "I believe that what Ornette Coleman is playing will affect the whole character of jazz music profoundly and pervasively," Williams editorialized a month before Coleman opened at the Five Spot.

Not all of Williams's colleagues shared his enthusiasm once they were given the opportunity to hear Coleman for themselves. In *Down Beat,* George Hoefer described the reactions of an audience at a special press preview at the Five Spot: "Some walked in and out before they could finish a drink, some sat mesmerized by the sound, others talked constantly to their neighbors at the table or argued with drink in hand at the bar." Many critics, finding Coleman's music strident and incoherent, feared that his influence on jazz would be deleterious. Others doubted that he would exert any influence on jazz at all. Still others, bewildered by Coleman's music and preferring to take a wait-and-see position on its merits, accused his supporters at *Jazz Review* of touting him for their own aggrandizement. Musicians—always skeptical of newcomers and envious of the publicity that Coleman was receiving—denounced him even more harshly than critics did. Some questioned his integrity as well as his instrumental competence; the outspoken Miles Davis went so far as to question his sanity.

"Every night the club would be jammed, with some people hating what I was doing and calling me a charlatan, and other people loving it and declaring me a genius," Coleman says. "I remember one well-established musician—a drummer, and I'm not going to name any names—becoming so upset he kicked down the door to the men's room, then coming after me and landing a punch on my jaw before the bartenders could pull him off. Incredible isn't a strong enough word for it."

"Many musicians were terrified that what Ornette was doing would render their music obsolete. That was the absurd part of it," remembers Martin Williams, now a Special Editor at Smithsonian Institution Press. It was Williams who landed Coleman the Five Spot engagement by playing an acetate of his music for Joe and Iggy Termini, the club's owners. "Some musicians had studied for years to learn everything it was possible to know about chord changes, and here comes a man whose approach was highly intuitive, reaping all that publicity, and telling them, in essence, that harmony wasn't as all-important as they assumed. He sounded like a primitive to them. Yet if you gave him the benefit of the doubt, it was obvious that he knew his instrument inside out. I remember hearing him at the Five Spot one night during a blizzard, when he played a blues exactly as Charlie Parker might have—and I mean *exactly*, the embouchere, the attack, all of it—and the few people who braved the weather that night just sat there with their mouths open in astonishment, because this was something he was supposed to be incapable of doing. Sonny Rollins was there, listening intently at the end of the bar, and I looked around at the end to see his reaction, but he had disappeared into the night."

Infighting over the merits of historical movements and geographical schools was nothing new in the jazz world. But not since the short-lived vogue for the decrepit New Orleans trumpeter Bunk Johnson (and perhaps not even then) had one musician split opinion so dramatically. Coleman was either a visionary or a fraud, and there was no middle ground between advocacy and disapprobation. The controversy raged, spreading from the music journals to daily newspapers and general-interest magazines, where it gradually turned comic. Every VIP in Manhattan, from Leonard Bernstein to Dorothy Kilgallen, seemed to have been to the Five Spot and to have emerged with wisdom to offer on the subject of Ornette Coleman. In Thomas Pynchon's first novel *V.*, there is a character named McClintic Sphere, who plays an alto saxophone of hand-carved ivory (Coleman's was made of white plastic) at a club called the V Note:

> "He plays all the notes Bird missed," somebody whispered in front of Fu. Fu went through the motions of breaking a beer bottle on the edge of the table, jamming it into the speaker's back and twisting.

This was the closest modern jazz would ever come to Beatlemania or the premiere of *Le Sacre du Printemps*.

The silver anniversary of Coleman's Five Spot opening passed virtually unnoticed toward the end of 1984. Coleman wasn't even aware that it was coming up, and if there had been an official commemoration, he would probably have been too busy to attend. As November 18 approached, he had just returned from a European tour with his band Prime Time. Following a 72-hour stopover in New York, he flew to Fort Worth, Texas (his birthplace), to mix two albums he hopes eventually to sell to an independent label—one a live performance by Prime Time, the other a eulogy for Buckminster Fuller with the Fort Worth Symphony. After running into endless financial roadblocks, filmmaker Shirley Clarke had finally completed *Made in America,* the bio-documentary on Coleman which she started shooting in 1968; Coleman was making plans to attend the world premiere in West Berlin early the following year. When he found a spare moment, he worked on "The Oldest Language," a piece calling for the participation of 130 musicians from Europe, North America, and the Third World, all of whom would have to live together for six months and reconcile their cultural and linguistic differences before learning Coleman's score. Coleman is no fool; he knows that the cost of such a project is prohibitive. "I've got to find an angel," he muses in his soft Texas drawl. "I know it can be done. Philip Glass has written things like *Einstein on the Beach* which must have cost a million dollars to stage. That proves it's possible."

The disarray of Coleman's loft, which occupies the top floor of a public schoolhouse on New York's Lower East Side and doubles as living quarters and rehearsal space, mirrors Coleman's vagabond lifestyle and his perilous financial station. One wall is nothing but windows looking out on grim streets still awaiting the first signs of gentrification. The sparsely and indifferently furnished room is dominated by professional-quality sound equipment, including a mixing board and speakers the size of small manned spacecraft, and by Coleman's own paintings, many of them photorealist renderings of his album jackets. In part, Coleman's interest in classical music, poetry, and the visual arts is the result of the interest classical composers, poets, and visual artists displayed in *his* work when he arrived in New York in 1959 (the Five Spot was a popular watering hole for artists long before the Termini brothers adopted a jazz policy). The open hostility of fellow jazz musicians wounded Coleman, but it was nothing new: he had been a pariah in Los Angeles in the 1950s and on the Southern chitlin circuit before that. At least in New York, he was able to make friends outside of jazz. The attention from famous artists surprised and delighted him. "You have to realize I wasn't trying to be an intellectual or anything like that. I had very little formal schooling, and coming from Texas, I had never even spoken as an equal to a white person until I moved out to California when I was 21," he says. As a self-made man, he is quite a piece of work.

For those of us who began listening to jazz after 1959, it is difficult to imagine that Coleman's music was once the source of animus and widespread debate. Given the low visibility of jazz today, a figure as heretical as Coleman arriving on the scene might find himself in the position of shouting "Fire" in an empty theater. Looking back, it also strains belief that so many of Coleman's peers initially failed to recognize the suppleness of his phrasing and the keening vox-humana quality of his intonation. Jazz musicians have always respected instrumentalists able to "talk" on their horns, and they have always sworn by the blues (although as jazz has increased in sophistication, the blues has come to signify a feeling or tonal coloring, in addition to specific forms). Coleman's blues authenticity—the legacy of the Texas juke joints he had played as a teenager—should have scored him points instantly, especially in 1959 when hard boppers were writing sanctified ditties with titles like "Work Song" and "Dat Dere," to celebrate their Southern roots (and, not coincidentally, to cash in on a trend). But Coleman was too much the genuine article; his ragged, downhome sound cast him in the role of country cousin to his slicker, more urbanized brethren—as embarrassing a reminder of their second-class status as a Yiddish-speaking relative might have been to a newly assimilated Jew. In 1959 the old country for most black musicians was the American South, and few of them wanted any part of it.

Still, what must have bothered musicians more than the unmistakable Southern dialect of Coleman's music was its apparent formlessness, its flouting of rules that most jazz modernists had invested time and effort in learning (as Martin Williams suggests). In the wake of bebop, jazz had become a music of enormous harmonic complexity. By the late '50s it also seemed to be in danger of becoming a playground for virtuosos, as the once liberating practice of running the chords became routine. If some players sounded at times as though they lacked commitment and were merely going through the motions, it was because the motion of making each chord change was what they had become most committed to.

In one sense, the alternative that Coleman proposed amounted to nothing more drastic than a necessary (and, in retrospect, inevitable) suppression of harmony in favor of melody and rhythm. But this amounted to heresy in 1959. It has often been said that Coleman dispensed with recurring chord patterns altogether, in both his playing and his writing. This is not entirely accurate, however. Rather, he treated a harmonic sequence as just one of many options for advancing a solo. Coleman might improvise from the chords or, as inspiration moved him, instead use as his point of departure "a mood, fragment of melody, an area of pitch, or rhythmic fragment," to quote Williams. Moreover, Coleman's decision to dispense with a chordal road map also permitted him rhythmic trespass across bar lines. The stealthy rubato of his phrases and his sudden accelerations of tempo implied liberation from strict meter, much as his penchant for hitting notes a quarter-tone sharp or flat and his refusal to harmonize his saxophone with Don Cherry's trumpet during group passages implied escape from the well-tempered scale.

Ultimately, rhythm may be the area in which Coleman has made his most significant contributions to jazz. Perhaps the trick of listening to his performances lies in an ability to hear rhythm as melody, and melody as rhythm, the way he seems to, and the way jazz pioneers did. Some of his phrases, like some of King Oliver's or Sidney Bechet's, sound as though they were scooped off a drumhead.

Coleman was hardly the only musician to challenge chordal hegemony in 1959. John Coltrane, Miles Davis, Sonny Rollins, Horace Silver, Thelonious Monk, and Max Roach, among others, were looking beyond Charlie Parker's harmonic discoveries to the melodic and contrapuntal implications of bop. Cecil Taylor and George Russell were experimenting with chromaticism and pantonality, and a Miles Davis sextet featuring Coltrane and Bill Evans had just recorded *Kind of Blue,* an album that introduced a new spaciousness to jazz by replacing chords with modes and scales. But it was Coleman who was making the clearest break with convention, and Coleman whose intuitive vision of the future bore the most natural relationship with jazz's pragmatic country origins. He was a godsend, as it turned out.

In 1959 Coleman's music truly represented "something else" (to quote the title of his first album). Whether it also forecast "the shape of jazz to come" (another early album title) is still problematical. Certainly, Coleman's impact on jazz was immediate, and it has proved long-lasting. Within a few years of Coleman's first New York engagement, established saxophonists like Coltrane, Rollins, and Jackie McLean were playing a modified free form, often in the company of former Coleman sidemen. The iconoclastic bassist Charles Mingus (initially one of the skeptics) was leading a piano-less quartet featuring alto saxophonist Eric Dolphy and trumpeter Ted Curson, whose open-ended dialogues seemed inspired by those of Coleman and Cherry.

Over the years, Coleman has continued to cast a long shadow as he has extended his reach to symphonies, string quartets, and experiments in funk. By now, he has attracted two generations of disciples. There are the original sidemen in his quartet and their eventual replacements: trumpeters Cherry and Bobby Bradford; tenor saxophonist Dewey Redman; bassists Charlie Haden, Scott LaFaro, Jimmy Garrison, and David Izenzon; and drummers Billy Higgins, Ed Blackwell, and Charles Moffett. They were followed in the late '70s by musicians who brought to Coleman's bands the high voltage of rock and funk, most notably guitarist James Blood Ulmer, electric bassist Jamaaladeen Tacuma, and drummer Ronald Shannon Jackson. Some of Coleman's early associates in Texas and California, including clarinetist John Carter and flutist Prince Lawsha, have gone on to produce work that bears Coleman's influence, as have Albert Ayler, Anthony Braxton, and the others whom Coleman put up when they first arrived in New York, and lent money to so that they could produce their own concerts. Coleman planted the seed for the free jazz movement of the 1960s, which in turn gave rise to a school of European "instant" composers led by guitarist Derek Bailey and saxophonist Evan Parker. Since 1965, Coleman has performed on trumpet and violin in addition to alto and tenor saxophones, and several young violinists have taken him as their model: Billy Bang, for example, whose jaunty, anthem-like writing also bespeaks an affection for Coleman. A relatively new form in jazz is the tempo-less ballad, the offspring of onrushing Coleman dirges like "Sadness," "Lonely Woman," and "Beauty Is a Rare Thing" (they could be described as mournful ballad performances, except that no one is playing in strict ballad tempo, and no one is mourning). And for all practical purposes, the idea of collective group improvisation, which has reached an apex in the work of groups affiliated with the AACM, began with the partial liberation of bass and drums from chordal and timekeeping duties in the first Ornette Coleman Quartet.

If one listens for them, one can hear Colemanesque accents in the most unlikely places: the maundering piano soliloquies of Keith Jarrett, the space age meditations of guitarist Pat Metheny, and the Socratic dialogues of young hard boppers like Wynton and Branford Marsalis. It is impossible to imagine how jazz might have evolved without Coleman, and he has even affected the way we listen to jazz that predates him. Yet for all of that, his way has never replaced Charlie Parker's as the lingua franca of jazz, as many hoped and others feared it might.

One reason could be that Coleman's low visibility has denied the jazz avant-garde a figurehead. "He hasn't played enough, especially in America," says Neshui Ertegun, president of WEA International and Coleman's record producer from 1959 to 1961. "I'm not saying that he's wrong to demand the things he demands from record companies and concert promoters, but it's made him invisible for long periods of time. As a consequence, his impact hasn't been as enormous as it might have been."

Coleman's Five Spot engagement, originally scheduled to last two weeks, ran six months; in all, he played a year and a half at the club between 1959 and 1961. But his failure to negotiate the controversy he caused into hard cash left him bitter and suspicious. "I was a patsy," he says now. "I never made more than two hundred dollars a week at the Five Spot, and when I would play a job in another city, I would wind up working for nothing after I paid travel expenses and hotel bills, even though there would be people lined up around the block waiting to hear me. Booking agents would tell me I wasn't in the business long enough to ask for top dollar, that I was just a creation of the press, a novelty that would pass."

"All of us were naive, not just Ornette," says bassist Charlie Haden. "All we cared about was music. Joe and Iggy Termini were sweet guys, nice guys, but they were paying us practically nothing. We couldn't even pay our rents. And they were making lots of money off us. That club was jammed every single night we were there."

"I started asking for good money when I realized how the system works," says Coleman. "You see Coca-Cola all over the world, right? You know what else you see? My records. Record companies tell me my albums don't sell, but if that was true, they wouldn't be all over the place. Somebody's making a living from them, and it isn't me. I haven't found one person in the record business willing to deal with me in an equitable way, as a person rather than a commodity."

Since the early '60s, Coleman has set a price for concerts and recordings that reflects what he perceives to be his artistic merit rather than his limited commercial appeal. Needless to say, he has had very few takers. Even with over 30 albums on the market (not counting bootlegs) some of the best music he has recorded (including a 1977 reunion of his original quartet, with Cherry, Haden, and Higgins) remains unissued. Despite receiving numerous grants, including Guggenheim Fellowships in 1967 and 1974, he has been insolvent for most of his career. In 1984, the Internal Revenue Service slapped him with a $5,000 fine for failing to file tax returns for 1977 and 1978.

Because he suffered net losses from bad investments for those years, he assumed he did not have to declare his earnings as a performer. The IRS was not charmed by his naiveté. The neighborhood he lives in is drug-infested, and he has been burglarized twice since moving there in 1982. The second incident was especially scary. Two neighborhood youths he hired to help him lug sound equipment up the five flights to his apartment broke in later that night when he was out. When he walked in on them, they hit him on the head with a crowbar and stabbed him in the back. Hospitalized with a collapsed lung, he was unable to play his saxophone for six months, and he says that the scar tissue still itches. Not that it would have made a difference to them, but it is unlikely that his teenage assailants had any idea that their victim was a celebrity of sorts.

Just a few years ago it appeared that Coleman's star was on the rise again. In 1977 his former sidemen Cherry, Redman, Haden, and Blackwell formed the band Old and New Dreams. Coleman compositions, old and new, accounted for roughly half their repertoire. If the myth that Coleman had to be physically present in order for his music to be played properly persisted in some quarters, Old and New Dreams dispelled it once and for all. They played his music with a joy and heart of purpose that bore witness to his omniscience as a composer. The reaction to Old and New Dreams showed that the music once both hailed and reviled as the wave of the future had taken a firm enough hold in the past to inspire nostalgia.

The rapture with which jazz audiences greeted the band's reinterpretations of vintage Coleman owed something to the fact that Coleman himself had moved on to other frontiers—appearing with two electric guitarists, two bass guitarists, and two drummers in a configuration he called Prime Time. This band provided the working model for a cryptic (and, one suspects, largely after-the-fact) theory of tonality that Coleman calls harmolodics, based on the premise that instruments can play together in different keys without becoming tuneless or exchanging the heat of the blues for a frigid atonality. (As critic Robert Palmer pointed out in *The New York Rocker*,

Coleman's music had always been "harmolodic" in a sense.) In practice the harmolodic theory functioned like a McGuffin in a Hitchcock film: if you could follow what it was all about, good for you; if you couldn't, that wasn't going to hamper your enjoyment one iota. What mattered more than any amount of theorizing was that Coleman was leading jazz out of a stalemate, much as he had in 1959. He had located indigenous jazz rhythms that played upon the reflexes of the body the way the simultaneously bracing and relaxing polyrhythms of funk and New Wave rock 'n' roll do.

"In jazz, it's when the drummer sounds like he's playing with everybody else that people say the music is swinging," Coleman says. "In rock 'n' roll and funk, it's when everybody else sounds like they're playing with the drummer." With Prime Time, he combined the best of both worlds. "In my band, all the instruments are independent and equal. Lots of drummers think that time is rhythm, but rhythm is independent of time. When I'm playing time, the drummers can play rhythm; when I'm playing rhythm, they can play time."

Unlike most of the jazz musicians who embraced dance rhythms in the '70s, Coleman wasn't slumming or taking the path of least resistance in search of a mass following. Nonetheless, a modest commercial breakthrough seemed imminent in 1981, when he signed with Island Records and named Stan and Sid Bernstein as his managers (the latter was the promoter who brought the Beatles to Shea Stadium in 1965). There is some disagreement among the principal parties about what happened next. "Nothing is simple for Ornette when it comes to money," says Stan Bernstein. "He made demands that are unrealistic in this business unless you're Michael Jackson." According to Coleman, "my managers sold *Of Human Feelings,** which was the first digital jazz album recorded in the U.S., for less money than it had cost me to make it, and I never saw a penny of the royalties." Coleman was paid $25,000 for the rights to *Of Human Feelings,* "not a terrific sum but not a modest sum, either, for a

* Antilles AN-2001, recorded in 1979 and released in 1982.

jazz artist," according to Ron Goldstein, who was at that time in charge of Antilles, Island's jazz custom label. "The figure was based on what we realistically thought we could sell, not what it had cost Ornette to record the album." Goldstein says that Coleman was given a $25,000 "one fund" advance to record a follow up to *Of Human Feelings*—one fund meaning that whatever was left over from recording costs was Coleman's to pocket. This much is clear: Coleman went over budget, asked for more money, and was refused. What should have been his second record for Island Antilles has never been released, and there is now some question of who owns the rights to the masters. The label did not pick up its option on him. In 1983, he severed his ties with the Bernstein Agency and again went into partial eclipse.

Lately, the task of shedding Coleman's light has fallen to his acolytes Ulmer, Jackson, and Tacuma. They have not sold very many records either, despite a greater willingness to accommodate public tastes—and despite reams of publicity from the intellectual wing of the rock press. When Coleman next makes a move, harmolodics may be an idea whose time has come and gone, so far as the critics and record companies are concerned. In photographer Carol Friedman's book *A Moment's Notice*, there is a haunting portrait of Coleman facing the camera with his hands up over his face. It is recognizably him, but for all he lets us see of himself, he might as well not be there. No doubt Coleman's grievances are real. But if he is a neglected artist, it is impossible to avoid the conclusion that he bears complicity for his neglect.

Several miles west of Coleman's loft, a new high rise condominium is going up at 5 Cooper Square, where the Five Spot used to be. Sometimes Coleman's influence is as difficult to trace as the club where he made his heroic stand. Still, in the final analysis, his failure to redefine jazz as decisively as many predicted he would is more the result of the accelerated pace at which jazz was evolving *before* he arrived in New York than of his relative lack of activity since then. During the 50 years before 1959, a series of upheavals had taken jazz from its humble folk origins and made of it a codified art music. It was as though jazz has imitated the evolution of European concert music in a fraction of the time. Just as the term "classical music" has come to signify European concert music of the late eighteenth and early nineteenth century, the words "modern jazz" have become synonymous with the style of jazz originally called bebop.

With Ornette Coleman, jazz established its permanent avant-garde, its "new" that would always remain new—comparable to the ongoing attack on tonality in classical music, on narrative in post-First World War fiction, and on representation in twentieth-century art. If one measures a player's influence solely by the number of instrumentalists who adopt aspects of his style (the standard yardstick in jazz), Coleman finishes a distant third among his contemporaries to John Coltrane and Miles Davis. Yet his accomplishment seems somehow greater than theirs, for they merely showed which elements of free form the jazz mainstream could absorb—modality, approximate harmonies, saxophone glossolalia, the sixteenth note as a basic unit of measurement, the use of auxiliary percussion and horns once considered "exotic"— and which elements it finally could not—variable pitch, free meter, collective improvisation. Coleman's early biography is replete with stories of musicians packing up their instruments and leaving the bandstand when he tried to sit in. If Coleman showed up now incognito at a jam session presided over by younger followers of Parker, Davis, and Coltrane, chances are he would still be given the cold shoulder. Bebop seems to be invincible, though Coleman and those who have taken their cue from him continue to challenge its hegemony. The bop revolution of the '40s was the last in a series of successful coup d'états. Coleman's revolution will never wholly succeed or fail. It is going to be a permanent revolution, its skirmishes marking the emergence of jazz as a full-fledged modern art, with all of modernism's dualities and contradictions.

And jazz is only part of it. Coleman's idiosyncratic symphonies and string quartets and his espousal of funk have helped demolish the barriers between what he calls "the three kinds of Western music— racial or ethnic, popular, and classical. I've transcended racial distinctions and stylistic divisions," he says, a tape of a recent performance of "The Skies of America" (the symphonic work that introduced the concept of harmolodics) booming out as he talks, doing more to warm up his chilly loft than the space heater in the middle of the bare floor. "I haven't had much material success, but I'm not a failure, either. I created music that's better than was there before," he says with the satisfaction of an artist who knows that his music has endured a quarter of a century and the wisdom of a prophet who knows it shall probably endure the ages as well. What does not change for him is the will to change, this man who seems bent on proving Bob Dylan's axiom: There's no success like failure, and failure's no success at all.

(NOVEMBER 1984/SEPTEMBER 1985)

# Don Cherry Sees the World

"I went to Morocco in 1964. That was my first big adventure, the first time I entered a foreign land and felt like I was entering an earlier period of history." The peripatetic pocket trumpeter Don Cherry is recalling for me some of the far-off places his travels have taken him, as he sits eating a breakfast of scrambled eggs on toast in a downtown Manhattan diner the morning after his forty-sixth birthday. "No, I didn't have any jobs lined up when I went. I just *went*, and that's the way to do it if you're going to meet all the musicians and learn melodies and rhythms from them, if you're going to see all there is to see.

"Two years ago, I did a State Department tour of West Africa. I played concerts, did workshops, but I didn't get to *see* anything." He scoops the ice out of his water glass, then drops in a crescent-shaped multivitamin he says is manufactured in West Germany. It fizzes like Bromo, looks like Tang, and Cherry reports that it tastes like mango, sadly adding that he has only two more tablets left. "I did that tour because I just had to get to Mali," he continues, "because that's where the guitar I've been playing the last five years—the *doussn' gouni*—comes from. A master had taught me the traditional rhythms, but I hadn't *been* there, so, you see, I had to go.

"But when I got there, all the *doussn' gouni* players were in the bush! It was their hunting season, and if I had gone on my own and gotten there two weeks earlier, I could have gone on the hunt with them. I met many *kora* players, many *balafon* players, but not one *doussn' gouni* player. So I'll have to return there someday soon.

"But anyway, at the first concert, as soon as I started playing that guitar, *right away* the people recognized that sound and started clapping the rhythm. Then, all of a sudden, they slowed it down, and their mouths just fell open. They were looking at me and wondering, 'But how it is possible for him to play our music if he's American?' Then after awhile, they just started clapping along again anyway," Cherry laughs. "They didn't care where I was from. It was so incredible!"

It's momentarily disorienting to hear Don Cherry say that he and his Swedish wife Moqui live with their youngest son Eagle Eye "right between the tunnel and the bridge, next to the river in Long Island City," even if he's not exactly telling me anything I don't already know. It's just that based on everything else I know about him I find it difficult to imagine this limber and wiry reddish-brown string figure living any one place in the world in particular.

Like most musicians, Cherry—born in rural Oklahoma and raised off Material Highway in Watts—has spent the greater portion of his adult life on the run. He first arrived in New York in 1959 as the diffidently lyrical trumpeter in the quartet with which Ornette Coleman forever distended the shape of jazz to come, and he gradually emerged as a confident if still cautious harbinger of change himself, serving as the sweet voice of moderation to Albert Ayler and Archie Shepp during their angry rampages through Europe and America in the matinal days of free jazz in the early '60s. Presently, Cherry divides his road time almost evenly between the superb Coleman alumni band Old and New Dreams and the World Music trio Codona. There are also special projects such as the tour of Europe with Charlie Haden's Liberation Music Orchestra from which he's just returned, and the tour of France with African pop star Manu

Dibango which will begin in two days. Not too long ago, Cherry even made all the stops on the rock circuit, in support of Lou Reed.

Most musicians are happy enough to go wherever business takes them, but Cherry has made a conscientious effort to see the world. Moving to Sweden in 1970, for instance, and setting up residence in an abandoned schoolhouse, he purchased a camper and embarked on what he describes as "an acoustic expedition" of Europe and the Middle East.

"I wanted to play different instruments in environments not man-made for music—natural settings like in a catacomb or on a mountaintop or by the side of a lake. I wasn't playing for jazz audiences then, you realize. I was playing for goat herders who would take out their flutes and join me and for anyone else who wanted to listen or to sing and play along. It was the whole idea of organic music—music as a natural part of your day. Moqui and the children and I would sing and play and camp out and live in the bus. We were never stationary the four years we were in Sweden." Given such a utopian, back-to-the-land philosophy, Long Island City seems like an especially incongruous place for Cherry finally to hang his hat. "I still live in Sweden three months each summer," he points out, "but living in Sweden to me is like living in the forest. Because that's what it comes down to, no matter where you live—either you're living in the forest or you're living in a metropolis, and I guess I need the balance of living in both. Everyone thinks of Long Island as a suburb, but the part I live in is more like an industrial city, and Manhattan is right outside my window.

"But if you were to go to our schoolhouse in Togarp and then come out to our loft, you'd see it was just like walking from one room of a house into another, because Moqui is a designer, and she creates the same environment no matter where we are. But, yes, it is hard adjusting all the time. At first, whenever you come back to New York, you get diarrhea!" A smile reapportions the furrows and long planes of his handsome, angular face, and his dark, prominent eyes dart quickly around as they do whenever he realizes he has said something funny or he wishes to underline a point. "I became very conscious of diet in Sweden. I was a vegetarian the four years we lived there year-round. I planted all my own food. Then I ate nothing but brown rice for a while, to remind myself there were starving people in the world. I'm still careful of what I eat, and I think you assimilate more energy by eating very little. But it's difficult to remain a vegetarian when you're on the road all the time, unless you're traveling the way we were in the camper.

"So I'm always adjusting to the pace of wherever I am at the time," Cherry sighs. "The impressions of being in the city are totally different, and I can hear that even in my compositions. Why I moved back here, it's difficult to say, except that I seemed to be here all the time anyway doing different musical projects around '74 or '75, and New York has always seemed like home to me, in a funny way, from the first day I came here with Ornette."

We're in a basement dressing room in the Public Theatre now; Cherry is due upstairs in an hour or so to begin rehearsal for the Liberation Music Orchestra's American premiere this evening. In the meantime, he's mugging for *Musician* staff photographer Deborah Finegold, using his tiny, battered, tarnished horn as a prop—tucking the pocket trumpet in the pocket of his coat so that it appears to be shyly peeking out; holding it up lengthwise to his chin and stroking it gently, rather as if he half-expected a playful, purring kitten to come pawing up out of the bell. Between rolls of film, he puffs his cheeks into giant bubbles and blows a few bars of Ornette Coleman's "Beauty Is a Rare Thing" through the horn. All the twisting motion and running colors of Coleman's classic meditation for quartet are hauntingly encapsulated in this impromptu solo rendition.

"I think of it as a tonsil," he says of the truncated horn. "I use it to *sing*. I mean, I wouldn't want to be thinking of playing trumpet to the point where the instrument begins to control *me*. This horn's a light instrument, and its timbre's close to the sound of my own voice.

"The first pocket trumpet I owned I got in the San Fernando Valley around the time I met Ornette. It felt good for my size and the kind of music I was playing. It was made in Pakistan, and I remember it cost a hundred dollars, and I only had twenty-five. But Red Mitchell, the bass player, loaned me the rest. I'll always be grateful to Red for that.

"This pocket trumpet I have now was made in France and used in a spectacular that Josephine Baker was in. Its bell is even smaller than other pocket trumpets, and as you can see, it has jade on the top. The first trumpet I *ever* owned was a Sears Silvertone—I guess everything Sears sells is named Silvertone. Fats Navarro and Clifford Brown were the trumpeters I adored around that time, but I realized that, small as I'm built, I would never be strong enough to get a big, full sound like theirs. Miles Davis became very special to me—he didn't need vibrato, his tone was so pure. And Sweets Edison impressed me a lot too; I especially liked his humor and his approach to accompanying singers."

Cherry was caught up in music even before settling upon these favorite trumpeters. As youngsters, he and his sister would roll back the living room carpet and jitterbug to the hits of the '40s, and on Sundays the entire family would sing in the Baptist church. His grandmother had played piano in a silent movie house before he was born, and his father tended bar in a Central Avenue jazz club. Still, Cherry's decision to become a professional musician met with some family disapproval. "From what he saw on the job, my father believed playing jazz was the first step to drug addiction," he affectionately jests.

Cherry was not so easily deterred, however. He learned chord changes from a bassist named Harper Crosby. "I was just improvising from the melody until Harper hipped me there was more. He taught me so well that Ornette used to call me the chord man, because I was always so fascinated by chord patterns.

"It was Jayne Cortez who introduced me to Ornette. Jayne was my guru when I was a kid, the one who would turn me on to the latest records and books. She later became Ornette's first wife, and now she's a highly regarded poet. Ornette was being persecuted even back then, and not just because of his music either. He was the first man I ever saw, white or black, with long hair. There's resistance to him even now, even from some black musicians, because of his electric band. It's amazing, isn't it?"

It's nothing compared with the controversy that circled over Coleman's head during his long stand at the Five Spot in 1959. If little of the debate surrounding Coleman extended to Cherry at first, it was because the trumpeter was initially deemed unworthy either of such approbation or advocacy. Understandably, Cherry let the leader dominate their unison skirmishes, and, to some listeners, Cherry's solos often sounded like timid paraphrases of the Coleman solos that preceded them. It became apparent only in retrospect that Cherry was commendably striving to maintain "the intensity and brilliance of Ornette's solos and his written lines, that sparkle Ornette's music has that is almost like a shining diamond and that you have to keep going from the beginning of the piece until the end," as he puts it. It has also become obvious in retrospect that Cherry succeeded in this objective more often than not.

Following an altercation long since forgotten by both men, Cherry left Coleman's group and returned to Los Angeles. "And it was Sonny Rollins who rescued me, who got me out of L.A. and took me to Europe for the first time. When I was in Paris with Sonny in 1963, I'd go sit in with the gypsies and play the standards Django Reinhardt had recorded. I'd find the dixieland groups and play with them too. And when we went to Denmark, I looked up Don Byas and Dexter Gordon, and I heard Albert Ayler for the first time there, too.

"My willingness to play different kinds of jazz is what led to my interest in ethnic musics, I guess. I've had so many wonderful experiences playing music in Europe, Asia, India, Africa, and South America, and I've been fortunate to study with the masters in all those places too. You know, to study with a man like Ustad Zia M'Digar in India, you have to humble yourself in a certain way. You have to demonstrate your respect for him and for the tradition that's been handed down in his family for two thousand years. It's like fine wine—you don't offer it to someone who isn't going to savor it, who can't tell the difference.

"It's funny. In many of the countries I've visited, the young people are more interested in Western music than in the music of their own culture. That's why it's important for me to go to Africa, say, and play the *doussn' gouni*. The young people realize the importance of their own music if they hear a Western musician playing it. It's happening here in America, too, with young black kids. If you look at the schools teaching improvisation, you'll see the students are mostly white. That's why I applied for a grant from the NEA last spring and went to work with the kids growing up now where I grew up in Watts. I tried to expose them to Charlie Parker and Thelonious Monk, both of whom I *revered* as a kid, and to Ornette Coleman, whose music I was able to contribute to.

"You asked me how it is that my kids are involved in music?" Cherry's eighteen-year-old daughter Nonah sings with the British punk band Rip, Rig and Panic, and his other three offspring all play instruments. "It's because they've been taught they're part of a culture and that they have a responsibility to keep it alive. Same thing with Jim Pepper, the saxophonist who went to West Africa with me. Jim's an Indian whose father is a singer in the pow wows," says Cherry, who is one-quarter Choctaw himself. "The response in Africa was tremendous when Jim would play one of the pow wow pieces he had written—from the people in the Embassy, especially. They realized that *here* was something truly American."

Western musicians have been infatuated with the musics of the Third World at least since the Great Mystical Awakening of the 1960s, and few have been able to resist the urge to conquer and colonialize. Don Cherry has been a notable exception. A kind of musical Marco Polo, he has introduced many exotic fabrics and spices to jazz. But it is not in Cherry's nature to plunder. He is determined always to offer something of equal value in trade for whatever bounty he decides to take on board. And most important of all, recognizing that a people's music is but one strand in the web of ceremony and custom that makes their experience unique, he is careful to leave that web intact.

Inevitably, some of what Cherry wants to tell us about the world is garbled in the translation. Sometimes he and his colleagues in Codona—Brazilian percussionist Nana Vasconcelos and American jack-of-all-instruments Colin Walcott—remind me of small children cupping seashells to their ears; they mistake the rush of their own hearts' excitement for the roar of the great ocean that washed such a treasure up. There are times when the sense of one-world optimism they labor to convey strikes me as wishful and self-deluded. And it's difficult for me to shake the long-standing prejudice that musicians like Cherry short-change themselves and their audiences when they put aside horns and disciplines years in the mastering to dabble with alien doctrine and instrumentation.

But it's possible to forgive the most lyrical trumpeter of his generation any amount of good-natured doddling the moment he finally lifts the trumpet to his lips. Blessed with an immaculate sense of form from the very beginning, Cherry's solos have gained even greater compression, I think, as a result of his examinations of musics in which the rules of improvisation are far more constricting than the make-it-up-as-you-go-along philosophy governing self-expression in too much contemporary jazz. If it seems that Cherry has been adrift on a musical odyssey these last 20 years, it's good to remember that an odyssey is a round trip, after all.

Homecoming is the theme that pervades his music now. One of the many pleasures of hearing Old and New Dreams, for example, is sensing the obvious pleasure Cherry, Dewey Redman, Charlie Haden, and Ed Blackwell still take from hearing one another, even after having played together off and on in various combinations for close to 25 years now. Each member of O&ND is an Ornette Coleman alumnus, and classic Coleman still accounts for roughly half of the band's live repertoire. "And some of those pieces I was playing with Ornette in California, long before we ever recorded," Cherry says. It is unlikely Coleman would ever have changed our perception of jazz as profoundly as he has, had he not enlisted players as sympathetic to his cause as Cherry and the others. Coleman's music is *their* music too, and they perform it with a keening edge that can literally make you tingle.

Tonight's concert is something of a reunion, too, of course. Few records of the era conveyed the musical and political upheaval of the late '60s as powerfully as Charlie Haden's *Liberation Music Orchestra* date did; now, many of Haden's original co-conspirators have begun to reassemble in this small room. Looking at them now, it's depressing to think how little the world has changed for the better in the intervening years, but heartening all the same to see that the rebels have aged so well. Obviously eager to greet old acquaintances and perhaps to have a few moments to himself before rehearsal, Cherry is growing restless with his interviewer, who asks one final question. Has Cherry ever played music indigenous to the part of the world he was in and gotten an angry or indifferent response?

"Yes, yes! With this very band in Spain, when we played one of the Spanish folk tunes that Charlie and Carla had arranged."

"The audience sat there thinking, 'We hear this crap on the radio all day, man. We came to hear *jazz*,'" explains Carla Bley, walking in on the conversation as if on cue.

"After it was over, someone yelled, 'SHIT,'" laughs Cherry, and something—perhaps the political content of the music he will perform this evening—reminds him of another story, which he tells Bley and me as he gathers his belongings to take upstairs. "I played a left wing festival in Milano once, and Gary Rubin? . . . Jerry Rubin? . . . Abbie Hoffman? . . . one of them . . . jumped onstage in his birthday suit just as we were ready to go on and started babbling for an hour at least. The promoters told us, 'Wait, wait,' but the audience—90,000 kids in a stadium, man, and some of them had been roughed up by the cops outside—started chanting, 'Play! Play! Play!' So I went up to the microphone and said in my best Italian, '*Senti, senti*, my name is Don Cherry . . . situation is simply music.' We started playing this lilting melody Nana Vasconcelos had written, and everyone out there started lighting pieces of paper and holding them up like torches. The whole stadium was *glowing*. It was one of the most beautiful reactions I've ever had, much better than people just applauding, you know?

"Then there was another episode in Italy when Moqui and I were wounded by the police during a student riot. But that's another story. I'll tell you about it next time I see you. . . ." And before I can register shock or curiosity, he is out the door and on the go again.

(MARCH 1983)

# Character Analysis

Talk about Warne Marsh—or talk with him—and sooner or later the subject of Lennie Tristano enters and begins to dominate the discussion. The tenor saxophonist remembers making his recording debut as a member of a Tristano sextet in March 1949, when he was 21, but his recollection of his second recording session, just two months later, is even more vivid. Indeed, it is unlikely that anyone interested in jazz, whether he was there that day or not, will ever forget the infamous session at which pianist Tristano had his group improvise two numbers—"Intuition" and "Digression"—without specifying keys, chord progressions, time signatures, or even tempos up front.

"It was the end of the session," Marsh recalls. "Lennie had gotten us together—me, Lee Konitz, Billy Bauer, who was the guitarist on the date, and the bass player Arnold Fishkin—and explained to us that we were going to improvise strictly from what we heard one another doing. Which was simple enough. The only thing that was set up in advance was the order of entrances, with Lennie starting off, setting the tempo and the mood. That and the fact that we'd play for three minutes, because we were making 78s. So we would give each other approximately 15 or 20 seconds and then come in. . . ."

Marsh wasn't caught off guard by Tristano's instructions. "This was normal for us, man. We had practiced it some and done it in clubs, and this was our second date for Capitol, so we were ready. When I listen to those sides now, I'm amazed at how far ahead Lennie was, at what great music he was playing. And it was *free* improvisation—free, right straight off the top of his head."

More than 30 years after the events Warne Marsh describes, and more than four years after the pianist's death in 1978, Tristano's rank in modern jazz and his role in its evolution remain points of some contention. The problem the critic inevitably encounters with Tristano is that he seems at once major and peripheral. As Marsh's comments suggest, Tristano was a trailblazer. Yet he can hardly be hailed as an innovator, for few among the jazz rank and file chose to follow his path. Certainly, the somber, ruminative music that the Tristanoites, chastened by their proctor's stern piano intro (and perhaps emboldened by the absence of a drummer), collectively and somewhat tentatively improvised in the Capitol studio that evening in 1949 bears little resemblance to free jazz as we understand the term today, in the fiery wake of Ornette Coleman and Cecil Taylor. But just as certainly, Tristano's music can stand on its own abundant merit, all questions of historical precedence aside, and Tristano should at least be credited with formulating a profound and wholly original system of linear improvisation based on the riddle of license and self-denial, and—more important perhaps—a school of thought to go along with it. Tristano's theories about jazz reach their apotheosis not so much in his own work as in his teachings and in the playing of two disciples who continue to spread his gospel—alto saxophonist Lee Konitz and tenor saxophonist Warne Marsh.

The sins of the father, both real and imagined, are often visited upon his sons even in jazz, and those who found Tristano's music rhythmically stillborn and too cerebral were quick to brand Konitz and Marsh as dispassionate, inhibited soloists. Konitz threw off that onus early on, soloing heatedly in almost every conceivable jazz context. But Marsh, who to some extent has remained secluded in the folds of the Tristano legend, ironically achieving a high level of visibility only when he reunited with Tristano and/or Konitz, has never really been able to shake the curse. Never fully accepted by the boppers of his own generation, he has been cited as a patriarch of free improvisation by no less an authority than avant-garde alto saxophonist and composer Anthony Braxton, who has dedicated at least one piece to him. Yet Marsh, whose musical values are firmly planted in the flowing rhythm of Lester Young and the harmonic vocabulary of Charlie Parker, expresses little interest in the doings of the post-Coleman avant-garde, and in any event, it is impossible to imagine him feeling comfortable in an AACM-like setting. If the younger generation of jazz listeners knows Marsh at all, it is by reputation or by the well-received two-tenor records he made in the late '70s with Lew Tabackin (*Tenor Gladness,* Inner City IC-6048) and Peter Christlieb (*Apogee,* Warner Brothers BSK-3236)—records which Marsh himself, a perfectionist in the Tristano mold, both arrogant and insecure about his own abilities, does not particularly like.

Laboring in relative obscurity, however, Marsh has matured into one of the most stimulating improvisers in jazz. His cool, liquid style is spiked with paradox. Playing a pop standard, he will frequently dissolve its melody completely in an attempt to isolate and purify its harmonic base. Yet the new melodies he stretches over the chords are usually appealing and memorable in their own right, and the *ideal* of melody is something he bears proudly and carefully aloft, as though it were a sacred chalice from which he were determined not to spill one sacred drop. Although he is a melodic player, however, he is not really a lyrical one in the conventional sense—his tone is one of the palest and brittlest in jazz. He has a knack for rhythmic displacement, and he uses silence and space almost as tellingly, if not as mischievously, as Thelonious Monk did—he speaks of "the ability to *play* the rests and give *them* meaning, too." But because he is not a virile, breast-beating swinger, many of his rhythmic subtleties are lost on all but his most attentive and sophisticated audiences. Above all else, there is an inner-directed quality to Marsh's best solos, a feeling of rigorous soul-searching as intense as that which one hears in John Coltrane, but more diffident in character. There is nothing purgative, nothing Promethean, or sheerly physical about Marsh's solos. Rather, one hears in them what critic Harvey Pekar has described as "the kind of intense concentration a scientist must feel when deeply involved in his work." No doubt it is this quality of passionate intellectual involvement which draws some listeners to Marsh at the same time it keeps larger numbers seeking simpler, more immediate pleasures away.

When Warne Marsh is playing, even his most abstract thoughts seem tangible—the notes seem to float in captions above the bell of his horn. In conversation, he is harder to read. Once a student of Lennie Tristano's, Marsh is now a teacher himself, commuting three days a week from his home in "a nice conservative Connecticut small town" to a one-room efficiency in a Broadway resident hotel where he sees his students. The first impression Marsh gives a stranger is of being guarded and rather distant. But it soon becomes apparent that he is painfully shy, almost jittery, as he paces around the small disordered room, lighting cigarettes he lets burn out, pouring coffee he doesn't finish, repeatedly adjusting the mouthpiece on the tenor saxophone that sits idle next to a drum set in the center of the floor. A slightly built man whose dark hair is just beginning to turn gray at the temples and on the chin as he enters his middle fifties, giving him a prematurely wizened look, Marsh answers questions slowly and thoughtfully, not venturing on to the next word until he is absolutely certain it is the one he wants.

He grew up in Los Angeles in a family he says cherished music. "My mother's musical through her fingertips. She's from that Russian-Jewish tradition where, hopefully, the first son will become a musician. But in this case, my mother was the firstborn, and the first son was not playing the violin the family bought for him, not at all, so she just walked in and took over. In the early '20s, she played in the string quartets rich Hollywood actors would hire to accompany the premieres of their silent films. I was *her* first son, so it came true there, I guess." But instead of violin, Marsh studied accordion, switching to tenor saxophone in his mid-teens.

"Like Charlie Parker out of Ben Webster," Marsh replies when

I ask him what he sounded like as a teenager. "I've got a tape some-one just sent me from when I was 19 years old in the army at Camp Lee, Virginia—a tape of the Special Services band we were in. But Tex Beneke was my very first inspiration. I was in a kid band that played for servicemen and young people at the Hollywood Canteen during World War II. We had Glenn Miller stock charts, with Tex's solos all written out, plus the harmony was given. I heard Tex on the radio quite a bit, too—'43, '44, his records were very popular. You know, young big bands—what else *were* they going to play? Besides the white dance band charts, maybe a little Duke Ellington. I was already playing 'Body and Soul' like Coleman Hawkins, and Ben Webster's solo on 'Cottontail.' My ambition was to become a studio musician. In Hollywood, that's the only way you're encouraged to think. By 17 I was serious, but what I was offered included no real *jazz* as a career. If you wanted jazz, you left L.A. and went to New York. It was quite clear-cut then."

The apprenticeship at the Canteen led to a job on CBS radio back-ing Hoagy Carmichael. By the time he was 19, Marsh was in uni-form himself, and it was through trumpeter Don Ferrera, a fellow G.I., that he heard about Lennie Tristano. When Marsh was trans-ferred to Fort Monmouth, New Jersey, he began formal study with the blind pianist.

Tristano changed his pupil's listening habits. "I became disen-chanted with Duke's band when I realized that no two saxophone players in that reed section played with the same vibrato." He began listening even more closely to Charlie Parker, and "I began hearing Lester Young, and really fell for his manner, on a quite conscious level. Now that I look back on my studies with Lennie, though, I have to admit that I came to him with my own feeling for a melody, my own way of playing. What he taught me was that you don't have to imitate your heroes or your idols. You have to accept responsibility for your own melody.

"Lennie brought me out. He always knew me at least two years better than I knew myself. I mean, he could sit and listen to me play and tell me what was original and what was derivative. I doubt my personal education would ever have gotten to where it has without him, because he presented it all so clearly to me when I was 20 that I've never been at a loss for ideas since, and if I want more ideas, I know from him exactly where to look—to 20th-century classical thinking, which is best heard in Bartók. It's a compound of 19th-century thinking, which is to say you can take the most advanced conventional harmony and meter and rhythm and begin compounding them, which is what the best composers have done in this century. Just add harmonies to harmonies and meters to meters, which is already being done in jazz, and rhythms to rhythms—polyrhythms—which has been done better in jazz improvisation than in classical composition.

"Lennie really knew music. My life would be a lot different if I had never met him. For one thing, I probably would never have taught."

Marsh began teaching by giving saxophone lessons to children and adult beginners in a Pasadena music store when he and his wife moved back to California in 1966. During his ten-year sojourn out West, he was also a founding member of Med Flory's Supersax, a group whose five-man saxophone section played orchestrated Charlie Parker solos. "Getting into Bird again was really meaningful at first," Marsh says, but ultimately the experience was frustrating for him (and for his fans) because he never got to solo on any of the group's records. "On jobs, everybody blew. Med's democratic, but he's also conservative . . . he's probably a Republican, come to think of it . . . and his thinking on the albums was that we should keep it to the format of the original records—trumpet solo, piano solo, and transcribed Parker solos by the whole section—no improvising by the saxes."

Returning to New York in the mid '70s, Marsh began his teaching career in earnest, continuing the peculiar mode of jazz pedagogy initiated by his mentor. Just as Tristano did not teach piano, Marsh does not teach saxophone. By the time a saxophonist or trumpeter or pianist enrolls with Marsh, he or she will already have studied his or her instrument for a number of years (and singers will have already studied voice). "They understand they'll be studying *improvisa-tion*. Your study of your instrument ceases, as far as I'm concerned, the moment you begin wanting to express yourself. The instrument should take care of itself after that." A good number of Marsh's students are women, including two singers who have released albums under their own names—Janet Lawson and Judy Niemack—and another singer he feels is especially promising—Carla White. There is nothing smarmy or opportunistic about Marsh's espousal of equal rights, according to one of his female students, who told me that one of the things she really appreciated about him was that "he treats me like a musician, not like a girl singer. And there are no sexual come-ons from him, either, the way there probably would have been from the other musicians who were eager to take me on as a student. I've studied with Lennie, too, as a lot of women did, and even though I'm sure he didn't mean to, he treated women differently. It was as though having so many women students and being so encouraging to them was proof of his sensitivity. Whereas the only thing Warne has ever said to me that I'm sure he wouldn't tell a male student was to warn me not to get married and start having babies, because it would interrupt my career." (Interestingly enough, early in our conversation, Marsh mentioned that his mother had put her violin away for good when she gave birth to him. "I understand why she felt she had to do it, but I don't know how anyone can give up music that easily," he said.)

When I ask Marsh how his teaching philosophy differs from Tristano's, he laughs. "It doesn't. I feel I was so well trained, it's a simple matter to turn around and give that training to someone else." The method involves "a lot of ear training at first—listening to records, transcribing and analyzing solos, a lot of that. One of the first things I expect [a student] to be able to do is to present a melody in a convincing manner. The next step is learning to improvise on that melody, and it becomes necessary to get into the other notes—the harmony. But it all proceeds from melody." As Tristano did with him, he has his instrumental students sing their exercises before attempting them on their instruments, the underlying assumption being that music comes from within and an instrument is merely that—a tool for bringing the music out. " 'A musician who can't use his voice!' Lennie used to say. 'How can that be?' "

With the arrival of the Tristanoites in the late '40s, jazz entered the age of anxiety, much as theater (and, subsequently, film) had with the Actors' Studio and the Stanislavsky Method. Lee Konitz once said of Warne Marsh, "He's had a big emotional thing going on within himself, and sometimes what he plays isn't what he's capable of, because he has trouble releasing his emotion. But when he does, it's really something to hear, I tell you." And Marsh himself has said of Charlie Parker, "Bird was able to get to the point where he played all music. I mean he got outside of himself by going through himself and eliminating everything in his personal character that might tend to distort his music."

What character armor did Marsh have to shed before he could get in touch with his feelings and create to his fullest capacity? *"Fear,"* he laughs nervously. Fear of what? "Fear of expressing myself. It's not exactly encouraged in American life. It can leave you exposed, but that can be your strength, too. I got over it once and for all around 1963 or '64. Suddenly, I just felt like playing all the time." Hadn't he felt like playing all the time before that? "No."

We both become aware that the interview is taking a strange turn when I ask him if he has ever undergone analysis. It is not a question I normally ask my subjects but I know that Tristano advised his students that they might become better improvisers if they submitted to psychoanalysis (his brother Michael was a practicing Freudian). An awareness of psychoanalytic terminology is reflected in the titles the Tristano school gave their compositions (it's a long way from "Livery Stable Blues" to "Retrogression"), in their acute self-awareness and their periodic lapses of faith in their abilities to perform. It is also reflected in their cryptic pronouncements about themselves and other musicians. "All emotion, no feeling," Tristano summed up his impressions of John Coltrane and Sonny Rollins for an interviewer from *Literary Journal* in 1964. "Their stuff is an expression of the ego. I want jazz to flow out of the id." Similarly, Marsh makes a distinction between personality and the deeper stuff of character in judging the work of his students and his peers. "Music that proceeds from a player's personality is superficial and transient and predictable, and it can become neurotic. Some players are more concerned with projecting their personalities than with the art of creating music, which involves the discovery of character, the quality that makes music sound eternal."

"No, I've never been in analysis," Marsh answers. "But all of us were pretty well-read on the subject, and there was some exchange of ideas. We took it seriously, man—Lee and Lennie and me—beginning with Freud and psychoanalysis and then progressing to Wilhelm Reich and character analysis, thinking of improvisation as a *form* of character analysis, in a way. But the problem with analysis is that it merely acquaints you with yourself. Once you know who you are, you're still faced with the problem of creating a life for yourself. I mean literally *creating*. And it's the same with music. You can become the perpetual student if you're not careful," he says, ironically echoing a charge often brought against him during his long apprenticeship with Tristano. "But at some point, you have to be prepared to do it—to perform. It's vital, man, if we're talking about jazz, which is a performing art. It fulfills its meaning, and you fulfill your meaning, only when you play it live in front of an audience."

Has the musician's life Marsh created for himself been easy or difficult? "Oh, I've had a wonderful life. I've had a lot of opportunity, a lot of work. There's a world of music I'm proud to be a part of, with the people I still consider my heroes—Bach, Bartók, Charlie Parker, Lennie, Lester." Does he ever wish he had pursued fame more aggressively? "Not in the least. I'm not oriented that way. I've got only the one career I've got. I've done mainly one thing for 30 years—music, my own music."

Still, "some of the best careers aren't very lucrative, though," Marsh admits. In California in the late '60s, faced with supporting a family for the first time in his life, Marsh supplemented his earnings from music by performing manual labor, but he is not bitter about the experience. He describes a job as a TV repairman as "paying four or five dollars an hour, great money in those days," and a job cleaning swimming pools as "a nice job outdoors." In New York, most of his income derives from teaching. If he has one regret, it seems to be that the close-knit, racially integrated jazz community he found in Manhattan when he first arrived there in 1947 has been torn asunder—he speaks of the long-defunct Birdland as though it were Eden, and there is a sense of loss in his voice when he recalls "a gig in Queens around 1950, a dance sponsored by probably a Communist-front organization, Youth for America or something like that, for $75 cash. Me, Bird, I think Kai Winding and Red Rodney, the four of us plus rhythm. A casual, you know? Jazz casuals, we used to call them."

I suspect that it frustrates Marsh that circumstances prevent him from playing in front of audiences as much as he would like to—four weeks or so a year at the Village Vanguard, scattered concerts around the five boroughs and New Jersey, and the occasional European tour must only whet his appetite. Still, I agree with him that he has created a wonderful life for himself. He hasn't always been able to call his own tune, and he has sometimes had to pay the piper, taking menial day jobs which at least afforded him the luxury of playing only the music he loved and could be proud to call his own. But he has always faced the music; he has accepted responsibility for his own melody, and however long it took to come, that melody finally came right straight off the top of his head.

(JANUARY 1983)

# An Intellect of the Heart

On the eve of his sixty-first birthday, George Russell was the one bearing gifts. It was mid-June, and Russell was in Philadelphia to conduct "The African Game," a panoramic extended work comparable to such latter Ellingtonia as "Three Black Kings" and "Afro-Eurasian Eclipse" in its textural sensuousness, its dynamic compass, its affirmative emotional capaciousness, its successful blend of Eastern stoicism and Western wondering why. "The African Game" lasted just under an hour, opening with a querulous rubato passage and climaxing with a rending, full-tilt unison roar with serrated brass and saxophone call and response figures, equine bass and synthesizer vamps, rupturous percussion salvos, and (a Russell trademark) earth-moving doublings and halvings of tempo in between. Although there were tentative moments here and there as Russell guided his youthful 14-piece Living Time Orchestra in and out of "The African Game's" mazes, by and large the band tore into the piece with a recklessness and precision that belied its complexity. Perhaps as a reward to the band for a job well done, Russell closed the set by giving his players an opportunity to blow freely and at length on a good set of changes. The piece was "Ezz-thetic," Russell's tangent on Cole Porter's "Love for Sale." Written for a Lee Konitz/Miles Davis date in 1949, "Ezz-thetic" sounded contemporary despite its vintage, and all the soloists pushed themselves to their limits in rising to its challenge, especially tenor saxophonists Bill Barron and George Garzone, who brought the piece to a rousing finish by going one-on-one as the other horns jeered them on.

It was an exhilarating concert, and the 35-year-span between "Ezz-thetic" and "The African Game" underlined not only George Russell's longevity but his continuing prescience. One went away that night convinced of Russell's genius and persuaded that there was indeed a sophisticated audience for jazz in Philadelphia, contrary to what previous bitter experiences had led this Philadelphian to con-clude—the tiny auditorium of the Afro-American Museum, which seats about 250, was packed for the first show, and there were long lines outside awaiting the second. But the comments one heard around town in the days that followed, after Russell had returned to Cambridge, Massachusetts, quickly deflated one's optimism. There were vague rumblings that Russell's performances had been "too academic"—a conditioned response probably owing something to the number of white faces in Russell's band and the fact that they read his difficult scores from sheet music.

Russell, who had been in Philadelphia two weeks earlier to deliver a lecture at Temple University, may have been anticipating such a parochial reaction when he told interviewer Terry Gross of radio station WHYY-FM, "We like to think that all this music we call jazz comes out of heart and feeling. And of course it does. But it also comes from an *intellect* of the heart—an intuitive intellect that can't remain intuitive if it's to survive and transcend the circumstances of its birth."

As the jazz avant-garde's most visible link to the past and its con-science against progress at any price, George Russell has clearly been one of the decisive figures in the ongoing development of modern jazz, even though the former big-band drummer and sometimes small-group pianist has made his greatest contributions from the wings, as it were, as a composer and theorist rather than as a performer. It was Russell who introduced bitonality and modal techniques to jazz with "Cubana Be" and "Cubana Bop," his visionary 1947 collaborations with Dizzy Gillespie and Chano Pozo. In 1959, Russell's inquiries into the nature of harmonic relationships culminated in the publication of the treatise *The Lydian Chromatic Concept of Tonal Organization.* Since 1969, he has taught courses in the Lydian Concept at the New England Conservatory of Music; long before that, even before the publication of Russell's book, musicians had studied the Concept informally, or absorbed its principles in the process of collaborating with Russell. It's no wonder that Russell's mark is all over *Kind of Blue,* for example, for among the musicians intrigued by his theories of tonal behavior were Miles Davis, John Coltrane, and Bill Evans; as a result of their influence upon wave after wave of younger players, Russell's own influence has become all-pervasive, if largely second-hand.

Attempts to elucidate the Lydian Concept invariably stray into musicological terminology beyond the ken of even the most well-informed layman and wind up making Russell's music seem more noetic than is actually the case. In essence, the Concept invokes the laws of physics to restore the ancient lydian scale to its former position of dominance over the diatonic scale, which has governed Western music only since the late 15th century. In categorizing tonal movement as vertical or horizontal, active or passive, outgoing or incoming, the Concept also embodies a philosophical critique of goal-oriented Western civilization which obfuscates matters even more. But if all this sounds rather forbidding, consider that (as Russell pointed out during his lecture at Temple) Michael Jackson's hit "Wanna Be Startin' Something" is based entirely on the intervals of a Lydian scale. And rest assured that in actual practice—which is to say in performance—Russell's charts subsume theory into rollicking swing, embracing tried values even while advancing iconoclastic vision. Moreover, like all great jazz composers and arrangers, Russell possesses a Midas touch; his shrewd juxtaposition of seesawing jazz harmonies and the smoldering rhythms he has become enamored of in recent years elicits powerful and to-the-point improvisations from even the most leaden of sidemen.

Russell has always gravitated toward visceral rhythms and bed-rock bass lines, and many of his best-known works—including "All About Rosie" (1958) and its precursor "Concerto for Billie the Kid" (1957); "The Day John Brown Was Hanged" (1956); and his pre-monitory adaptation of "You Are My Sunshine" with singer Sheila Jordan (1963)—have integrated grass-roots folk and gospel motifs. The son of a college band director, he was raised in a foster home in Cincinnati. "My foster mother was an avid church-goer," he says, "though ours was hardly the jump-and-holler kind of church. It was the sort of church that had doctors and lawyers as deacons. I don't even think we had a gospel choir. But as my mother became more involved in evangelical religions, she would take me to hear the evangelical preachers, and, even before that, I would sneak over to those holy roller churches and lay outside for hours listening to those people rock—and I do mean *rock*—the earth as they sang."

He made his stage debut at age nine, singing "Moon over Miami," accompanied by "a friend of the family"—Fats Waller, no less. "As a member of an oppressed race, I had the good fortune to have joyous music all around me as I was growing up," Russell says. "Our next door neighbor for a while was Jimmy Mundy, the arranger who wrote 'Five O'Clock Special' for Benny Goodman and 'Travellin' Light' for Billie Holiday. I heard all the bands that came up the Ohio River from the Mississippi on the big riverboats, and as I got older, I would walk down to the section of Cincinnati they call the black bottom to hear all the big bands at a place called The Cotton Club and all the great blues singers like T-Bone Walker at all the little joints I would pass along the way.

"The Lydian Concept evolved out of all that—the music I listened to all my life and the knowledge I picked up from people on the street," says Russell, who bristles when he hears himself described as a theorist, "because that implies I'm an intellectual, and I'm not. If I possess knowledge, it's come intuitively from a healthy respect for ideas as living entities and an absolute reverence for the learning process, not from cramming facts in my head in order to attain this or that degree. Schools and knowledge are not always compatible, you know," he says, ignoring the fact that he is himself a tenured academician, like it or not. "Many of the greatest contributions to American culture have been made by people with little formal education and very little respect for formal education, either. No, the Concept grew out of an intuitive feeling I had that conventional music theory was subjective, biased, fragmented, and not holistic, though I wasn't necessarily able to put it in those terms when I first started work on the theory in 1953. Long before that, I had realized that if I was going to learn everything I want to know about music, I was going to have to teach myself."

The intuitive feeling that Russell had about the inadequacy of the conventional music theory he had been taught at Wilberforce University was helped along by a chance remark by another autodidact, Miles Davis; and a long convalescence in a New York tubercular sanitarium gave Russell ample time to study on his own: "Back in the mid-'40s, Miles told me his ambition was to learn the ins and outs of all the chords, and thinking about that, I reasoned that for every chord, there must be a scale closer to that chord than any other scale. Its scale of unity, in other words. So for the first movement of "Cubana Be" and "Cubana Bop," I chose a C seventh with an augmented ninth and a flat fifth, and—not to get too technical—I already knew by that time that the scale of unity in this case was a B-flat auxiliary diminished scale—whole step, half step, whole step, half step, whole step, half step, whole step. So I based the movement not on the chord but on its mode of unity, under the assumption that you could convey the harmony of the chord without *sounding* the chord. And I had written my first modal composition.

"Thinking about it, I realized that there were really only two basic forms of jazz improvisation, one vertical in nature, and the other horizontal, one exemplified by Coleman Hawkins, the other by Lester Young. Coleman Hawkins addressed the task of negotiating a credible melody on a given set of chords by enunciating the tones of each chord, and, as he soloed in that vertical manner of his, he would take liberties by going just outside the chords. But the point is he would meet each chordal deadline as it occurred. Lester Young did not—his chief tendency was to float over the top of the chords, using scales to telegraph to the listener the direction in which the chords were moving on their way to resolving in a tonal center. It occurred to me that musicians were really like physicists or mathematicians in the way they went about solving the problems of improvisation.

"Then came the big shock when I realized that the tone on the fourth degree of a major scale—the step we normally call 'fa'—prevents the major scale from achieving unity with its tonic chord, it's 'do,' because that 'fa' is itself so tonic. If there's a reason for calling the major scale diatonic, that 'fa' is the reason. It keeps the C-major scale in a constant state of goal seeking, of seeking unity with its tonic chord. The diatonic scale achieves a finality in the sense that it reaches resolution with its tonic, but it never manifests *self-unity,* unlike the lydian scale, which is at peace with itself all up the ladder of fifths. It's a provable, objective fact, and it's not just important musically, either. It's central in understanding the sociological development of the Western world."

In pointing out that the Western diatonic scale was originally a "plagel" (or derivative) mode of the lydian scale, which predated Western civilization by some 2000 years, Russell infers that the use of the lydian puts one back in touch with "a vertical force, a passive force" sacrificed by "our horizontal, goal seeking society," and it is this attempt to press harmonic terminology into philosophical service that ultimately undermines Russell's formulation. In what sense is hierarchical Western civilization "horizontal" rather than "vertical?" It's also debatable whether music can serve the ameliorative purpose of putting one back in touch with primal forces. Still, these are semantic issues, not musicological ones. Overreaching philosophical implications aside, what rescues the Lydian Concept from arcania is the almost physical ardor of Russell's obsession with it (he describes it as "my life's work—it's the debt I owe the forces that are responsible for my existence," and is currently revising the 1959 tome that first outlined the Concept's ruling principles), and what marks it as a breakthrough is the fact that it gives improvisers the freedom to combine both vertical and linear strategies without risking false moves or "wrong" notes (a point John Coltrane grasped intuitively—and perhaps independently—around the time he started superimposing chords and scales in pantonal "sheets of sound"). "It's the first systematic theory of music that poses no rules, no dos and don'ts, but instead offers a limitless variety of possibilities, because it encompasses all of equal temperament and is based on the principle of gravity, the assumption that all music has a tonal center," Russell says. "It doesn't matter whether that tonal center is audible or inaudible; it doesn't matter if it's artfully disguised, as in twelve tone music. Even in the most chromatic music—even in Schoenberg or Stockhausen or Cecil Taylor—there's always a little slice of tonality that serves as a tonal center."

Since, as Russell puts it, "Rhythm behaves much the same way the harmony does," one recent outgrowth of the Concept is a related system of polyrhythmic organization that Russell calls Vertical Form, comparing it to the drum music of West Africa, in which one drummer lays down a ground rhythm (a tonal center, if you will) as others gradually layer interlocking rhythms on top. Russell cites "The African Game" as an example of the method. " 'The African Game' expresses my admiration for the enormously sophisticated music Africa has given us since the dawn of history," he says, adding that the title conveys underlying speculations about the origins of man. "Eight million years ago, give or take a few million, along the shores of what is now called Lake Rudolph near Kenya, 'God said grace, then rolled the dice on the human race' ('The African Game's' evocative subtitle). He—or she—took a gamble as nature always takes a gamble when it creates a new species, because there's always the possibility that species will annihilate itself or otherwise preside over its own extinction, which seems to be the direction humanity is heading in now. I'm not one of those people who rejects every new innovation, but I see in advancing technology the danger that we're on the verge of eliminating ourselves. That's what steers me away from electronic music, though I have experimented with it" (on the 1969 *Sonata for Souls Loved by Nature,* and elsewhere).

"People assume 'The African Game' is about black evolution, but it's not. It's about *human* evolution, because we're all Africans at the core, when you trace these things back. It's ironic, in a way, that I'm playing the Afro-American Museum, because there are so many white players in my band, it'll probably look like Buddy Rich's band to some people. But I've never bought that theory that says only black people have soul or essence or whatever—that does nobody any good. I don't care where a musician comes from or what he looks like. I listen for that electricity you get from certain players. If I sense an affinity for someone else's music, I know he'll have an affinity for mine. I mean, I heard Jan Garbarek in Norway when he was just eighteen, and he had never even heard of 125th Street and Lenox Avenue, but he had the *fire.* Same thing with Terje Rypdal and Jan Christensen and all the musicians I worked with in Europe."

America's racial unrest, in fact, was one of the factors that drove Russell to seek haven in Stockholm in 1965; what lured him back to the U.S. four years later was Gunther Schuller's offer of a faculty position at the New England Conservatory of Music, along with a nagging feeling that he had been neglecting his responsibilities as an American artist. "I consulted the I Ching both times, and both times the oracle said it was time to cross the great waters. I left America because I felt great hostility directed toward me as a black man and as an artist, and I was somewhat reluctant to return to America at what seemed to be a time of violence and turmoil. On the other hand, that in itself seemed to be the best argument for return- ing. It created an opportunity for me to contribute something of value to my homeland in a period when it was going through relentless self-examination. That's a perfect climate for the artist.

"What worries me now, though, is the survival of jazz, and all the values it has come to stand for, in America. After all, the pattern suggests that as America goes, so goes the world, and here in this country at the present moment, it looks as though the media are arresting aesthetics, and the individual artist is losing all control over his art form. You no longer have people enamored of jazz at the major record companies. There seems to be less and less room being made at the corporate level for the Orrin Keepnewses, the Milt Gablers, the Alfred Lions and Francis Wolffs—the men of conscience and patrons of the arts who have traditionally assumed a protective stance toward the artist. It's significant that Giovanni Bonandrini [of Soul Note/Black Saint], the one man in the world who has shown the greatest interest in recording not only me but all kinds of jazz, lives in Milan. How many record companies are recording jazz in the United States? One? Two? You can't count the smaller labels because you can't even find them in the stores."

Uncertainty regarding "The African Game's" fate may have been one reason for Russell's pessimistic ruminations. We spoke a week after Bruce Lundvall resigned his position as head of Elektra Musician, the label to which Russell had consigned a self-produced 1983 concert recording of "The African Game." With Lundvall gone, jazz was in limbo at Elektra, and Russell feared that "The African Game" would never be released.

The story has a happy ending, however, one which Russell could not have foreseen in June 1984. "The African Game" has followed Lundvall to EMI and is scheduled to be among the first batch of new releases on the reactivated Blue Note label in 1985.* Once the record finally comes out, "The African Game" should be hailed as a masterpiece and win Russell the place in the pantheon he has long deserved—assuming his delicately poised and uniquely American balance of pure knowledge and blood pumping speculation, of intellect and heart, doesn't fall on ears deaf to one or the other or both, as seemed to happen in Philadelphia last summer, and has happened all too often throughout his long, exemplary career. If as robust and

---

* *The African Game* (Blue Note BT-85103) was released in February 1985.

stimulating a work as "The African Game" fails to arouse jazz listeners, one will be forced to share its composer's concern for the survival of jazz. But one will also be forced to conclude that it is the complacency of the jazz faithful, rather than the indifference of the mass media, that may ultimately plant the seeds of destruction.

(DECEMBER 1984)

# Maintaining the Structure

Now that the charges of willful primitivism and novelty-for-novelty's-sake have abated, and now that the shock waves of its influence have been registered in hemispheres some distance removed from the territorial boundaries of jazz, the Art Ensemble of Chicago is generally conceded to have been the signal jazz band of the '70s and to remain one of this decade's vanguard outfits. Seguing from the raucous to the cerebral, from the primal to the post-modern without so much as skipping a beat, the typical Art Ensemble performance is equal parts African fertility ritual, turn-of-the-century minstrel show, dinner theater of the absurd, political filibuster, free-form endurance contest, and cross-cultural bricolage—this is the band that gave eclecticism a good name. But the Art Ensemble's high standing as a unit has tended to overshadow some of its members' individual accomplishments—those of Roscoe Mitchell in particular.

A cogent soloist and a distinctive ensemble colorist on all of the numerous reeds and woodwinds he plays, Mitchell makes more telling use of accent and space than any saxophonist since Sonny Rollins, and his odd fingerings, "off" intonations, and broad, slightly flattened vibrato recall Nigerian music in an oblique, non-proselytizing manner. But perhaps even seasoned listeners sometimes find it difficult to distinguish Mitchell's wry voice from that of the more voltaic Joseph Jarman, the Art Ensemble's other all-purpose multi-reed and -windsman. (Difficult on record, at any rate. Live, it has never been a problem telling them apart: Mitchell is the one wearing neither costume nor warpaint.) Or perhaps—the more compelling explanation—Mitchell's most ambitious writing for the Art Ensemble (most notably on the epochal 1969 *People in Sorrow*) subsumes itself so completely in group improvisation as to seem to be the work of five authors instead of one. Mitchell's structuralist sensibility so dominated the Art Ensemble in the group's formative years that, when all is said and done, it is easier to pinpoint the elements of street-corner theatricality, gallows humor, pan-African tribalism, and percussive tintinnabulation brought to the band in varying measures by Jarman, trumpeter Lester Bowie, bassist Malachi Favors Maghostut, and percussionist Famoudou Don Moye than it is to isolate the more deeply ingrained values of group purpose and order instilled by Mitchell. Let us not forget that the Art Ensemble of Chicago evolved out of what was originally the Roscoe Mitchell Quartet.

According to Mitchell, necessity mothered the bewitching tribal percussion passages that became the trademark of the Art Ensemble sound, just as it was necessity that forced the Roscoe Mitchell Quartet to go co-op. "The original members of the mid-'60s quartet were myself, Lester, Mal, and Phillip Wilson on drums. When Phillip left the group, we doubted that we'd ever be able to replace him, because most of the drummers who were equipped to play free music were very heavy-handed, and we required someone who could play more sensitively. A lot of the so-called avant-garde music coming out of New York around that time was, like, triple fortissimo all the time, and the music we were playing was more delicately shaded than that. So we decided to investigate percussion ourselves, playing little, sometimes homemade percussion instruments behind each other, and that seemed to work out fine."

Joseph Jarman, who had played with the Mitchell Quartet off and on throughout the '60s, became a full-time member in 1969, and Famoudou Don Moye, a drummer who met the unit's exacting specifications, came aboard during a European sojourn a year later, by which point the Roscoe Mitchell Quartet had evolved into the Art Ensemble of Chicago. "It was my band, right? But I wasn't working enough that I could afford to pay those guys what they deserved, and expect them to be there whenever I called. Plus, even though I was still doing most of the band's writing back then, a lot of my pieces called for collective improvisation, so everybody was shouldering an equal amount of responsibility. We became a co-operative unit in order to remain committed to one another and in order to survive.

"I tried painting my face once like some of the other guys, but I started sweating when I got out onstage, and when I wiped my brow, the paint smeared all over my hands," Mitchell confides one spring morning over breakfast in a diner across the street from the midtown hotel where he has set up temporary quarters for the two weeks he is scheduled to play New York (with the Art Ensemble at the Village Vanguard, and with his own group at the Public Theatre). A small, tidy man in his early forties whose soft brown eyes sharpen when he discusses music, Mitchell lives with his pre teenage daughter on a 365-acre farm about 30 miles from Madison, Wisconsin. An early riser, he repeatedly voices dissatisfaction with the late hours and fast pace expected of a musician on the road.

"So for me, the paint is not all that practical. Plus, I worry what the long-term effects are, of filling up the pores of your skin with makeup. But the makeup reflects the concern some members of the Art Ensemble have for tradition and theatricality. When you see the Art Ensemble in concert, you're conscious of witnessing a ceremony with certain people enacting certain roles. You're right about the blend of musical personalities, by the way. Jarman has definitely incorporated concepts related to theater and politics, and it's true Malachi is well-versed in African custom. There generally is a streak of humor to the things Lester does, and, yes, I *do* insist on structure.

"Because, look, even if you just start right off improvising, it'll end up having some kind of structure, if you're doing it right, because the same rules that apply to composition apply to improvisation. Say you and I are improvising together, and you're developing a very intricate motif, and—BAM—here I barge in playing something that's not very provocative in itself and isn't even an acceptable counterpoint to your line. To a perceptive listener, it's going to sound the same as if we were playing a piece of *written* music that you're reading correctly and I'm not.

"As a composer, you never really have that much control over what happens to your piece once the part you've written comes to its conclusion and the solos begin. All you can hope for is that the improvisers will be having a good night and stay within the guidelines you've provided. Usually, that doesn't happen, especially in free music. Cat's playing and you don't know *what* he's playing! It may be a fine solo in terms of its own vocabulary but not relate at all to the piece you've written. To me, this is a sign of immaturity, both as a player and as a human being. You can't even suppress your ego long enough to concentrate on the task that's placed before you."

While Mitchell was growing up in Chicago in the mid-'50s, "music wasn't divided into categories the way it is now, with one age group listening to this and the next age group listening to that, and so on. I liked what my parents liked—Nat Cole and other pop singers, as well as Charlie Parker and Lester Young. You were exposed to all kinds of music on the radio in those days, and when you became a musician, it was just a matter of deciding which kind of music you wanted to play."

As a fledgling musician, Mitchell was "into a conventional style of playing—Wayne Shorter, Blakey-Messenger tunes like 'Moanin,' the kind of thing that was popular then, around 1959 or 1960. I enlisted in the army right after high school and that proved to be a mindopening experience. The three years I served in the army, music was a 24-hour obligation. I had the luxury of being a full-time musician, with none of the petty distractions you have in civilian life. I was stationed in Heidelberg, Germany, and there was a club there called The Cave, where I was exposed to some very interesting European musicians like Albert Mangelsdorff and Karl Berger. Plus, I heard

Albert Ayler for the first time. Albert was in one of the military bands, and I remember everyone was putting him down, because we were all so obsessed with playing correctly. But at this one session, Albert led off with three or four choruses of the blues and then went off into his own thing, with that awesome sound he had, and everything became clear to me. I had already heard Ornette Coleman on records and couldn't quite grasp what he was doing. But hearing Albert live was an enlightening experience. I went back and listened to Ornette and to things like Coltrane's record of 'Out of This World,' and Dolphy's solos on Max Roach's *Percussion Bitter Suite,* and all sorts of possibilities seemed open to me."

Returning to Chicago following his discharge, Mitchell located another source of strength in pianist/composer Muhal Richard Abrams. "I was taking music education courses at Wilson Junior College, studying the classical literature. No college had a jazz curriculum then, but every Monday, there was a free period and I would jam with guys like Malachi, Henry Threadgill and Jack DeJohnette. And every day after classes, I'd go over to Muhal's house. I certainly think I learned more from my sessions and discussions with Muhal than I learned in school. Muhal is about ten years older than I am; he had come on right at the end of the bebop era; he had several compositions to his credit; and he had chosen to continue exploring music from a creative perspective. There was a great wealth of musical information passing back and forth among all the younger musicians in Chicago around that time, but Muhal was the one who had all the practical experience and organizational skills, the one we all felt we could count on and respect."

Abrams's philosophies regarding creativity and economic self-determination—together with the passing of a restrictive nightclub entertainment licensing act that threatened to make the professional musician an extinct species in Chicago—ultimately led to the formation of the Association for the Advancement of Creative Musicians (AACM), an organization which was to have lingering impact far outside Chicago. One immediate benefit of the AACM, however, was that the spirit of solidarity it fostered among its members gave talented young Chicagoans like Roscoe Mitchell reason to forgo the once obligatory move to New York.

On the basis of his writing for the emerging Art Ensemble of Chicago, we can applaud Roscoe Mitchell for intuiting, long before most of us, that stamina and inspiration could not always be counted on to sustain lengthy free collective improvisations. The advances made on behalf of improvisational self-expression and rhythm section independence cried out for similar bold initiatives in the areas of compositional forethought, development of motifs, stage presentation, and inner-group dynamics, lest solipsism and chaos inevitably reign. Mitchell's minimalistic, incremental sound collages (beginning with "Little Suite" in 1967 and continuing up to the present) have had a profound effect on the thinking of fellow Chicagoans Anthony Braxton and Leo Smith, and—via Smith—the still-emerging New Haven school, which has already spawned such promising young players and writers as George Lewis, Dwight Andrews, and Anthony Davis. "Tkhke," Mitchell's pioneering anti-virtuosic 1968 solo alto improvisation, pointed the way for Braxton, Steve Lacy, and the European *tabula rasa* "instant composers." In addition, Mitchell is one of a handful of Chicago saxophonists responsible for retrieving the bass saxophone and the curved soprano from the dustiest recesses of the jazz past.

One can also mount a convincing argument for Mitchell as an innovative figure based on current activity. During the Art Ensemble's increasingly protracted layoffs, he fronts three provocative bands: the first is Space, an epigrammatic post-serialist trio with low reed player Gerald Oshita and singer Tom Buckner; the second is Sound, a vital quintet with guitarist A. Spencer Barefield, bassist Jaribu Shahid, percussionist Tani Tabbal, and either trumpeter Hugh Ragin or his replacement Michael Mossman; the third is Space and Sound, trio and quartet co-mingled. Mitchell also performs solo saxophone concerts and composes ambitious works for ensembles of virtually every size, configuration, and musical persuasion.

Like many other contemporary composers, Mitchell has devised his own systems of "scored" improvisation. The tools for Mitchell's "cut out" method (illustrated on *3X4 Eye* [Black Saint BSR-0050] and *More Cut Outs* [Cecma 1003], both reasonably easy-to-find Italian imports) are the mental equivalents of scissor and paste. "You take the specific materials the composition is based on and rearrange selected elements of them for the improvised situation that follows, placing them on a score sheet each improviser can refer to when needed—the conceptual equivalent of chord changes, almost."

He views his improvised solo concerts as "staged" improvisation. "I often play *practiced* solo improvisations. The point of playing solo is to prove you can sustain a structure for longer and longer periods of time, so I develop exercises to increase my powers of concentration, starting off with small sections at first, and while I'm doing that, I'm also working on technique—things like circular breathing and fingering. It would be nice if every time you started playing, all of a sudden, the heavens open up and the light comes shining down, and you can't do wrong. And you *reach* that point sometimes—but not every night. So there's always at least a germ of a thought I start off with, even on a completely open improvisation."

Mitchell's intellectual immersion in composition often results in music that strikes most ears as cold and forbidding, and can leave even the gamest listener groping in vain for an easy way in. A rationalist in a world that wishes its composers would surrender themselves over to rapture, Mitchell readily admits most of his pieces are tabular and non-impressionistic, "about" nothing save their musical coordinates and variables. Not surprisingly, he composes without necessarily worrying about how his pieces will *sound* in performance; as a consequence, his is the kind of writing that is often more rewarding to contemplate than to actually hear. But 1981's *Snurdy McGurdy and Her Dancin' Shoes* (Nessa N-20), with its delirious invocations of '20s jazz and its premonitions of a kind of heavy-bottomed abstract expressionist R&B, seemed to signal an unexpected turn to the sensual in Mitchell's music. Several of the pieces followed a conventional theme-solos-theme scenario, although the solos functioned more like "breaks" in early jazz and swing than like the extended soliloquies of bop or free jazz, and the most satisfying improvisatory passages of all were those created simultaneously by Mitchell and Hugh Ragin, an expressive young trumpeter equally adept at conveying baby-faced lyricism and five-o'clock-shadow growl and menace. And "Jo Jar" (from *3X4 Eye*) rocked out harder than anything this side of Ronald Shannon Jackson, even though it was all-acoustic and rolled on the doo-wack-a-doo rhythms of vintage jazz and pop rather than on the polyrhythms of '80s funk. "Jo Jar" had some of the randy propriety of Jelly Roll Morton's music, some of the structural implacability of Ornette Coleman's "Ramblin'."

"There are references to Morton there, that's right. I was trying to make the statement that there's a lot of strong music back there that no one knows about, and everybody will be discovering it after they've exhausted bop. But now I wonder if that kind of thing is worth my time, frankly. I feel like I take a step backwards when I play certain kinds of music. I remember once after the Art Ensemble had established ourselves as the more avant-garde musicians of the day, we'd sometimes go out and play nothing but jazz standards for our first set. But that first set was enough. It wouldn't have proven anything, and it wouldn't have been fun, to go on doing that all night.

"See, I feel like I'm back in the point on the circle where I can start learning again, where I can go without sleep for days and still be on top of the situation. Sometimes I think I push myself and my musicians too hard in demanding that we learn an infinite amount in a finite amount of time, and I know I risk bad performances that way, but what else can I do? I see cats folding up all around me, retreating into conventional modes of playing and writing, and I think, 'is this the time for me to push on my creative button or what?' Because five years from now when those guys look up, or whenever it is that they look up . . .'"

The Art Ensemble of Chicago is now together only a few months each year because, as Mitchell puts it, "we all feel as though we've devoted a good part of our lives to the group at this point, and we all have other projects to do." If Mitchell had his way, he would probably spend most of his time writing in his Wisconsin farmhouse. "I don't see myself spending this next period of my life running up and down the road like I have, always feeling too wiped out to write. I'd like to reach the level where I don't have to be physically present in order for my music to be performed. I'd like to walk to my mailbox and get a check from some ensemble that was performing one of my compositions, and all my energy would be focused on the work that still lies in front of me.

"There are some great people in the music department at the University of Wisconsin. I've been commissioned to write a piece for the Windmer Ensemble there, and I had hoped to have it finished before I rejoined the Art Ensemble, but I just couldn't do it. I told them I'd have it ready in the fall. Then I got a call from Chicago asking if I could have an orchestral piece in the mail by June 24. I couldn't turn that down, because who knows when I'll ever be offered an opportunity like that again?"

It would be a pity if the vivacious *Snurdy* proved to be no more than a brief time-out in Roscoe Mitchell's quest, an even greater pity if his outside activity made him odd-man out in the Art Ensemble of Chicago, a band which will always bear his mark. Still, one wishes Mitchell luck in his efforts to break free of the shackles of jazz. A revolutionary who knows the taking of the palace means the struggle has only begun is always worth giving the benefit of the doubt.

(DECEMBER 1983)

# Apples, Oranges,
# and Arthur Blythe

"The first time I came to New York—this was in 1968—I got smacked
in the face," Arthur Blythe says, and then—"BAM"—pantomimes an
open-handed whack across his kisser, and—*"oooh"* rubs his jaw as if
it still smarts. Realizing from the look of concern on my face that I
think he's recounting a mugging, he shakes his head no and laughs,
*"New York* smacked me in the face," and then his soft drawl quickens
and rises a megaton in volume until he has become Bill Cosby scold-
ing a moppet for playing with her stringbeans, "New York said 'KID!
what you doin' here, KID—you think you're comin' to the city, KID?'
And I said, 'Yeah, I'm coming to the city, what of it?' The city said
'TAKE THIS,' and *oooh* . . .

"You know how New York can be overwhelming when you've
come from a slower paced region? New York is so professional. I was
green and couldn't keep up with the pace. It seemed like I had come
from a country town to a big town. I had come to a cultured place
and I didn't have any culture. I did have some culture—I had something valuable of my own to contribute, but I wasn't confident of
that yet, and the city just overwhelmed me, and I ran back home."

It's incredible to hear Blythe talk about himself so self-deprecat-
ingly, impossible to believe that he was really the bumpkin he is

making himself out to have been. If New York City is the entire world—as many people who live there and all the people who fantasize living there secretly believe it is—then it must now seem at times to Arthur Blythe that he has the world at his feet. As rush hour begins in the streets below us and as bright lights pop on to outline the electric New York night, Blythe and I face each other across a desk in the 12th-floor publicity department of CBS, Inc., the steel and glass monolith people in arts and communications call The Black Rock. It's a busy day at CBS. In a much larger room across the hall, a Southern kickass rock 'n' roll band I had no idea was so popular is conducting a press conference. New releases by Elvis Costello and Earth Wind & Fire have just shipped, and from all appearences the cheerful but harried CBS publicity staff is experiencing a Christmas rush, even though it is only the last week in October. Blythe, a short, stocky, compact man whose photographs and Buddha-like concentration on the bandstand give him the appearance of being fleshier than he actually is, seems poised and self-assured in the center of all this industry.

Blythe is probably the one unanimously praised soloist to emerge in jazz during the pluralistic 1970s, an alto saxophonist whose choice of sidemen and restless explorations of counterpoint and extended harmony link him to the radical avant-garde, but whose plump ripe tone, irreproachable swing, and regenerative use of the standard jazz literature have won him acceptance even from hard-bop conservatives. He may well prove to be the magic figure of reconciliation, the force for consensus, that modern jazz has been looking for in vain since the death of John Coltrane in 1967. He has distinguished himself on records and on world tours with the Gil Evans Orchestra and with the small groups of Lester Bowie and Jack DeJohnette, and he now leads not one but two bands of his own: a mainstream alto-plus rhythm quartet he calls In the Tradition and a unit of more unusual instrumentation—alto, tuba, cello, guitar and drums—which sails more uncharted waters and which has no trade name, although those familiar with Blythe's music usually call this spunky quintet "the guitar band." Each new release by Blythe sells better than the one before it, and *Blythe Spirit* (Columbia FC-37427), his fourth effort for CBS, is the only unadulterated jazz record on the tradepaper "jazz" charts as we talk. Blythe is on the brink of artistic break-through, and if CBS remains solidly behind him—if the company refrains from the kind of advertising copy ("The greatest alto player since Charlie Parker") which "embarrassed and pressured" Blythe upon the release of *Lenox Avenue Breakdown* in 1979, if it is patient with him as it was patient with Miles Davis 25 years ago, if it honors his desire to be marketed and remains sensitive to his refusal to let himself be sold—if everything goes just right for him, he may be on the verge of worldly success as well. Blythe is not likely to be asked to endorse Blackglama minks, as Luciano Pavarotti has done, nor will he in all probability be the subject of a Dewar's Profile. He will be written about in *The New Yorker* only if Whitney Balliett decides to write about him. He will inhabit an all-too-real New York which is frequently squalid, frustrating, and, worst of all, humdrum. But in the socially circumscribed world of modern jazz, he may one day soon be able to crow (to himself most likely, since he is a modest man, not given to rodomontade) that he's A-number one, king of the hill, top of the heap.*

The "slower paced" region Blythe abandoned for New York wasn't really a "country town" at all, but Los Angeles. He was born in L.A. in 1940 and lived there from the time he was 19 until he settled in New York for good, on his second bob at the Apple in 1974. Many of us who live in the East still use the phrase "West Coast Jazz" as an epithet, a synonym for "cool" or "progressive," the diluted styles of swing and bop that were more popular than the genuine articles for

---

* Much has happened since this was written, and my comments now strike me as naive. Although Blythe remains under contract to CBS, the label has decided to place its bets on Wynton Marsalis, who has achieved the celebrity I predicted for Blythe and then some. Meanwhile, Blythe has been the victim of critical backlash, and in 1985, he finally caved in to pressure and recorded a blatantly commercial album—*Put Sunshine in It* (Columbia FC-39411). Still, rash or not, I have decided to let my original comments stand, because they convey something of the excitement surrounding Blythe in 1981.

a period in the middle '50s, when an in-group of musicians, most of them white, clannishly monopolized the Los Angeles studios. But logic should tell us that less aberrant kinds of jazz were also being played in Los Angeles then. Resident there at the time, if languishing in obscurity, were some of the architects of the bop revolution— Dexter Gordon, Howard McGhee, Gerald Wilson, Wardell Gray—as well as some of the most vital of the second wave of boppers—Harold Land, Art Pepper, Hampton Hawes—and the city's location, its large native black population, and its status as a media center made it a lure for the players from the Southwest and Prairie States who would prove to be the spiritual heirs of those men. Ornette Coleman and Ed Blackwell migrated to L.A. from Texas, Charlie Haden from Missouri, and Paul and Carla Bley from Northern California, joining natives like Don Cherry, Billy Higgins, and Eric Dolphy to form a nucleus of musicians who would help determine the direction of jazz in the next two decades, although, typically, all had to move East in order to be heard.

Arthur Blythe came to Los Angeles from no further away than his parents' home in San Diego. He had begun playing alto saxophone at the age of nine, and his first love had been rhythm 'n' blues ("no one called it rock 'n' roll back then"). Discovering jazz when he was 15 or 16, he began taking lessons from Kirtland Bradford, a former lead altoist with the Jimmie Lunceford Orchestra who had retired in San Diego. That was the extent of Blythe's formal training, but he had resolved to listen to everything he could and to learn something from everything he heard. It was his determination to unearth the ancestral roots of jazz—and his tendency to proselytize his discoveries— that earned him a distinctive nickname from his new friends in Los Angeles.

"I was expounding on some facts that I had learned about black musical history, some things that I hadn't known before about Scott Joplin and James Reese Europe—I was expressing myself so heavily and bending everybody's ear, and they said 'okay, man, we love it, we love to see your pride in yourself and in your history, but WILL YOU PLEASE STOP TALKING SO MUCH.' But I was so wired

up and excited I just went on, blah, blah, blahblahblah. They said
'please Black Arthur, please black *man,* can we talk about something
else?' It was a term of endearment from some of my closest friends,
a nickname like Fat Boy or Toby or Duke—Black Arthur. I think a
couple of writers heard me called that, and it just got out. The use of
the word was to connote pride and love of self, you know, but it did
have to some white people at the time an offensive connotation which
wasn't intended. I figured in order not to be misinterpreted I should
back off the 'black' a little bit and I started using Arthur Blythe instead of Black Arthur Blythe. But now it's accepted more or less that
'black' doesn't mean 'hate white people,' so sometimes it's used, and
sometimes it isn't. I have no qualms either way."

Blythe's musical circle in Los Angeles included trombonist Lester
Robinson; trumpeters Bobby Bradford and Walter Lowe; clarinetist
John Carter; pianists Horace Tapscott, Raymond King, and Linda
Hill; bassist David Bryant; and drummers Everett Brown, Jr., and
Stanley Crouch. In the mid-'60s, these players and others from the
area, spurred on by the innovations of Coltrane and Coleman, the
Black Power rhetoric of Malcolm X and H. Rap Brown, had the organizing energy of Horace Tapscott, banded together in the Underground Musicians Artists Association. UGMAA resembled the
Chicago AACM insofar as it represented an attempt to win political,
economic, and aesthetic self-determination for its members. Ultimately, however, the developments in Los Angeles were not as historically crucial as those in Chicago; the AACM members evolved a
unique collective approach to improvisation which offered a radical
alternative to the frantic solo-oriented style of free jazz in fashion in
New York during the '60s, while the players in UGMAA tended to
echo Coltrane, Coleman, Ayler, Taylor, and other New York heroes.
But UGMAA membership at least gave a musician a sense of purpose within the black community. The state and federal monies that
poured into Watts following the 1965 riots allowed UGMAA to stage
regular concerts at the Watts Community Coffeehouse and the Im-
manuel United Church of Christ for a few years in the late '60s. But
by 1974, long after all this activity had subsided, Arthur Blythe found

himself approaching middle age with no money, few press clippings, and little opportunity to play his music outside of Watts.

"I got fed up with California. I was about to suffocate out there; I couldn't see any light. If I was serious and wanted to partake of the music on a higher level, I had to be in New York. I didn't want to be thinking back later and saying 'what if . . .'

"So I didn't know anybody the second time I got here, either. I had a possible thing of some recordings with people which didn't manifest. But I just had to get out of L.A. 'Up against the Wall,' that tune that Trane wrote? That's how I felt."

Blythe was a mature stylist when he set out for New York the second time. Even with an artist of the calibre of Miles Davis or John Coltrane, we can chart an awkward, imitative, even painful growth on the basis of recorded evidence. Blythe's lack of early recording opportunities on the West Coast (one 1969 LP with Tapscott and some 1973 tracks with Azar Lawrence, as well as "some scab work on rock 'n' roll sessions," which were never released for all he knows) worked to his advantage, in a way—by the time anyone outside of Los Angeles heard him, he was fully formed. He was like a ray of sunshine on the blustery New York mid-'70s energy scene. Within months of his arrival, he became a regular in the downtown lofts, and within a year, an offer to go out on the road with Chico Hamilton enabled him to quit his day job as a security guard at a Broadway porno house and send for his wife Mamie and their three children. Soon he was leading his own groups in the lofts and recording for independents like Adelphi and India Navigation, and not much later, he was under contract to Columbia and playing the Kool Festival and the Village Vanguard.

The notion of regionalism, so widely endorsed in contemporary painting and literature, goes only so far in jazz—young players hear the same records and start off imitating the same idols no matter where they live. But Blythe happily asserts that his is a "California" sound, "not only the sound, but the ideas and the overall projection. It has connotations probably of the geography, the weather, of space,

mountains, ocean, sea, semi-tropical climate. It might be the dialect—
we're all American, but it's a big country. You go down South, you
go to Boston, you go to the Western part of the United States and
the Midwest—Indiana, Ohio—and everybody says the a's and the r's
just a little different. That's reflected in your music, because your
music is a direct reflection of your speech."

The hallmark of Blythe's sound—the thing you notice first—is his
vibrato. It's a wide vibrato of the kind that has not been in favor in
jazz since the swing era, but it's a rapid vibrato too—a sleek vibrato
for all its heft—and it's always under pinpoint control. It is the result
of a happy accident that occurred when Blythe was still toiling with
teenage rhythm and blues bands in San Diego. "Part of the reason I
wanted a big sound was that I was playing with electric guitars and
drums, and I had to struggle just to be heard. A friend of mine and
I used to go down to this music store and act as though we were going to be buying some new horns so we could play all the horns they
had there. We must have been 15 or 16, I guess. So anyway, once I
left the hard rubber mouthpiece I had been using at the store, and I
had a gig that night—all the stores were closed, and I needed a
mouthpiece to make the gig. My friend had this metal mouthpiece—
he said 'I got this Berg Larsen and I can't play it, man, I can't control it, but you're welcome to try.' Well, it was a medium open
mouthpiece, and I couldn't control it either, but it was broad and it
was loud and it cut right through those guitars, and I thought, you
know, this might be the one. Kirtland used to talk to me about tone,
about getting a big sound and a quality tone. So I started thinking
more about control, about diaphragm usage, embouchure, throat—
things like that—and I think that accounts for the way I play now,
thinking about sound in those terms."

His early experiences in ryhthm and blues may also have something to do with his flair for making dramatic entrances (he will
sometimes begin a solo with a note held over several measures, or a
furiously double timed passage, or a penetrating falsetto break) and
with his knack for exiting before he has worn out his welcome.
"With the bands I played with, the saxophone had time for a little

quicky and no more. I don't think everyone should play long solos. I mean when Trane did it, he was an exceptional person, and he could keep the spirit up that high that long, and [pianist] McCoy [Tyner] and [drummer] Elvin [Jones] and [bassist] Jimmy [Garrison], too—all of them sticking right in there with him. But I've listened to the 78s that Charlie Parker and Dizzy Gillespie and them made, and they'd have just a few choruses but they'd be smoking; they'd get out there and speak and you'd think WOW! That makes me realize you don't have to stay out there a long time to say what you have to say. I think the trick is to maintain interest and forward motion, from the listener's point of view and especially from *my* point of view, to keep the spirit of the music up and alive. When the spirit starts to decline, that's when you get out—the music is telling you it's time to end your say."

Like most musicians of his generation, Blythe was inspired as much by John Coltrane's moral rectitude as by his music. But even when playing the kind of reverential and sweepingly elegiac breath-measured ballad that Coltrane introduced to jazz, Blythe sounds earthy and full of impudent good cheer; his head may be in the clouds, but his feet are still planted on solid ground. He is also a resourceful composer whose riffing heads are deceptively simple, surprisingly tuneful, reassuringly familiar sounding on a first hearing, for all their intensity and originality. Frequently, his pieces are built from the bottom up. "What came to me first was the bass line—deedle de-do/deedle de-do," he says of the lilting "As of Yet," a piece he has recorded twice, most recently with the In the Tradition band on *Illusions* (Columbia JC-36583), "then the melody came. I was thinking about balance, like a legato line over a syncopated line, breaking it down and having that blend, and that contrast, and that was the melody that came out. I didn't really think about what it sounded like until my sister-in-law heard it and mentioned that it sounded like 'Spring Is Here.' I hope it doesn't sound so *much* like it that I'm stealing something, you know?" I assure him that in the event of litigation, I can testify in all honesty that it sounds like "I Should Care" to me.

"Counterpoint and repetition—repetition without monotony, with variation, that makes interest happen," Blythe says, and it is an ideal I think he best realizes in the guitar band, where the pattycake between Blythe's alto and Bob Stewart's tuba, the pungent crosstalk between Kelvyn Bell's guitar and Abdul Wadud's cello, and the spread rhythms of Bobby Battle's drumming all work to create a balance of contrast and continuity. It is the guitar band which Blythe takes on tour with him and which currently seems to occupy his thoughts—he is considering adding "a voice—not a word singer but a voice as an instrument—and an organ—just the top part of the organ, the keyboard, not organ as bass. I'm thinking of asking Amina Claudine Myers to join. I haven't talked to her about it yet; I guess I'm telling everybody *but* her." But it is the quartet—In the Tradition—which has won Blythe the greater notoriety.

A movement in jazz can be a reflex, an almost imperceptible twitching of a nerve or muscle. All of a sudden, as the '70s yawned to a close, many of the musicians associated with the avant-garde began to seek a healing with the jazz past rather than continuing to stress their rupture from it. Of the reasons most frequently offered for this phenomenon—that jazz had ventured so far out a return to basics was the only hope of maintaining an audience; that, with no sweeping change on the horizon, musicians were looking back—neither seems accurate to me. But for whatever reason, we found the trio Air recording Joplin and Morton; pianist Anthony Davis and flutist James Newton fashioning suites around fragments of Mingus and Monk; Chico Freeman rhapsodizing in the manner of middle Coltrane; Sun Ra playing reasonably faithful Fletcher Henderson adaptations; and Cecil Taylor improvising, for a few dazzling moments on 3 *Phases,* over Ronald Shannon Jackson's Baby Dodds-like shuffle beat. When Arthur Blythe formed a quartet with pianist Stanley Cowell (later to be replaced by John Hicks), bassist Fred Hopkins and drummer Steve McCall (both from Air) and began mixing tunes by Ellington, Waller, Monk and Coltrane in with his originals, he gave a movement—or more precisely, a moment—its name and unintentionally became its figurehead. Any performance that swings or follows a chord sequence or makes an overt reference to the past is now said to be in the tradition. And any performance which doesn't do any of those things isn't.

Blythe's love and respect for his jazz forebears is evident in every note he plays with either band and in every sentence he utters about Parker, Young, Hawkins, Armstrong, Ellington, and Coltrane. What distinguishes a Blythe reading of "Caravan," for example, or "In a Sentimental Mood," from desultory readings of such pieces with similar instrumentation on blowing dates from the '50s (or the '80s, for that matter) is his emotional investment in the material. But if I distrust the slogan In the Tradition, it's because I fear that such sloganeering ultimately plays into the hands of the jazz equivalent of the new right—the hard liners for whom jazz is bop and nothing else, King Oliver and Albert Ayler both be damned. And if I prefer Blythe in the context of the guitar band, it's because I think his contributions to an ongoing tradition are more powerfully evident in a radical setting in which he comes across as a relative conservative than in a conventional setting in which he seems the relative firebrand. I think it is significant that the most convincing In the Tradition performances occur not on Fats Waller or Ellington material but on the Blythe originals in *Illusions*. It is significant, too, I think, that Blythe's most forcefully inventive reading of a standard so far on record is *Blythe Spirit*'s "Just a Closer Walk with Thee," on which he is accompanied not by a piano trio but by Bob Stewart's tuba and Amina Claudine Myers's organ.

But I am willing to concede that In the Tradition has been poorly represented on disc. The only LP the band has to itself, the eponymous *In the Tradition* (Columbia JC-36300), was bedeviled by an excessively bright and epicene recording, for which Blythe himself is willing to shoulder much of the blame: "It was the first time I was involved in the production, and I was trying to develop my sound on record. I didn't hear it properly. I didn't hear the way it would sound outside the studio." Who knows what heights of creativity the quartet reached at the Vanguard when I wasn't there. And I am willing to admit, finally, that comparing Blythe's two bands is like comparing apples and oranges, as they say, or comparing the East Coast to the West. I once heard John Cage say, during a question-and-answer period following a performance of *Empty Words,* that when you compare two things as though you had to choose between them, you wind up with one thing rather than the two you might have had. I am glad that Arthur Blythe, although he is willing to compare the two bands, sees no reason to give up one or the other.

"With In the Tradition, I tend to *sing* a little bit more; I tend toward a more legato kind of phrasing. In the guitar band, I'm more staccato because of the breathing"—because even a tuba player as fluid and dependable as Bob Stewart can't sustain long notes the way a bassist can—"but I have to sing there, too. With the guitar band I have to be more emphatic. I'm emphatic with the piano band, too, but not *as* emphatic. They're still following me when I play a solo or play the melody, but there's a little stricter adherence to tonality as it moves in a certain direction. I have to give them cues, but it's a different kind of cue than I give the guitar band. With that group, it's not just cues for in or out, but maybe a cue to let them know I'm at the end of a phrase, or I'm beginning the next eight bars, or I'm going to the bridge, or I'm coming out of the bridge, or I'm going to slow it down here or pick it up there. I mean there are different musical things happening in each band, and the way I respond to those things is different. It's like a good baseball player adjusting his stance for different pitchers, or different pitchers making adjustments for various batters. It's that kind of adjustment I have to make. But I definitely feel that anything that feels good to me, I ought to play it."

His baseball analogy leads me to ask Blythe if he's a fan, and he says that he enjoys the game without following the standings. As we walk to the elevator, I ask him if his loyalties are divided between the Yankees and Dodgers in this World Series (this is before the Yankee bullpen collapses and the Dodgers breeze to victory in game six).

"You mean because I was from L.A.?" he says, "No. I'm a New Yorker now."

(FEBRUARY 1982)

# Leading Lady

When singer Abbey Lincoln gives her autograph, she appends the name *Aminata Moseka*. During her pilgrimage to Africa in 1975, the president of Guinea christened her "Aminata" in recognition of her inner strength and determination, and Zaire's minister of education likened her to "Moseka," the god of love in female form. "I love Aminata Moseka. I've added her to myself. But I can't say that's my one and only name," says Lincoln, who has taken many names, experienced several rebirths, in her fifty-five years, and who invests as much thought and feeling in conversation as she does in her songs. "It's more like a title—something to live up to. That's why I recorded Stevie Wonder's 'Golden Lady.' It gave me the opportunity to sing to a female god. But I'm still Abbey Lincoln—I still like to wear makeup and glittering dresses and look attractive for an audience. And in many ways, I'm still Anna Marie."

Anna Marie Wooldridge was the name she was born with in Chicago in 1930, the tenth of twelve children. Before she started school, her family moved to rural Calvin Center, Michigan. "My parents were city folk, but the story goes that because my mother insisted that the country was the only place to raise children, my father saved up and built a house for us on the eleven and a half acres he bought.

I still remember the sound of my father's voice as he sang lullabys to me and my baby sister. He was a fine singer who might have become a professional if he and my mother hadn't had so many children. But they had a wonderful, lifelong love affair, and we were the result. He did odd jobs around the community, taking care of people's gardens and such, and my first exposure to music was from the records that neighbors would give to him instead of throwing them away. The one I remember best went 'Take them up in the air, boys. Take them up in the air.' It was by [black vaudevillian] Bert Williams, and I guess it was recorded just after air travel became commonplace. The point was that's how men could impress women—take 'em up in the air.

"I sang in school pageants and in the church choir, though I never much enjoyed that. I preferred to sing alone—to be the centerpiece, for lack of a better word. The living room piano was my private space, once I discovered that singing could win me attention and admiration."

At nineteen, she began her professional career as Gabby Wooldridge. "I was Gabby for two years, because the owners of the Moulin Rouge in Los Angeles wanted all their girls to have French-sounding names. They didn't realize that Anna Marie *was* French; it was Wooldridge that was the problem. They knew less about their European heritage than I knew about my African heritage, which was nothing." She discarded the surname soon after an aged white millionaire also named Wooldridge spotted a mention of her in a newspaper and wrote to inquire whether she was his long-lost heir. "That's when I realized that although Wooldridge was the name my father handed down, it wasn't really ours."

At that time, her manager was Bob Russell, best known for his lyrics to Duke Ellington's "Do Nothing 'Til You Hear from Me" and "Don't Get Around Much Anymore," and pop standards including "Time Was" and "Crazy, She Calls Me."

"Recognizing something potentially fierce and proud and independent in me, Bob renamed me Abbey Lincoln. He said, jokingly, 'Well, Abe Lincoln didn't really free the slaves, but maybe you will.'

When I signed with Liberty Records, as a promotional gimmick, they sent the disc jockeys a photo of me wearing one of Marilyn Monroe's skin-tight dresses superimposed over President Lincoln's face on a penny. It was ridiculous, and, of course, nobody got the joke. But the name worked magic on my life. As Abbey Lincoln, I acquired a reputation as a woman warrior."

> But for the painted lady,
> There is a point and stare,
> And eyes that ask a question:
> Is she going anywhere?
> (*Painted Lady*, Moseka Music, BMI)

The covers of Lincoln's first few albums (most are still available in facsimile editions) mirror her growing self-awareness. *Affair,* her debut, released in 1957 and subtitled *A Story of a Girl in Love,* shows her lounging centerfold-style, like a sepia Julie London, a come-hither look in her eyes, her breasts barely contained in her low-cut blouse. "That was the way they packaged women singers then, and I went along with it because I didn't know any better. I didn't yet think of myself as a serious artist—or as a serious person, either. All I wanted was to be thought of as beautiful and desirable."

Although the covers of the three albums she made for Riverside in the late '50s after becoming romantically involved with drummer Max Roach (whom she married in 1962) made no secret of the fact that she was a shapely woman, the fortitude that was coming to light in her singing was also becoming manifest in the poses she struck for the camera. Gaining a sense of herself as a black woman, she took herself off the sexual auction block. "Through Max, I met a circle of black artists—not only musicians, but actors, novelists, poets and playwrights. It was the early days of the civil rights movement, and we were all asking the same questions. But they were questions that glamour girls weren't supposed to ask. As I toured the country, I noticed that black people everywhere were living in slums, in abject poverty. I wanted to know why."

Gone were the strings that had accompanied her on *Affair.* Her delivery never really changed, but she was recording with jazz pace-setters like Roach, Sonny Rollins, Wynton Kelly, and Kenny Dorham now, often performing topical material. Although she continued to do standards, she banished from her repertoire songs about unre-quited love and "no-good men who didn't know how to treat women. I discovered that you *become* what you sing. You can't repeat lyrics night after night as though they were prayer without having them come true in your life."

By 1961, when she collaborated with Roach and lyricist Oscar Brown, Jr., on *We Insist: The Freedom Now Suite* (the original cover showed a reenactment of a sit-in at a segregated Southern lunch counter), she'd been branded an outspoken, intractable militant. Rec-ord companies considered her too hot to handle. "I would run into my old show-business associates who would be surprised to see me looking pretty much the way I had always looked, and they would say 'Abbey, we heard you were living in Greenwich Village, wearing black wooly stockings, and sleeping with musicians.' The word was out on me, and I was in plenty of trouble. But at least it was trouble of my own choosing. As the woman of easy virtue I was encouraged to portray earlier, I was on the road to loneliness and despair."

Over the last two decades, Lincoln's records have been few, less the result of a lingering backlash than of the American record indus-try's antipathy toward jazz. The records that have originated from Europe and Japan since *We Insist* and its companion album *Straight Ahead* show Lincoln wearing her hair natural or in dreadlocks or cornrows. "My straightened hair was the last curse left on my body. I started wearing a natural long before it became fashionable, and people would tell me I was a pretty woman, why didn't I make my-self more presentable? But I was determined to find my hair beauti-ful, to find myself and the people I was representing up there on stage beautiful just as we were—even if no one else did."

> *I think about the life I live,*
> *A figure made of clay,*
> *And think about the things I lost,*
> *Things I gave away*

*And when I'm in a certain mood,*
*I search the halls and look.*
*One night I found these magic words*
*In a magic book:*

*Throw it away!*
*You can throw it away.*
*Give your love,*
*Live your life,*
*Each and every day.*

*And keep your hands wide open,*
*And let the sun shine through,*
*'Cause you can never lose a thing*
*If it belongs to you.*

(*Throw It Away*, Moseka Music, BMI)

In concert, with her regal bearing and forthright declamation, Lincoln conveys an actress's riveting stage presence, without indulging in salacious flirtation, histrionic bathos, or sociopolitical cant. Jazz critic Martin Williams once saluted Billie Holiday as an actress without an act—and that accolade also describes Lincoln, who did in fact enjoy a sporadic film career, singing one number in the 1956 rock exploitation flick *The Girl Can't Help It*; co-starring in the acclaimed, independently produced 1964 civil-rights-of-passage film *Nothing But a Man*, and playing Sidney Poitier's love interest in the 1968 romantic comedy *For Love of Ivy*.

"With *Ivy*, my life reached a peak," she says. "Then it slid right into the valley again." *Ivy*'s producers optioned the rights to Billie Holiday's autobiography *Lady Sings the Blues* for Lincoln, but finally they were resold to Motown's Berry Gordy, who cast his own star, Diana Ross, in the lead. "I always loved Billie," Lincoln says, "but I was scared of her, too. She came to hear me once in Honolulu and just sat at the bar staring at me without saying a word. Years later, she came to Birdland one night when Dizzy Gillespie was playing and Max and I were in the audience. 'I'm so lonely,' she told me. 'Louis is in California on business, and I'm sitting at home washing my hair and polishing my nails and going crazy.' And everybody in the club knew that Louis McKay, her husband, was a few blocks away living it up with a woman who called herself Broadway Betty. That's the worst lie they told in the movie version of her life. Why give her one husband, when in real life she had four or five? If she'd had a man as faithful to her as the Billy Dee Williams character in the movie, her life might not have been so tragic. The problem was that although she could have had any man she wanted, she was only attracted to men who mistreated her.

"In a way, it's best that I didn't play Billie, because I don't know how to do anything half way. I was in such a sorry state myself at the time that portraying Billie's sorrow might have killed me. Max and I were divorced in 1970, and I was like a wounded animal. It's difficult recovering from a broken marriage, especially when it throws your career up into the air. I needed sanctuary, so I signed myself into a psychiatric hospital in upstate New York for five weeks, which turned out to be one of the best things that's ever happened to me."

Moving to Los Angeles to care for her ailing mother in 1973, Lincoln laid low for eight years, rarely performing. "I went underground, though I never intended to. I did community work and taught drama at Northridge University, where I felt a little out of place because I hadn't attended college myself. The good part about being in California was spending my mother's last years by her side. Oscar Brown, Jr., had shown me how to use the *I Ching,* and I would take comfort in the hexagram that said you cannot lose something that belongs to you *even if you throw it away.* I had thrown away my career, my relationship with Max—and I thought I had thrown away my life."

> I'm a world away, it seems,
> From the one who haunts my dreams,
> Like the distance that
> The earth is to the sun.
>
> And he holds me in his love,
> Like the light that shines above,

*And he's everywhere*
*and everything to me*

*He makes the day begin,*
*Just like the rising sun,*
*An elemental fellow*
*Who gets the job done*

*He's simple and he's super,*
*Oh, and what I wouldn't do for*
*Just a smile from the early rising sun.*

(Moseka Music, BMI)

"I wrote a love song to a man not of this world, a man who doesn't even exist," Lincoln says of the title track of her 1984 album *Talking to the Sun* (Enja 4060), the implication being that no lover under the sun could be as steadfast. Although her lyrics generally strive for social uplift, she does not consider herself a message singer. "Gil Scott-Heron is a message singer, not me. My songs are autobiographical, about the world as I encounter it. For example, 'People on the Street' [also from *Talking to the Sun*] is about the plight of the homeless, but it's based on personal observation—and sometimes I think I should be doing more to help those people than just singing about them. When I moved back to New York in 1981, I was shocked to see women younger than I was huddled on the streets like zombies, and my friends laughing at them, as if there was anything to laugh about. In the '60s, people used to at least feign social conscience, even if they didn't have any. It proves that we've taken more steps backward than forward since then. We demanded a say, and it was given to us. But some of the very people the revolution was fought for have sold it out. Black people like to wear the white hats—we're very good at pointing our fingers at others and pretending that we can do no wrong. But we can."

As a songwriter, Lincoln's greatest gift is her knack for hearty melodies and quick, pointed, telling observations. *The people in the houses ain't got long,* "I cried when that line came to me, because I realized I could wind up out there someday too. Composing music is

the difficult part for me. I've come to think of lyrics as poems, some
of which I find melodies for and some of which I don't." She has
written an unpublished volume of poetry called *In a Circle, Everything Is Up* and an unproduced play called *A Pig in a Poke* "about
an odd jobs man who stumbles on to a large fortune and doesn't
know what to do with it. The character is partly based on my father
and partly on myself. In my case, the fortune is my career, the musical gift it's taken me this long to figure out how to use properly."

Lincoln reclaimed the career she had thrown away in 1979, when
Inner City Records released *People in Me* (IC-6040), an album she
had recorded with Miles Davis sidemen in Japan six years earlier.
Since 1983, her backup band has included alto saxophonist Steve
Coleman, pianist James Weidman, bassist Billy Johnson, and drummer Mark Johnson, all promising young musicians in their late twenties. "Even though I don't perform often enough to give them steady
work, they're there for me whenever I call, and that thrills me. I
worry about them, though—whether they can hold out against the
commercial pressures that young musicians face today. Nobody pays
them any attention, and I'm afraid that's going to make them bitter
and discouraged. That's why I'm glad I arrived on the scene in the
'50s, when things were better. In those days, a lot of decisions were
made for you by your management, and you just played along. But
now that I'm out here by my lonesome, I miss that in a way—someone
to hold my hand and tell me everything will be all right."

She lives alone now, in an apartment building on Central Park
West, ten floors below her ex-husband, still a trusted friend. She has
no children. "I never intended to. What sort of mother would I have
been, travelling all the time? My mother was always there for me,
and I knew I couldn't do that. I've gone through so much madness
that I'm glad I didn't drag anyone else through it.

"That's why I'm thankful I've got my music. In a sense, it's all I've
ever had. After *For Love of Ivy*, people predicted a big film career for
me, but I knew it wouldn't happen. It wasn't even something I
dreamt about, because it wasn't practical, and you have to temper
idealism with practicality in real life. There are no roles for a black

woman unless you're willing to play the buffoon, like Nell Carter in *Gimme a Break!*—not to knock her, you understand, because she has to make a living. I was offered plenty of parts as the sassy maid, but I turned them all down. I decided that if I was going to be in the movies, it would have to be as a leading lady. Because that's what I've been off-screen, for better or worse—the leading lady in my own life."

(MAY 1986)

# *Patron Saint*

"Part of what has deranged American life in this past decade is the change in book publishing and in magazines and newspapers and in the movies as they have passed out of the control of those whose lives were bound up in them and into the control of conglomerates, financiers, and managers who treat them as ordinary commodities," *New Yorker* film critic Pauline Kael wrote in 1980. "This isn't a reversible process; even if there were Supreme Court rulings that split some of the holdings from these conglomerates, the traditions that developed inside many of these businesses have been ruptured. And the continuity is gone."

Kael's lament is just as applicable to the jazz record business. As they fell into the hands of corporate lawyers and accountants, the small, independent labels of the '40s and '50s folded or lost their identities. The industry has become a high-stakes numbers game, and the big numbers just aren't there for jazz. Of course, pop is a gamble, too, but the payoff can be enormous. The most a hard-core jazz album can hope for is slow but steady sales, and that simply isn't enough to excite corporate decision-makers, few of whom have any personal enthusiasm for improvised music anyway; rock is the music that people in the industry listen to for pleasure, and the glamour and high-stakes excitement of the rock scene was what lured many of them into the record business in the first place. Every so often—usually as a perk to a company executive who happens to be a jazz fan—one of the majors will debut a jazz line. Generally, these custom labels survive only two or three years, because the masterminds behind them lose interest or are fired or defect to other companies. Majors that take a fling with jazz tend to react like spurned suitors once they discover how slowly jazz moves—they want nothing more to do with the music.

It's a gloomy picture, all right, but jazz still has a few things going for it. It's much cheaper to produce than pop, and, thanks to decades of neglect, even some of its top names can be had for a song. New labels have sprouted and survived after a fashion: Muse, Xanadu, Gramavision, and India Navigation in New York; Pablo, Concord, and Palo Alto on the West Coast; Timeless, Steeplechase, and Hat-Hut, among others, in Europe and Scandinavia. These upstarts are rarely able to conduct business in the grand style they might wish, and their life expectancy is anybody's guess. But, for the time being, they set the tone for jazz in the '80s, much as Blue Note, Prestige, Riverside, Contemporary, Atlantic, and Savoy set the tone in the '50s and '60s.

The feistiest and most prolific of the new independents are the Milan-based sister labels Soul Note and Black Saint. Producer Giovanni Bonandrini—padrone and sole arbiter of taste for both—came to New York earlier this year to talk sales strategy with his American distributors and to supervise recordings by a number of artists, including Archie Shepp, Jimmy Knepper, and Ray Anderson. We met at a Clifford Jordan and Barry Harris session. As he stood tapping his foot to a Harris piano solo, it was plain to see that this is a labor of love for him. Sooner or later, jazz seems to demand active participation from everyone who falls under its sway; to hear Bonandrini tell the story in his serviceable, Mediterranean-flavored English, his transformation from collector to producer was the logical consummation of an enduring passion.

A scholarly looking type who did in fact teach French and English literature in Italian high schools for 25 years, Bonandrini began collecting 78s in the late '40s. Jazz remained a hobby, though, until 1974, when he pooled resources with four other investors to start IREC, a record distribution company that eventually came to represent over a hundred small American and European labels in Italy. Shortly before he retired from teaching in 1978, Bonandrini and his partners purchased Black Saint, a three-year-old Italian label with an adventurous international image and a checkered financial history.

At the time of sale, the label had a mere 13 releases in circulation. Six years later, the catalog has burgeoned to more than 60 titles, including landmark releases by David Murray, Muhal Richard Abrams, Anthony Braxton, Roscoe Mitchell, Leroy Jenkins, Sam Rivers, John Carter, and the World Saxophone Quartet. No label, foreign or domestic, has been more vigilant in tracing the movements of the post-AACM Chicago diaspora and the post-Coltrane New York avant-garde. But Bonandrini's interest in jazz does not begin with the avant-garde, nor have his contributions to the welfare of contemporary jazz ended there. "Giacomo Pellicciotti, who was in charge of production from the beginning and is now no longer with the company, wanted to go only in the direction of the avant-garde," Bonandrini explains. "He thought that to record mainstream artists like Billy Harper and Max Roach was to regress—Max Roach with Anthony Braxton was okay, you see, but not Max's quartet. I agreed with him that if you love jazz you follow its progress. But you also have to remember jazz is everything, from the beginnings on."

So one of Bonandrini's first moves after taking control of Black Saint was to launch a mainstream affiliate he christened Soul Note (in memory of Blue Note). With just over 60 releases to its credit since 1979, Soul Note has borne witness to the resurgence of hard bop, in addition to providing a badly needed outlet for such uncategorizable mavericks as George Russell, Jaki Byard, Bill Dixon, Walt Dickerson, and Ran Blake. Bonandrini admits that the distinction between his two labels is often fuzzy: "Many artists today, you take them into the studio with no way of knowing whether they will want to play bop or free." But the point is that in addition to nurturing revolutionary new talents, Bonandrini has also been ensuring that marginally more familiar yet scarcely less incendiary voices will not be ignored. Two years ago, he proved himself as shrewd a businessman as he is a talent scout, singing a worldwide distribution pact with Polygram that has resulted in greater visibility for his labels and his constellation of recording artists.

"I knew nothing about record production when I started, but I knew jazz," Bonandrini says. More important, he knew what he liked. There are producers who think of themselves as facilitators—Norman Granz, for example, or Blue Note's team of Alfred Lion and Francis Wolff—and those who think of themselves as *auteurs*—ECM's Manfred Eicher or CTI's Creed Taylor. Bonandrini counts himself among the former, which means that his productions are recognizable by their standard, not by their sound. While no one is likely to mistake a Soul Note or a Black Saint for a state-of-the-art recording, their evident lack of varnish belies the forethought that goes into them every step of the way.

First come the decisions: whom to record, when to record them, and where. "Musicians are skeptical by nature," Bonandrini points out, "and in dealing with record companies, they have had good reason to be." At first Bonandrini had to cajole artists into working with him; now that he has established a reputation as a square-dealer, musicians approach him.

The last two decades have witnessed a proliferation of European import recordings by American jazz artists, as foreign labels have endeavored to take up the slack left by the demise of American independents. Many of these releases, particularly those from France and Italy, are poorly mastered, indifferently edited concert performances. Realizing that great concerts don't necessarily yield quality recordings, Bonandrini prefers studio dates, though he has released live tapes submitted to him by musicians whom he wanted in his catalog (usually with the tacit understanding that a studio date would follow at some unspecified point). Unlike many European producers, he will not record a band at the beginning of a tour, before it has had a chance to fine-tune its material. And with American musicians becoming less eager to play in Italy as the dollar value of the lira continues to plummet, Bonandrini works more frequently in the U.S.

In Milan, the engineer he swears by is Giancarlo Baragozzi, who meets the one prerequisite Bonandrini has for that job: some experience as a working musician. "He must be able to think like a musician in order to splice without interrupting the flow of the rhythm." Bonandrini admits his own knowledge of music is rudimentary but claims that's no drawback to being a producer. "Musicians will listen to your objections as long as you have sound reasons for them," he says. Generally, Bonandrini has few objections because few surprises await him when he enters the studio. He and the leader have discussed such matters as sidemen and choice of material months in advance, and there has usually been a rehearsal the day before—prudential measures overlooked by a surprising number of jazz record producers. There are fewer agonizing delays than at most jazz functions, because Bonandrini will not tolerate lateness or errant behavior once on the job. "I am serious and I do my job, and I expect the musicians to be serious and do their jobs, too," he says. Owners of small jazz labels tend to be idealists these days, and artists often suffer their own quaint illusions about what the public wants; on two or three occasions, Bonandrini has had to dissuade musicians from recording material he deemed "too commercial." Yet he has never supervised a session that did not yield a release.

Such pragmatism is crucial: While Black Saint and Soul Note may qualify as the growth story of the '80s in the downscale world of jazz, they are still marginal enterprises in the larger scheme of things. Bonandrini's production costs per record range from $7,000 to $20,000 (studio time, advances for leaders and session fees for sidemen, covers, pressings, labels, graphics, and liner notes). Sales average 3,000 to 7,000 copies worldwide, with North America accounting for no more than 30 percent of that piddling sum; five top sellers—*Old and New Dreams*, Max Roach and Anthony Braxton's *Birth and Rebirth*, David Murray's *Ming*, George Adams's and Danny Richmond's *Hand* *to Hand,* and the World Saxophone Quartet's *WSQ*—have passed the 10,000 mark.*

Although the affiliation with Polygram will no doubt increase American penetration, it also entails compromise: The conglomerate has persuaded Bonandrini to stagger his release schedule here in order to allow more time for promotion. As a result, some titles are now available in Europe and Asia months before they reach the U.S. And one of Bonandrini's artists (unofficial sources say it's David Murray) is under exclusive contract to him because Polygram would not flex its promotional muscle without such an arrangement.

Clearly, no one is getting rich from Soul Note or Black Saint, not the artists who record for the labels (they draw 6 percent royalty of list price on every unit sold—roughly 60 cents), nor Bonandrini himself. But the first function of music is pleasure, not profit, and the pleasure of taking matters into your own hands to document the music you love is inestimable. At one time or another, every jazz fan dreams of owning his own label, and those who realize that ambition often do so only by risking financial disaster and the enmity of the musicians they most admire. Bonandrini has somehow found a way to make it all work. His labels are solvent and show no signs of swerving from their commitment to quality. And he is trusted: most musicians conduct business with him on the basis of a handshake.

In an industry where scruples are often regarded as a luxury, Bon-

---

* Compared with figures provided by Bruce Lundvall, former president of CBS Records and Elektra Musician, now charged with reviving the Blue Note label for its corporate owner EMI, these numbers offer testimony to Bonandrini's thrift. According to Lundvall, the average major label jazz album costs upwards of from $20,000 to $35,000 to produce: "This is assuming we're talking about a pure jazz album by a well-established artist like McCoy Tyner or Dexter Gordon, and not an album intended for crossover. That figure includes sideman fees, advances on royalties for the leader and studio rentals for rehearsals and the actual recording sessions. It doesn't include the cost of pressing the discs or art work or advertising or promotion." As a result, Lundvall says, a jazz album released by a major label must sell from 35,000 to 40,000 copies worldwide to break even, and most hard jazz albums are lucky to sell between 7,000 and 20,000. On the basis of these figures, it is tempting to attribute the reluctance of major labels to record jazz to their inability to think small.

andrini sounds almost too good to be true. But before canonizing Bonandrini, it is wise to remember that—like Alfred Lion and Francis Wolff, who kept Blue Note afloat for 30 years only to sell the label to a conglomerate for a handsome profit in 1966—he is an entrepreneur, not an altruist. In fact, at least one of his American business associates, a fellow small-label owner whose records Bonandrini distributes in Italy, characterizes him as "aggressive and opportunistic. He took advantage of circumstances that existed in jazz in the mid-1970s, when no one else was recording the music—and when those few of us who *were* were scrambling. He begged all of us to sell him our records at the lowest possible price so that he could get his distributorship started, and then he took the money he made and started his own labels, which he imports to the United States in direct competition with us. It's conflict of interest." The label owner in question was hesitant to be identified in print "because Bonandrini has a virtual monopoly on jazz record distribution in Italy, and it could be costly for me if I were to antagonize him. He's a very powerful man in jazz."

Yet, within the jungles of commerce, aggressiveness and an ability to recognize opportunity when it arises are not necessarily deplorable traits. If Bonandrini is a businessman, at least he is a good businessman, which is more than can be said for most of the small-timers in jazz. And at least it is his sole business, not merely a foolproof tax write-off or a temporary bid to diversify. Indeed, the lesson to be learned from CBS's decision to drop James Blood Ulmer despite rave notices and slowly building sales is that the problem of hooking up with a major label is nothing compared to the problem of staying with one.

With profits that once trickled down to jazz now being funneled into rock videos and other loss leaders, the immediate future looks bleak for jazz on the corporate level. No matter. One suspects that Giovanni Bonandrini and others like him—Xanadu's Don Schlitten, SteepleChase's Nils Winter, India Navigation's Bob Cummings, Concord's Cal Jefferson, and Gramavision's Jonathan Rose, to name a few—will tough the hard times out, just as Blue Note's Lion and

Wolff and Prestige's Bob Weinstock did before them, and for much the same reason: they can't afford not to. Bonandrini has too much invested in jazz to pull out now, and money is only half of it. In the long run, jazz figures to prosper from the willingness of fans like Bonandrini to let money follow faith, even if they and the artists who record for them fail to prosper here and now.

(DECEMBER 1984)

# III

## *JUDGMENT*
## *CALLS*

# Henry Threadgill Leads
## the Parade

Saxophonist Henry Threadgill—the most commanding soloist as well as the most prolific writer in the collective trio Air—claims no special privilege for himself when he moonlights as leader of his own sextet (which usually numbers seven pieces, but who's counting?). Indeed, he is frequently upstaged by the sextet's impudent brass duo, cornetist Olu Dara and trombonist Craig Harris. But the sextet's three-horn front line and double-layer rhythm section (two percussionists, bass, cello) enlarge Threadgill's resources as a writer, and it's the expansive writing that makes *Just the Facts and Pass the Bucket* (About Time AT-1005) one of 1983's most provocative releases.

Along with such recent albums as Muhal Richard Abrams's *Blues Forever*, Roscoe Mitchell's *Snurdy McGurdy and Her Dancin' Shoes*, Anthony Davis's *Episteme*, Leroy Jenkins's *Mixed Quintet*, David Murray's *Ming* and *Home*, and Threadgill's earlier *When Was That?*, *Just the Facts* points jazz in a direction it was for a long time regrettably reluctant to explore: toward the writer as band helmsman. Notwithstanding the vogue for narcissistic loners like Keith Jarrett, the belated recognition of benevolent dictators like Sun Ra, and the cult adulation accorded leading lights in fusion and recombinant bebop, it was collectivism that set the ideological tone for jazz in the '70s.

Now, as the above-mentioned records suggest, far-sighted composers are breaking ranks with leaderless co-ops and reestablishing their sovereignty; and with *Just the Facts*—its writing painterly in its tonal abstraction and cinematic in its emotional spread—Threadgill has sprinted to the head of the field.

*Just the Facts* is a six-part album-length suite whose unifying motif—to judge by its cover, its selection titles, its recurring references to New Orleans funeral bands and African sun dances, and its diametrical stances of resignation and pixillated defiance—is Afro-American attitudes toward death and deliverance. Although an air of lamentation pervades the slower movements (notably the title track, with its echoes of Dvořák, Mingus, and gospel; and "Cremation," in which a waltzing, hard-won optimism finally prevails), the tone is hardly grim. In the boisterous "Black Blues," for example, the mood turns festive, even flippant. Like so many other Midwesterners associated with the jazz avant-garde, Threadgill has a lingering affection for marches, and "Gateway" is the loosest-limbed jazz march yet, with the three horns parading past one another in contrapuntal formations that recall a Grambling State halftime.

Some of Threadgill's more voluptuous voicings suggest Duke Ellington (or more accurately, Charles Mingus's Ellington evocations), but the resemblance goes deeper than mere tonalities. Although the Threadgill Sextet is largely a writer's band, the leader calls on the soloists to further his narratives, much as Ellington did. Traditionalists who complain that modern soloists sacrifice the idiosyncrasies of sound for speed are advised to hear Dara's half-valve catcalls on "Black Blues" and his plungered sobs on "Just the Facts." And Harris plays the title role on "A Man Called Trinity Deliverance" in wonderfully villainous fashion, blaspheming merrily over a 3/4 hambone rhythm. Lithely muscular and enjoyable as these improvisations are in their own right, what's most impressive about them is their structural kinship with Threadgill's writing. Next to Dara and Harris, Threadgill seems positively circumspect, but his brief alto solo on "Gateway" neatly encapsulates and accelerates the number's bracing theme, and his svelte flute lines anchor the moody "Cover." The four-member rhythm section never sounds bottom heavy. Cellist Deidre Murray displays a handsome sonarity on "Cremation," the horn's striping her liturgical reading of the melody. Bassist Fred Hopkins, Threadgill's compatriot in Air, is as flexible and stalwart as usual, and drummers Pheeroan Aklaff and John Betsch soft-shoe around each other nimbly.

*Just the Facts* is not without minor flaws. The album begins and ends with drum dialogues, thereby ensuring symmetry at the cost of climax—Harris's "Trinity Deliverance" solo and the Ellingtonian dissolve that follows are tough acts to top. The solos might have been allowed to go on longer, since in the band's live performances, all three horn players have demonstrated their ability to sustain lengthy thematic improvisations. But these are quibbles. *Just the Facts and Pass the Bucket* offers writing that is fanciful and exacting, improvisations that are feisty and compact. The engineering is crystalline, with each instrument judiciously placed in the mix. One can't ask much more of an LP.

(AUGUST 1983)

# Woman's Work

Singers—can't live with 'em, can't live without 'em. Those of us who dote on jazz delight in extolling our favorite soloists as "storytellers," but we realize perhaps better than anyone that only singers have at their disposal *the words* that can charge a story with the shock of recognition, the emotional weight of concrete detail. The ever-short supply of committed jazz vocalists ensures that you'll find albums by whorish singers having little or nothing to do with jazz in the collections of listeners of otherwise impeccable taste. At the same time, we seem to begrudge even exemplary singers the hosannas we lavish only too gratefully on the humblest instrumentalists.

For many of us, singers are a guilty pleasure, a secret vice. As defenders of a minority, somewhat déclassé position, jazz fans can become self-righteous in self-defense. Jazz elitists who scorn all pop songs are especially scornful of the tonier forms that are still the most logical sources of material for jazz singers—the Broadway musical and American popular song (or Tin Pan Alley, as it was called before gentrification). We're just now emerging from a period in which soloists were ranked on their manly stamina and revolutionary ardor. A predilection for singers (especially women singers) who do show tunes and standards and don't scat is still considered damaging proof of homosexual tendencies (or bourgeois decadence at the very least) in some quarters—witness the omission of the names Mildred Bailey, Connie Boswell, Lee Wiley, Maxine Sullivan, and Ethel Waters from standard roll calls of great jazz singers, though no survey of jazz singing styles can be complete without homages to those stars of vaudeville and cabaret.

One reason we undervalue singers is that compared with playing a horn, singing *looks* too easy—we've all sung at one time or another, so we know how it's done. But much of our distrust for singers stems from the mean uses that musicians have found for them. On one level, the human voice is just another musical instrument, particularly in jazz, a music which has long cherished the notion that is most compelling instrumentalists are those whose lines refract the hue and cry, the piths and gists, of human speech, while its only authentic singers are those whose syllabification triggers visions of fingers traveling merrily over a row of valves or keys. Although soloists who walk it like they talk it continue to command respect, modern jazz has become an instrumental music in conception as well as execution, having loosened if not severed its ties to vocal blues, gospel, and pop song with the coming of bebop. Once tolerated as the carrot-before-the-stick (the squares'll listen to my original compositions if I sucker them in with pretty show tunes sung by a pretty girl in a pretty dress), the singer is now all too often the spoonful of sugar that helps the medicine go down (someone has to mouth those inspirational messages some musicians think the people need to hear, all about how the creator has a plan that a man must be a man before he can lend a hand). Musicians often envy singers for the direct pathway words grant vocalists to audiences that instrumentalists must approach in a more abstract language, and sometimes they despise singers for reminding them jazz is still show business, like it or not. It shouldn't go unmentioned that virtually all jazz instrumentalists are men, while a disproportionate number of jazz singers are women; the theory of penis envy that Freud projected upon women finds a musical analogue in the accepted wisdom that what makes an improviser an improviser is his ax, and she who would sing jazz had better learn to phrase like a horn.

No, singers have not had an easy go of it lately, so it's not surprising that so few of the singers who arrived in the '50s and '60s have been able to sustain productive careers into this decade. One of those who has is Sheila Jordan, who gained an underground following on the strength of two records she cut in 1962 (a thawing rendition of "You Are My Sunshine" with the George Russell Sextet for Riverside; and *Portrait of Sheila,* one of the few vocal albums ever released on Blue Note) but recorded so little in the years that followed that listeners outside New York knew her by reputation only.

Following the 1980 American release of *Sheila* (SteepleChase SCS-3081)—an excellent duet album she recorded with bassist Nils-Henning Orsted-Pedersen in Denmark in 1977—Jordan finally surfaced as surrogate horn in pianist Steve Kuhn's Quartet. "You Are My Sunshine" had established Jordan as a gritty, emotional singer, but Kuhn's gnomic lyrics and doomy melodies pushed her uncomfortably close to melodramatic self-caricature—Liv Ullmann for beboppers. The choice standards on *That Old Time Feeling* (Palo Alto PA-8034), Jordan's new album of voice-and-bass duets with fellow Kuhn group member Harvie Swartz, allow Jordan more leeway for impulse and caprice. She is one of those rare singers who can scat without sounding coy, mechanical, or grotesque (nicely demonstrated on her swoops up and down the Charlie Parker line "Quasimodo" on a reworking she calls "Tribute"). She has a see-through voice it's a pleasure to hear used instrumentally (the astral falsettos that punctuate the rubato portion of "Lazy Afternoon," for example, or the reed-like beeps and overtones that heat "Whose Little Angry Man Are You?").

But what Jordan does best is to re-imagine the familiar lyrics of faded pop standards, declaiming them over and over in and out of tempo, sliding them up or down a quarter-tone until they begin to make sense for her, and the performances in this vein on *That Old Time Feeling* are among the most audacious she has ever recorded. "Let's Face the Music and Dance" (reprised from *Portrait of Sheila*) tempers gaiety with just the right note of desperation. And "Lazy Afternoon" interweaves the woozy confusion of depleted hope and persistent lust implicit in the lyric. "How Deep Is the Ocean" and "The Thrill Is Gone," both powerful songs to begin with, gain deepened character and vitality from the urgent double-timing and modal distentions they undergo. Although Sheila Jordan is a singer no jazz listener need be embarrassed to listen to, at her best she transcends jazz to join the company of those women singers who have brazenly demanded that their audiences identify with them and have left themselves (and their audiences) vulnerable in the process—Judy Garland, Edith Piaf, the vanquished Billie Holiday of the later Verves. But Jordan's commitment to jazz values—her readiness to put musicianship at risk as well as personality—rescue her from the longueurs and artifice of high-camp chanteuse/existentialists like Jane Oliver, Morgana King, and Barbra Streisand. *That Old Time Feeling* leaves Jordan's mark on the listener, despite its sprinkle of catchy trifles like "Tribute (Quasimodo)," and some self-referential intrusions the singer should have resisted (the "You Are My Sunshine" coda to "Lazy Afternoon"; the substitution of "songs" for "things" in the line "Haven't done half the things we want to" in "Some Other Time").

I don't mean to praise Jordan at risk of making it seem as though bassist Swartz is merely her dutiful accompanist. Voice-and-bass duets make harsh demands on a singer, but they are an even greater test of the instrumentalist's resourcefulness and restraint, and busy and full as Swartz's counter lines are, they never limit the singer's rhythmic and harmonic stretch. Swartz's co-conspirator role is especially evident on the Duke Ellington chestnut "It Don't Mean a Thing," which is taken at a much slower tempo than usual. Swartz's goosy slides, ostinatos, and double stops combine with the vampish cackle of Jordan's "hey-ho"s to conjure the panache of a Cotton Club floorshow.

Jordan has been named female singer deserving wider recognition in five of the last seven Down Beat International Critics Polls, which underlines the diminished power of us jazz critics to make our will be done, but also underlines the dearth of new woman singers. Scatters are suddenly a dime a dozen but who can take them seriously? DeeDee Bridgewater, the most promising singer jazz nurtured in the

'70s, has drifted to funk, where she's not going to make anyone forget Patti Labelle or Aretha Franklin. Amina Claudine Myers focuses her energy on piano and composition. Jay Clayton patrols the wilderness between new music and free jazz. The recent attempts by Carly Simon and Rickie Lee Jones to sing evergreens hardly inspires hope that a new flock of jazz singers will soon cross over from soft rock.

But there are singers who bear watching. The aforementioned Clayton has performed with leaders as diverse as neo-bop alto saxophonist Bob Mover and minimalist composer Steve Reich, and—as befits a singer holding dual citizenship in jazz and experimental classical music—her wordless vocalizations usually fall somewhere between scat and sound text. But *All Out* (Anima 1J35), her first record under her own name, is all too obviously a jazz record, with compositions (by Clayton, pianist Larry Karush, saxophonist Jane Ira Bloom, and producer Heiner Stadler) that serve as either pointillistic frameworks for group improvisation or modal blowing vehicles with the singer lining up as another horn (as on the hypnotic but overextended "7/8 Thing," where three other female voices set hers off). Having relinquished the singer's traditional storytelling advantage (except on a brilliant reading of someone named Guryan's lyrics to Ornette Coleman's "Lonely Woman," which is far and away the album's best track), Clayton is often left with literally nothing to say. Her taste in syllabification, her timbral purity, her unerring intonation, her taunting way with rhythm, and her readiness to go out on a limb all make her freewheeling singing amply rewarding in itself, but she comes across more vividly with an autocratic composer calling the tune (her virtuoso turn on "Inneroutersight," from Muhal Richard Abrams's *Spinhumonesty* [Black Saint BSR-0032], for example). Still, *All Out* is well worth hearing, and not merely because Clayton is a visionary singer, the closest thing jazz has to Meredith Monk or Diamanda Galas. The musicianship of pianist Karush, drummer Frank Clayton, and bassist Harvie Swartz (him again) is impeccable, and Bloom's alto and soprano improvisations are passionate and involving, if somewhat over deliberate.

Kim Parker—daughter of Chan Richardson, stepdaughter of both Charlie Parker and Phil Woods—made an inauspicious debut singing pianist Larry Gelb's jejune lyrics on *The Language of Blue* (Cadence Jazz CJR-1012). On her own *Havin' Myself a Time* (Soul Note SN-1033), Parker reveals an ingratiatingly screwball persona, biting into songs by Arlen, Ellington, Porter, and Robin and Rainger as though they were deliciously sour pieces of fruit. A trio led by expatriate pianist Kenny Drew paces her nicely. On the more recent *Good Girl* (Soul Note SN-1063), the pianist is Tommy Flanagan, so the accompaniment is even firmer and more chivalrous. But an erratic choice of material, most of it recently derived from jazz, makes *Good Girl* one of those unbalanced records in which you notice the singer not the songs. Stick with *Havin' Myself a Time*.

Then there is Susannah McCorkle, whose first loyalty is to pop songs of the '20s, '30s, and '40s, but who favors songwriters who figured jazz phrasing into their melodies, reminding us of a bygone time when jazz and pop weren't the two distinct camps they are now. A sensitive interpreter of lyrics whose voice recalls Peggy Lee and Rosemary Clooney (with the young, still relatively carefree Billie Holiday audible parenthetically). McCorkle has great promise. But she also has great potential, which is not necessarily the same thing. Her first three albums, all of which can be highly recommended, were songbook-styled tributes to lyricists Johnny Mercer, Yip Harburg, and Harry Warren.* The fourth, *The People You Never Get To Love* (Inner City IC-1151) is a mixed bag of standards and what those in the biz call "more contemporary material"—Sedaka and Greenfield, Rupert Holmes, and the dreaded Bergmans, Allan and Marilyn. Pianist Keith Ingham's arrangements are a bit too peppy, and the quartet instrumentation is a bit too spare. Too often the singer sounds do-

---

* *The Songs of Johnny Mercer* (Inner City IC-1011), *Over the Rainbow: The Songs of E. Y. "Yip" Harburg* (Inner City IC-1131), and *The Music of Harry Warren* (Inner City IC-1141). Little did I know when I wrote this that McCorkle's best was yet to come—1985's *Thanks for the Memory: Songs of Leo Rubin* (Pausa 7175).

mesticated. But it's possible to forgive her any lapse when she turns around and swings Jobim's "No More Blues" or sings an old song as beautifully as she does "I'm Pulling Through." Can't live with 'em, can't live without 'em, either.

(SEPTEMBER 1983)

# Back in Time

Too much significance is generally attached to the fact that the original members of the Modern Jazz Quartet first played together in the rhythm section of the Dizzy Gillespie Big Band—too much irony drawn from the information that the most temperate, most buttoned-down small group to convene in the '50s had a decade earlier manned the boilers in the most fevered, most gloriously disheveled of the bop orchestras. On the basis of such circumstantial evidence, the MJQ has traditionally been credited with expanding bop's frontiers in the direction of greater group intimacy and precision. But the same evidence is also frequently employed to advance the ludicrous proposition that the MJQ's formal excellence amounts to little more than a corsetting of modern jazz, a sheathing of bop's pointed anger in exchange for concert hall respectability.

There is some logic to this complaint only so long as we narrow discussion of the MJQ's lineage to bebop and the Gillespie Big Band. But I think we gain fuller measure of the MJQ's impact by zeroing in instead on the activities of John Lewis, the problematical figure whose composer's sensibility pervades the group's music. And we gain deeper insight into Lewis's values, I think, if we remember that in addition to serving time with Gillespie, Lewis was also the pianist

227

and one of the more prolific arrangers with the 1949 Miles Davis Nonet, a short-lived ensemble whose influence nonetheless proved decisive in the following decade. Like fellow Nonet arrangers Gil Evans and Gerry Mulligan, like the young Miles Davis, and like several other seemingly incongruous movers and shakers who helped advance jazz beyond bop in the '50s (Horace Silver, Thelonious Monk, Charles Mingus, George Russell, and Jimmy Giuffre chief among them), Lewis was a counterrevolutionary in at least one crucial sense: it fell upon him and the others to reacquaint jazz with felicities the insurgents had renounced in their struggles for improvisatory freedom during the previous decade.

Lewis addressed this necessary and difficult task with wit and ingenuity. Though couched in the phraseology of Parker and Gillespie, Lewis's writing for the MJQ reveals an intimacy with the secrets of tension and release, the tenets of dynamic shading and dramatic pause more characteristic of jazz of the '20s and '30s than jazz of the '40s and early '50s. Critic Martin Williams has praised Lewis's cheery contrapuntal stop-time piece "The Golden Striker" (from his score to the film *No Sun in Venice*) as a kind of up-to-date if somewhat fussy "Bugle Call Rag." We are also indebted to Williams for the revelation that King Oliver's 1926 recording of "Snag It" may have been the unlikely source of the whopping bass line that walks the soloists through their choruses on Lewis's "Django." Lewis himself has frequently expressed admiration for the seamless interaction between the horn soloists and the All-American Rhythm Section in Count Basie's big band of the '30s. But Lewis's revitalization of jazz traditions goes far deeper than casual appropriation of such trademark devices of early jazz as contrapuntal theme statements, group tremelos, stop-time solo breaks, and gradual accelerations of tempo that relied on nothing so obvious or so disruptive as double time. It's often forgotten that it wasn't until late swing/early bop that the improvised solo—or the string of improvised solos—became the raison d'être of jazz performance. Jazz had been an ensemble music in its infancy and remained so for a time, despite the emergence of such imperious soloists as Louis Armstrong and Lester Young. For the most part, the great soloists had enjoyed their privileged moments within the larger mise-en-scène of arrangements; they strutted their stuff within the choreography of collective impromptus. But with the advent of bop, the soloist reigned supreme, and the ensemble had some catching up to do. John Lewis was one of the musicians who consciously or unconsciously set out to restore the balance.

Fashioning a group music in which the improvised chorus and all that surrounded it were of equal importance, Lewis performed a feat of magic only a handful of jazz writers, including Duke Ellington and Jelly Roll Morton, had ever pulled off—he reconciled the composer's belief in predetermination with the improviser's yen for free will. The MJQ's best performances plumb tensions deep at the wellspring of jazz, tensions personified by the uneasy alliance some listeners have long perceived between Lewis and vibist Milt Jackson. There are still those who argue that Lewis's insistence upon group order and structural coherence audibly inhibits Jackson's self-expression. Quite the contrary, I think. Lewis's stagings generally heighten the dramatic impact of Jackson's soliloquies, particularly on the slow ballads and medium tempo blues Jackson is likely to favor in any setting. It's worth considering that the MJQ rescued Jackson from a career of blowing sessions and spared him the dilemma of competing with horns—worth considering, too, that Jackson's philanderings have inevitably led him to pianists as strong willed as Lewis, in their own ways: Thelonious Monk, Horace Silver, Oscar Peterson.

Not to ignore the virtues and historical primacy of the MJQ's early Prestige sides with drummer Kenny Clarke, I think the group reached its apotheosis in the years immediately after replacing Clarke with Connie Kay and signing with Atlantic—a period more or less beginning with *Fontessa* in 1956 and climaxing with the flawless *European Concert* retrospective in 1960. Not coincidentally, this is the period in which Lewis most exerted himself as composer and captain of the MJQ's destiny. While Kay is by no means as buoyant or bracing a timekeeper as the pioneering Clarke, he is, for Lewis's purposes, the more complete percussionist, the more efficient colorist. With bassist Percy Heath holding steady compass on the meter, Kay is free to create shimmering effects with finger cymbals, triangle, and tympani. Kay's multiple percussion anticipated the AACM more than a decade, while also evoking in spirit the very earliest jazz drummers, who were never satisfied to confine their tapping and jingling to their traps. But the actual model for Kay's tintinnabulation (which Atlantic's superior engineering made possible to appreciate in living color) was undoubtedly the symphonic percussion section, as James Lincoln Collier points out in *The Making of Jazz*.

Lewis's fascination with the music of the Renaissance, the Baroque, and the Romantic periods made him a source of some controversy during his most productive period as a composer. His European borrowings were so central to his work they could not be dismissed as momentary aberrations like Art Tatum's "Humoresque" or countless other attempts by jazzmen to "swing" the classics. Several of Lewis's most celebrated pieces for the MJQ are fugues, including "Concord," "Vendome," "Versailles," and "Three Windows." (Whether or not they are "true" fugues is another matter. Wilfred Mellers protests not; Max Harrison and Martin Williams vote yes. But I think we can at least say such pieces are fugues in the same general way "Lonely Woman" or "All Blues" is a blues; the Lewis pieces make liberal use of fugal motion and countermotion much as a piece by Ornette Coleman or Miles Davis might partake of blues tonality without observing strict blues form.) *The Comedy*, a Lewis suite for the MJQ, follows the conventions of the Italian commedia dell'arte, and "In Memoriam" is a concerto grosso for the MJQ and a symphonic orchestra. The aria-like "One Never Knows," from the *No Sun in Venice* score, concludes with a rubato passage that—with Connie Kay's brush strokes sounding like the slap of oars in the water, and Percy Heath's 6/8 strumming sounding as lyrical and noble as a gondolier's—simulates an Italian barcarola. The MJQ's book has always included classical adaptations (from Bach and Rodrigo, among others), and a cultivated air of European gentility hangs over the group's performances, sometimes more a question of ambience than specific reference. The European echo is even more discernible in Lewis's work away from the

MJQ, his scores for large orchestras and brass and string concerts in particular.

Lewis was not the first prominent jazz musician to face charges of social climbing for his European leanings, nor is he the latest. The sticky issue of what we might call European intervention in jazz began with Duke Ellington (more specifically with John Hammond's attack on "Reminiscing in Tempo"), and led to the temporary devaluation of Scott Joplin and W. C. Handy, and the early resistance to Cecil Taylor; Anthony Davis seems to be the currently popular whipping boy from a stellar field of postmodernist candidates including Anthony Braxton, Leroy Jenkins, James Newton, and Roscoe Mitchell. White jazz musicians have come in for their share of abuse too, but, interestingly, when a Dave Brubeck or Stan Kenton or Lennie Tristano manifests a classical influence, the gravest charge he faces is pretentiousness, or pomposity, or bad music. A black musician betraying similar inclinations is accused of cultural treachery.

The issue is larger than John Lewis and is never likely to be settled once and for all. But it might be good to remember that Lewis (like Ellington, Taylor, and Anthony Davis) is a product of the black bourgeoisie. In a sense, men like Lewis, through their interest in things European, are maintaining a status their families have long enjoyed within the black community. Americans are an inquisitive people, after all, obsessed with self-improvement—black Americans no less than any other group, jazzmen no less than musicians in any other field. One characteristic of a democracy is that Everyman feels obliged to prove he's just as good as the next guy. One might also raise the point that, from its very beginnings, jazz borrowed its instrumentation and its rough notions of harmony from Europe (granted, the earliest jazz musicians were given little choice); that jazzmen have always been inclined to judge facility by European standards (why else would so many have admired Art Tatum more for his velocity than for his harmonic daring; why else would so many have acclaimed Oscar Peterson a virtuoso and denigrated Monk as a "functional" pianist?).

I think we can credit John Lewis with intuiting that the ultimate benefit of his European borrowings might be to impose order and a sense of permanence upon a music which otherwise might become solipsistic and fatally spur-of-the-moment. I think, too, that the same conservative lust for simplicity of form that draws Lewis to the Renaissance and the Baroque draws him inevitably to the blues, another form of music permitting endless variation only within the logic of rigid boundaries. Significantly, the most memorable theme from *The Comedy* is "Harlequin," a scherzo accumulating its humor through fits and starts more evocative of the Kansas City barrelhouse than the Roman piazza. And the *No Sun in Venice* soundtrack summons up the antic shades of New Orleans even while painting a serene Turner-like sound portrait of Venetian seas and skies.

I will concede that there are occasions when Lewis courts pastiche (the majority of his "third stream" experiments and the disappointing *Blues on Bach*), occasions when the naiveté of his string writing suggests a tourist gaping at magnificent ruins. I'll concede that Lewis often manacles his drummers, that segments of *The Comedy* trade swing for a fey, musicbox sonarity. But Lewis's assimilationism has also produced its share of masterpieces, as well as its honorable failures and tantalizing near misses. Among his vehicles for the MJQ, I would single out *No Sun in Venice* (or *One Never Knows*, to use its popular subtitle) six pieces which can be appreciated individually or as a suite, much like Ellington's *Such Suite Thunder* or *The Far East Suite*. I admire the staccato bustle and modest proportion of "Sketch," at least in its original recording by the MJQ and the Beaux Arts String Quartet. Lewis's most triumphant encounters with larger ensembles are long out-of-print. The original recording of "Three Little Feelings," with a brass choir bleeding iridescence into Miles Davis's fuliginous timbre and rolling kettledrums emboldening his brooding matador eloquence, achieves an integration of soloist and orchestra that places it in a league with Ellington's "Concerto for Cootie" and such Davis/Gil Evans collaborations as *Miles Ahead* and *Sketches of Spain*. Other neglected Lewis treasures include a 1956 recording of "The Queen's Fancy," with orchestral heraldry dovetailing lovely solos by J. J. Johnson and Stan Getz, and the 1962 "Donnie's Theme," with Eric Dolphy shearing the barbed strings of Orchestra USA.

Whatever their rococo flourishes, these works sting with the emotional immediacy of jazz, while conveying their author's intimacy with principles of organization set down over the decades by the most resourceful jazz composers. By the late '50s, John Lewis had been admitted to the pantheon—it was not unusual to hear him mentioned in the same breath with Morton, Ellington, and Monk. Over the last decade, however, his stock has plummeted to the point where he is now accorded the begrudging respect due an historical but peripheral figure. His relative inactivity between the MJQ's breakup in 1974 and their reformation in 1981 is one explanation for his fall from grace, the unavailability of so many of his major records another. But I think the flirtation with Europe took its toll on Lewis's reputation, and no wonder. Hindsight shows Lewis to have been swimming against the musical currents of his time. Heard in the context of ongoing jazz history, Lewis's experiments of the '50s and '60s sound timid indeed in light of what was just beyond the horizon. Lewis may have been Ornette Coleman's first benefactor, but it was hardly a matter of like attracting like, to judge from the MJQ's bowdlerization of "Lonely Woman." It isn't only within the confines of jazz that Lewis now seems anachronistic, either. By the late '50s, the Southern Baptist hymn and the Appalachian ballad had usurped the operetta and the canzione as the tacit model for the popular song. Cruelest irony of all, while Lewis was indulging fantasies of Harlequins and Columbines in the salons of ancient Europe, contemporary European composers were enduring the rigors of dissonance and atonality, total serialism and chance.

In recent years, Lewis has regained visibility, and a twist of fate suggests it's time for reappraisal, what with the "return to romanticism" being proposed in academia by George Rochberg and David Del Tredici, what with the arrival in jazz of left conservative/romantic structuralists as close in sensibility to Lewis as Anthony Davis and James Newton. Lewis is again writing for the MJQ; the group's

1983 Carnegie Hall recital witnessed the premiere of several major new works. A series of imports from Europe and Japan suggests that Lewis has become a more extroverted soloist over the years (*Statements and Sketches for Further Development* is especially enlightening, with the pianist gently knocking the starch out of several of his more venerable themes, including a "Django" that might warm the hearts of Donald Lambert and Willie "The Lion" Smith). On 1982's *Kansas City Break* (Finesse FW-38187), Lewis unveils a working sextet with an unusual front line of violin and flute. Some of his scoring for this combination is prissy and overdressed, but Joe Kennedy's weeping gypsy violin contrasts nicely with the leader's economical piano, the way Jackson's vibes do in the MJQ.

But I witnessed a unique dramatization of the best service a John Lewis can render jazz one afternoon last summer, when he coached three local saxophonists through a reading of his winsome "Afternoon in Paris" at a free workshop held in Philadelphia's Afro-American Historical and Cultural Museum. "You have to put yourself at the service of the melody," Lewis kept insisting. "Your solos should expand the melody or contract it." But the young saxophonists initially approached Lewis's melody as a succession of chord changes. To the man, they were haunted by Coltrane's vigor but not possessed of his logic. If Coltrane often sounded like he was clearing long rows of high hurdles, these Philadelphians—like most young Coltrane followers—sounded as though they were running in place. But after an hour of tussling, they finally gave in to Lewis, and their solos gradually took on a lovely tone. Afterwards, they seemed visibly surprised that so simple and straightforward an approach to a melody could have put them in touch with such complexities of feeling, and the audience seemed to share their surprise. Only Lewis acted as though he knew it would work out that way all along.

If every improviser were a Louis Armstrong or a Sonny Rollins, jazz would have no crying need for a John Lewis. But since few improvisers are blessed with Armstrong or Rollins's intuitive sense of form, mediators like Lewis serve a crucial function. Some might regret that Lewis consults the past rather than the future for inspiration, and might wish that he confine his inquiry to native soil. But Lewis is so rare a musician and his contribution to jazz so valuable, we'd be foolish not to accept him gratefully under whatever conditions he chooses to impose.*

# II

The Modern Jazz Quartet disbanded in 1974 (temporarily, as it turned out), presumably to allow the group's members to pursue individual goals. But the MJQ seemed to have outlived its usefulness anyway. In the decade before the split, John Lewis's reputation had been sliding. On the MJQ's classic recordings, Lewis had masterminded a music at once "created by the players *and* fully shaped by the composer," as British critic Francis Newton put it. In the process, Lewis located affinities between bop and the Baroque, between 18th-century European romanticism and the emotional extravagance of the blues. But by the late '60s, the dissenting view that Lewis had accomplished all this at too high a cost was gaining favor, as the MJQ's performances settled into predictability (and, too often, preciosity). Just as Lewis's unapologetic European bias worked against him in an era in which jazz increasingly looked to Africa for inspiration, so his primness and economy began to seem quaint to audiences cued to hear long improvised solos as tests of manhood and flashes of technical exuberance as epiphanies of Soul.

Ten years is a long time in jazz, however, and now that the MJQ

---

\* Catalog numbers for records mentioned here in passing, some of which may be out of print: *No Sun in Venice* (Atlantic SD-1284), *Fontessa* (Atlantic SD-1231), *European Concert* (Atlantic SD-2-603), *The Comedy* (Atlantic SD-1390), *Blues on Bach* (Atlantic SD-1652), *Statements and Sketches for Further Development* (CBS Sony SOPO-126 [Japanese]). The MJQ's performance of Ornette Coleman's "Lonely Woman" is the title track of Atlantic SD-1381. "Sketch" is on *Third Stream Music* (Atlantic SD-1345). "Three Little Feelings," with Miles Davis is included in the reissue *Jazz Compositions* (Columbia FC-37012). "Donnie's Theme" was on *Orchestra USA* (Colpix SCP-448). The MJQ's Prestige recordings are collected on P-24005, a two-record set.

is back together more or less full time, it has again become evident that the integration of soloist into ensemble that represents the MJQ's—and John Lewis's—clearest virtue is both timeless and ever in peril. Lewis has been rescued from ignominy by Muhal Richard Abrams, Anthony Davis, James Newton, and others who have tipped the balance away from the soloist back to the composer. So it is not surprising that *Echoes* (Pablo D-2312 142), the MJQ's first album since its re-formation, sounds as fertile as its first recordings must have sounded in the early '50s, though it is essentially just more of the same. Nor is it surprising that Lewis's sensibility governs even the material written by Milt Jackson and Percy Heath. What is surprising is that Lewis, not Jackson, walks away with top honors as a soloist.

This is not to say that Jackson's playing is subpar. With its preponderance of slow- and medium-tempo blues, *Echoes* is custom tailored for Jackson, and he is in handsome form, clearly gaining momentum at times from Lewis's riffing accompaniments and teasing antiphonal queries. Still, it's Lewis's simpler thematic variations that steal the show. Always a witty and amiable pianist with a shapely and personable touch, Lewis became more outgoing during the MJQ's layoff, perhaps as a result of performing solo and with pick-up groups in which he couldn't leave as much to inference. His pulse was always sure, but now it's more insistent, and despite their surface decorum, his solos speak their piece with a bluntness worthy of Count Basie.

The material on *Echoes* is drawn from the newer pieces the MJQ has been mixing in with its standard repertoire since reconvening, and numerous performances have polished these numbers to a high shine. The three Lewis compositions, which are among the most sprightly he has ever written, will be familiar to those who have followed his solo career—he has already recorded both the curvaceous single-note melody "That Slavic Smile" and the jig-like "Hornpipe" with a quartet featuring vibist Bobby Hutcherson (on *Slavic Smile,* French RCA PL-45729), and the strutting "Sacha's March" has appeared in no less than five previous versions, including a solo piano interpretation on the 1980 anthology *I Remember Bebop* (Columbia C2-35381). Although Jackson and the composer are the featured soloists on "Sacha's" (Jackson fleet choruses gradually kicking the performance into higher gear), the arrangement is essentially a grand showcase for Connie Kay's tubby parade drumming, and Kay's dynamic conjuring makes you realize the crucial role this most under-rated of drummers plays in the MJQ's equality of voices, even when he is less prominently featured than he is here. This "Sacha's March" is a perfect example of Lewis's cunning in reshaping a piece for the players on hand.

In emotional timbre at least, all three of Lewis's contributions to *Echoes* are blues, however cleverly disguised. Heath's "Watergate Blues" and Jackson's two compositions are blues which make no secret of it, but even these numbers owe much of their charm to patrician temperance. In cloaking the primal in the regal, the MJQ is heir to the legacy of the Ellington Orchestra—and it shares Ellington's knack for programming, too. Heath's "Watergate," a flatfoot-floogie variation he has also recorded with the Heath Brothers, is little more than a throwaway, but coming as the last track on side one, it supplies a welcome change of pace from Lewis's more intricate melodies and Jackson's more straightforward blues. It also provides an opportunity for the nonpareil team player Heath to come to the fore, and his earthy lines are as infectious in solo as in support of Lewis and Jackson.

To call *Echoes* one of 1984's finest releases hardly does it justice—this has been a great year for good records but a miserable year for great ones. But to say that *Echoes* recalls the MJQ's seminal work of decades past begins to capture its luster. Music created by the per-formers *and* fully shaped by its composer still represents achievement of too rare and high an order to be taken lightly, or taken for granted.

(SEPTEMBER 1984)

# Yankee Ingenuity

Perhaps it means no more than that I have finally learned how to listen to him, but the music of pianist Ran Blake seems to have undergone a profound transformation in the last few years, and I can only assume that this miracle has proceeded from a leap of faith in his audience. Always something of an interloper in jazz (an improviser who draws on the vernacular and legerdemain of jazz but makes no claims for himself as a jazz musician), Blake continues to essay music rooted in abstract supposition rather than tangible sensation, a music not merely introverted but almost *secretive;* and he continues to regard improvisation as a vehicle for relentless self-examination rather than revelry or virtuosity. Yet beginning with the aptly titled 1976 release *Breakthru* (Improvising Artists IAI-373842), he has somehow learned to voice even his most tentative and circuitous musings in a lucid, forthright, positively airy manner, as though communicating to an audience hanging on his every thought. Of course, like the audience for most visionary performers (especially those who don't fit into any particular genre), Blake's is largely proverbial, peopled by the handful listening now and the larger numbers a performer must trust will listen eventually. But this renders his commitment to communication all the more exemplary, and the mere act of making such a quixotic commitment seems to have elevated his music to a state of grace few performers as cerebral as he ever achieve.

As the chairman of the Department of Third Stream Studies at the New England Conservatory of Music, Blake has modified the original definition of third stream (the confluence of jazz and European concert music) to signify temporary alliances of serious, popular, and ethnic musics. His third stream is also a stream of consciousness enveloping not only a body of music but whatever impressions of politics, literature, film, philosophy, and nature happen to be floating through his mind when he sits down to play or compose. This broad framework rescues his performances from insularity.

"Duke Dreams," the foreboding original which raises the curtain on Blake's album of the same name (Soul Note SN-1027)—a tribute to Duke Ellington and Billy Strayhorn—also draws the curtain in a way. Listening to it and to all that follows (six Ellingtons, two Strayhorns, Dave Brubeck's whimsical and deftly drawn sketch "The Duke," and "Animal Crackers," a novelty tune covered by the Ellington Orchestra in 1926), I feel I am attending a seance. I *think* it is Ellington's shade guiding Blake's fingers as they form chords with one note ominously protruding on "Something To Live For," or toss unexpected splashes of bright color on to the bleak canvas Blake has chosen for "Black and Tan Fantasy," or tickle both takes of "Me and You" to rousing stride finales. But if it is Ellington, it is an apprehensive Ellington we have not encountered before, an Ellington born of Blake's dark speculations on Duke's music—an Ellington finally as real and valuable as any other. And when the record is over, I know that only Blake's hands touched the keyboard, that he is, as the skeptic John Corbit says of the spiritualist Mrs. Henderson in W. B. Yeats's "The Words upon the Window-Pane," an accomplished actor and scholar and no medium. But I know, too, that I could be wrong, just as Corbit was wrong.

What I *am* certain of is that *Duke Dreams* is a remarkable album. Blake has gained self-confidence and artistic generosity over the years: his almost rhapsodic, surprisingly literal reading of "Sophisticated Lady" announces that he no longer feels compelled to play devil's advocate with a pretty tune, to cast it forcibly against tempo and mood as he once used to do. And though he doesn't exactly swing, there are moments here when his slippery grasp of time reminds one that Ellington had nothing so tangible in mind as a steady four beats to the measure when he declared it don't mean a thing if it ain't got that you-know-what.

Given Blake's reputation as a cineaste, it's tempting to use filmic metaphor to describe *Suffield Gothic* (Soul Note SN-1077), his album of solos and duets with tenor saxophonist Houston Person. Indeed, when Blake quotes "Come Sunday," "Onward Christian Soldiers," and his own "Sister Tee" during his introduction to the gospel tune "There's a Change in My Life," the effect is closer to montage than to interpolation. But if analogy is in order, *Suffield Gothic* is more like the literary journals of a crusty 19th-century New England transcendentalist, an attempt to recapitulate "the experience of the race . . . In the experience of a single man, the scope of the globe concentrated in the microcosmology of a few acres," as Norman Holmes Pearson said of Thoreau's *Walden*. I doubt that Blake was reading Emerson or Thoreau when he recorded *Suffield Gothic,* but what brings the comparison to mind is the record's vivid sense of Blake's native New England as repository of personal memory and national fable. Not a "tone parallel" to New England or an impressionistic watercolor in any sense, *Suffield Gothic* nonetheless plays upon the myth of a self-reliant Yankee temperament born of a chilly climate and a belief in accountability in the beyond.

However one chooses to perceive it, *Suffield Gothic* is an evocative album full of disquieting external signifiers. Blake has been so beautifully recorded that even his thoughtful silences acquire the weight of audibility, and every subtle gradation of touch registers cleanly. Gospel supplies the tropes, and functions as an emblem of salvation, throughout the album, most notably on "There's a Change in My Life," "Old Man River," and a tripartite homage to Mahalia Jackson. But this is gospel from a skeptic's perspective, as the Monkish deviltry of the left hand's figurations on the Jackson tribute make clear. Probing around in the folds of the melody of "Old Man River,"

Blake discovers an echo of "Yesterdays" in the infamous "tote that barge" phrase and milks the revelation for grim, exquisite irony. His interpretation of the theme from the film *Pete Kelly's Blues* is all lowlife ambience and pummeled chords, a vision of the jazzman's travail at once more harrowing and more optimistic than that depicted in the film; and "Stars and Stripes Forever" juxtaposes dissonant clusters and a boogie-woogie bass line to posit a thornier brand of patriotism than John Philip Sousa ever intended, without lapsing into satire or otherwise debunking this thumping, stirring march.

*Suffield Gothic*'s most buoyant tracks are those teaming Blake with the underrated Houston Person, a tenor saxophonist typecast as a barroom lothario, all balls and no brains, on his own Muse LPs (the tight, leering close-ups of female anatomy on his album covers haven't helped his image, though he probably isn't responsible for his label's sexism). Person is in his element on Blake's preacherly blues "Midnight Train to Tate Country," but he proves himself equally adept on two other Blake originals—the wistful and perky "Curtis" (the album's most haunting melody, thanks to its swirling "Last Tango in Paris"-like bridge) and the teasing, "Indian Winter" (which annotator J. R. Taylor says he first mistook for a neglected standard, and no wonder—it's a delightful pastiche of "Indian Summer," "I Won't Dance," "It's a Sin To Tell a Lie," and perhaps a half dozen other popular songs, and Person sounds as if he were fashioning lyrics as he goes along, so songlike is his phrasing). Person has Blake's "Vanguard" all to himself, and if his improvised choruses are a mite too sequential in outline, his straightforward reading of the melody is absolutely incandescent. Some of *Suffield Gothic*'s glory should go to Person, though the lion's share belongs to Blake for conceiving such an unlikely setting and presenting the tenor saxophonist in such a flattering light.

Collaboration is also a key element of Blake's *The Portfolio of Doktor Mabuse* (Owl 029), one side of which is given over to a sprawling orchestral rumination (arranged by Blake, Daryl Lowery, and Michael Linn) on Fritz Lang's classic silent film, incorporating jazz and classical soloists, quizzical Blake interludes, dense string writing for the massive New England Conservatory Symphony Orchestra, the standard "You Stepped Out of a Dream," a Greek singer, and a theme by Theodorakis, with nothing rounded off or reduced to the lowest common denominator. Recorded in 1979 but not released domestically until 1984, *Mabuse* actually predates Blake's *Film Noir* (Arist/Novus AN-3019)—a more successful orchestral LP, and a more successful attempt to reproduce the sensation of film from the flicker of memory. Although it lacks *Film Noir's* sleekness and easier accessibility, *Mabuse* is an intriguing piece of music nonetheless, if only for its further evidence that Blake the accomplished miniaturist is willing to experiment with larger forms. The other side features seven shardlike piano solos recorded in Paris in 1977, including "Smoke after Smoke," a gesture of solidarity with Thelonious Monk (it even ends with Monk's familiar repeated-note signature phrase), and "Interrogation at Logan Airport," which is almost suffocating in its scrupulous depiction of terror and despair. Although the aphoristic brevity of these pieces is a point in their favor (most are between one and two and a half minutes), they're over before they've begun. Blake's owlish soliloquies need the three-and-a-half-minute running time of a pop single (or an early jazz 78) to sink in. Still, at his best, he can thrill you with the passion of pure reason, give ideas shape and heat; and he accomplishes this feat on *The Portfolio of Doktor Mabuse* no less than on *Suffield Gothic* or *Duke Dreams*.

(SEPTEMBER 1982/NOVEMBER 1984)

# Like Attracts Like

In jazz, like is attracting like more than ever these days, and the various clarinet summits, bass-violin choirs, and percussion tribes that have come our way lately are all progeny of the World Saxophone Quartet. Indeed, you can hear the WSQ's echo even in saxophone-dominated ensembles led by drummers and pianists, like Jack De-Johnette's Special Edition and Dollar Brand's Ekaya, and in saxophones-plus-rhythm collectives like the Microscopic Septet (although this may be simply a matter of fans' sudden propensity for attributing WSQ influence to juking riffs and bleeding unisons that would have been cataloged as Ellingtonian or Basie-ish less than a decade ago). The World Saxophone Quartet has had such a profound bearing on the philosophy and sound of jazz in the '80s, sometimes it's difficult to remember that the band started off as a kind of busman's holiday, that it remains essentially a part-time alliance, and that it has recorded only five albums, the best of which dates back to 1980, though it wasn't released until 1983.

Even if it lacks some of the earlier album's feeling of breakthrough, *Revue* (Black Saint BSR-0056) represents a considerable advance over *WSQ* (Black Saint BSR-0047), in terms of making such long-postponed ideals as true collective improvisation and the reconciliation of traditionalism and experimentation seem finally within reach. *Revue* announces in no uncertain terms that the WSQ is one of the few contemporary ensembles to catch on to the trade secret of the great little jump bands of the '30s and '40s: that precision is the quickest and surest method of inducing ecstasy. And through trial and error, the members of the World Saxophone Quartet—post-modernists to the core—have come to realize that precision is never more necessary than when everyone is improvising simultaneously, with no holds barred. It's easy to understand the attraction these four multi-instrumentalists, all rooted in the solo-wind concept pioneered by Roscoe Mitchell and Anthony Braxton, felt for one another upon forming their group in 1978; easy, too, to appreciate why they trusted their federation would work and why it almost did not. On *Revue*, Oliver Lake's cutting a cappella solo intro to his "Hymn for the Old Year," Hamiet Bluiett's bittersweet baritone prologue to David Murray's "Ming," and Murray's own smeary tenor build-up to "David's Tune" all reflect the WSQ's origins in the unaccompanied-saxophone field, while avoiding the bluster that has capsized so many similar endeavors, some of this band's included. But aside from Julius Hemphill's bobbing stoptime choruses on Bluiett's gangbuster blues "I Heard That," these intros are the only solo passages on *Revue*, and in each instance, the soloist makes his greatest impact the moment the other horns collide with him. The level of invention is highest, in fact, on the pieces on which no single voice dominates at any time, in particular the four Hemphill compositions on side one. Hemphill exploits the ability of each group member to double on flutes or clarinets to optimum advantage on both "Little Samba" and "Affairs of the Heart," and proves himself a master of illusion on "Slide" and "Revue," stacking the four saxes in such a way as to suggest a big band's dynamic contrasts, variegated textures, and houserocking heat. Even in this assembly of equals, Bluiett's wedge-like section work stands out, and his lovely vignette "Quinn Chappel A.M.E. Church" brings the album to a reverent conclusion.

A disappointment only in terms of the unreal expectations it arouses coming after *Revue*, *Live in Zurich* (Black Saint BSR-0077), recorded in 1981, fades in with the WSQ members marching on from the wings (presumably decked out in formal attire) tooting their roundhouse signature theme, Bluiett's "Hattie Wall." This attempt to capture the delicious visual irony of a WSQ live performance just sounds badly recorded until one catches on; otherwise, *Live in Zurich* is boffo, with five previously unrecorded Hemphill compositions that achieve the Quartet's earmark motion of line and meld of voices and a whistling rendition of Hemphill's "Steppin'" so rigorous in its counterpoint yet so whimsical in execution as to make its earlier version on the homonymous, and justly celebrated, 1979 album (Black Saint BSR-0027), sound unduly measured by comparison. Although each member of the WSQ has proved himself as a composer in a variety of other contexts, it is Hemphill who best mines this particular outfit's rich resources, on textured pieces like "Bordertown" (which shanghais the hook from "Don't Cry for Me, Argentina," of all things) and the bustling "Funny Papers" (which suggests the contours of a Charlie Parker line before exploding into dense four-part free improvisation). The most attractive new Hemphill composition is "My First Winter": basically a cameo for Murray, it also boasts an ear-catching theme, a ballad that skirts the sentimental by incorporating scalar suspensions into its arrangement. Hemphill distinguishes himself as a player, too, threading the ensemble on the bluesy "Touchic" and setting a moody keynote with his lovely soprano introduction to "Bordertown." Neither Lake nor Bluiett is featured individually this time out, but each makes his presence felt, Lake with penetrating alto and soprano leads, Bluiett with the sheer athletic bulk of his barking pedal tones.

If the demise of the big bands precluded saxophonists from bonding together in sections after the 1940s, it hasn't prevented them from practicing together over the years; and the jazz avant-garde's gradual blurring of distinctions between practice and performance probably made the formation of an all-saxophone line-up seem an ideal move when the WSQ first came together. But on their debut (*Point of No Return* [Moers Music 01034]), Hemphill, Lake, Murray, and Bluiett still sounded more like four onanistic virtuosos practicing together than like a band. To their great credit, they have since come to think of themselves as a big-band reed section bereft of the big band, and therein lies both the secret of their alchemy and an explanation for their vast influence, which clearly strikes deeper than the recent proliferation of saxophone quartets and three-or-four-sax front lines. (The Berkeley-based Rova Saxophone Quartet, formed before WSQ, is a different story, however.) By discovering thematic advancement as well as rhythmic propulsion in the most basic patterns, the WSQ has restored the riff to the dominance it enjoyed in jazz before the arrival of bebop and the cult of the self-fixated soloist. The great swing bands knew that riffs were a way of getting carried away while remaining in control, and so did the audiences that dances to those bands. But with significant exceptions like the Modern Jazz Quartet and the Ornette Coleman and Albert Ayler groups, this approach skipped several generations before inexplicably turning up in recombinant form in the delirious riffing of the World Saxophone Quartet.

All of which makes the newly formed 29th Street Saxophone Quartet seem more a missing link than still another WSQ clone. In any case, *Pointillistic Groove* (Osmosis 6002), the 29th Streeters' debut, is one of 1984's surprise delights. Mirroring the WSQ in basic instrumentation (tenor, baritone, dual altos) but eschewing soprano, clarinet, and flute "doubles," the 29th Streeters achieve a harsher and more monochromatic blend, as befits a hard-bop orientation that also reveals itself in rhythmic accent, repertoire, and the favoring of solo statements and unison blowing at the expense of contrapuntal interplay. But the solos are freer in conception that you might expect, and the riffs that set them up and keep them in motion generate heat that rivals that of the WSQ. The alto chases on "Anthropology" underline the contrasts and similarities between the angular and Colemanesque style of Ed Jackson and the more harmonically anchored but no less vocalized style of former Jazz Messenger Robert Watson. Both altoists have contributed tangy originals to the Quartet's book, Watson again scoring points for his directness and simplicity with the tone poem "One Chance at Life" and the infectious "The Curious Child," and Jackson impressing with his adventurousness in this relatively conservative setting (though the "groove" passages of Jackson's title cut work better than its "pointillistic" ones). Baritone saxophonist Jim Hartog, a selfless team player throughout, weighs in as a promising writer with "Still" (waltzlike in lilt if not in meter) and a clever reharmonization of "Love for Sale," on which the syncopated handclaps of Watson and Jackson goose a Rich Rothenberg tenor solo into high gear as it threatens to flag. Rothenberg's pale, indolent tone pleasingly recalls Warne Marsh and early Jimmy Giuffre, and his "Bigfoot" (no relation to Charlie Parker's) stalks along playfully on its way to a blaring crescendo. *Pointillistic Groove* is a sleeper, but it's a record you don't want to miss. In addition to heralding the arrival of an immensely likable new group, it also signals that the World Saxophone Quartet is making inroads on the jazz past as well as the jazz future, and that not even bebop is inviolate.

(APRIL 1983/DECEMBER 1984)

# The Unsure Egoist
## Is Not Good for Himself

Although it's beset with galling inconsistencies, *Star People* (Columbia FC-38657) finally delivers the testimony his more optimistic fans have been anticipating from Miles Davis ever since the tarnished trumpet idol broke his long silence two summers ago. The wait has been painful. The gameness of Davis's solos on 1981's *The Man with the Horn* (Columbia FC-36790) compensated neither for a puffy tone symptomatic of six years of inactivity nor for the numbing clamor of the two electric guitarists he had taken under his wing. And 1982's live double *We Want Miles* (Columbia C2-38005), which reeked of the stale odors of sports-arena fusion and heavy-metal exertion, sounded especially ponderous compared with the sleeker, friskier, funk-influenced jazz of Ornette Coleman, Ronald Shannon Jackson, and James Blood Ulmer. Of course, many listeners who felt exactly as I did about *We Want Miles* bought it anyway. And I should talk—I bought it, too, which only goes to prove that the Miles we want and the Miles we're willing to settle for are often entirely different creatures. The set did have its moments, though they were few and far between. "Jean Pierre" 's doddering nursery-rhyme theme was oddly contagious, even if the leader was the only soloist who really seemed to "catch" it either time around (his "Lullaby of Broadway" quote on take one was especially wry).

There was a boldly phrased, going-for-the-limit trumpet solo on "Back Seat Betty," and soprano saxophonist Bill Evans (not to be confused with Yusef Lateef) tried valiantly to sustain the mood of Davis's improvisations, though the effect wasn't always pleasurable when he succeeded. (It's impossible to say at this point whether Evans is a player of rare sensitivity or just Fashionable Mr. Hybrid.) What was most distressing about both *The Man with the Horn* and *We Want Miles* was how dated their licks sounded in light of all that happened in jazz and pop during Davis's withdrawal—no wonder he had Ulmer's group bumped from the bill at his 1981 Kool Jazz Festival comeback concert, and no wonder that wags were suggesting he title his next LP *The Unsure Egoist Is Not Good for Himself*, from a line by the poet Robert Creeley.

With *Star People*, though, Davis has partially regained his confidence and his knack for telling understatement. The centerpiece of the album is the title track, a 19-minute slow blues as basic and as savoury as any Davis has ever recorded and a proving ground for his continued eloquence with Harmon mute. "Star People" gathers power as Davis and his resourceful drummer Al Foster (whose shadings gave both *The Man with the Horn* and *We Want Miles* the illusion of swing) up the improvisational ante on each of the trumpeter's three solo turns, until the suspense is its own payoff. Parceling out notes in a conversational mid-range, Davis stirs excitement not with blinding speed or stratospheric bolts but with mounting rhythmic complexity and tensile-strength in his ever-lenghtening phrases; all the while, Foster's terse (post-dubbed?) afterbeat, distant at first, is encircling wider areas of rhythm, growing denser and more combustible. As "Star People" opens, Davis is spraying notes on the Oberheim organ, a ploy he repeats to dramatic effect following an edit 12 minutes into the cut; along the way Evans preaches briefly on tenor, and guitarist Mike Stern boomerangs BB King-like blue notes so grand you hardly notice how derivative they are.

The title cut dwarfs the rest of the album, but there are two other notable workouts. Davis and Evans supply lightly dancing horn solos on the engaging "U 'n' I," a breezy melody bumping along on the fat bottom of Marcus Miller's Fender bass lines. "It Gets Better" is another slow blues, with sly Davis choruses and savvy fills by John Scofield, the subtler, warmer-toned guitarist who alternates with Stern. The rest is uneven. "Come Get It" boasts a fine Davis solo based on the fanfare from Otis Redding's "Can't Turn You Loose," but the band vamps endlessly before sliding in gear behind the leader and thunders off track completely once he has spoken his piece. "Speak" is an elephantine dance riff that stumbles under its own weight, and "Star on Cicely" fails to exploit a misterioso guitar-and-soprano-saxophone voicing contributed by Gil Evans, who attended the recording session in a troubleshooting capacity, according to the liner notes (another full-scale Davis/Evans collaboration is always rumored to be on the drawing board, but don't hold your breath).

Davis's reign as an avatar might be over; jazz has splintered into so many factions that no single album can reverberate the way *The Birth of the Cool* did in 1949, or *Kind of Blue* in 1959, or *Bitches Brew* in 1970. Still, *Star People* reassures us that one of the greatest living improvisers is still committed to and capable of making soul-nourishing music—something that didn't seem at all certain just a few months ago.

(MAY 1983)

# II

In jazz circles, *You're under Arrest* (Columbia FC-40023) has gained instant notoriety as the album on which Miles Davis plays, among other things, tunes associated with D Train, Cyndi Lauper, and Michael Jackson. The Jackson hit "Human Nature" is little more than glorified filler, but D Train's "Something's on Your Mind" is the album's most spirited workout, and Lauper's "Time after Time," with its pellucid melody and mournful harmonic suspensions, proves to be a surprisingly effective vehicle for Davis, who, come to think of it, has long nurtured an affection for slow-motion ballads of just this sort. But unlike his classic showtune interpretations of the 1950s, which begged comparison to nothing save one another, "Time after Time" is essentially a jazz instrumental cover of a recent pop vocal smash—Cyndi Lauper, not Miles Davis, supplies the context, and it's ominous to realize that the most cocksure of jazz musicians no longer feels he is in a position to call his own tune, at least not when radio programmers might be listening in.

*You're under Arrest's* original material (by Davis, guitarist John Scofield, and synthesizer player Robert Irving III) also tilts in the direction of pop—more specifically, what the trade papers call urban contemporary—with reinforced guitar and synthesizer licks which suggest that, like the rest of us, Miles spent last summer listening to *Purple Rain.* It's tempting to dub this music post-fusion: though it might seem like one more permutation of the jazz/rock synthesis Miles presaged with *Bitches Brew,* it's slinkier, brighter, and infinitely more enticing—only "Katia," with its keynote John Mc-Laughlin guitar hyperbole echoes the murk and tumult of Davis's mid-'70s concert LPs and last year's wretched *Decoy* (Columbia FC-38991). There are a number of attractive melodies here—most notably Davis and Irving's hooky "Ms. Morrisine"—and Davis plays superbly. Still, though his solos wound deeply, their pensive melancholy is frequently out of whack with the orgiastic bumping on the rhythm tracks, and the contrast is jarring in ways that seem unintentional. This is party music for stay-at-homes: it might be good dance music, but it's hardly likely to get anyone up on the dance floor.

Poor Miles. As a thinking man's pop star, he's unbankable in a market that increasingly depends on conditioned reflex. As a jazz panjandrum, he's been trading on credit for far too long. To judge from the leather and embroidery and mascara he affects in the cover photograph, even his fashion sense has deserted him: fine Italian silk is in again, thanks to his anointed heir and label mate Wynton Marsalis. It's easy to say that music is music and categories don't count—the standard line of Miles apologists—but it's difficult to imagine either a jazz or pop audience being thrilled with *You're under Arrest,* modestly diverting though it may be.

(JULY 1984)

# Index